For Ann and Ellen

with love and appreciation

CONTENTS

List of Illustrations

ILLUSTRATIONS

PREFACE

Americans in the era of the New Republic found themselves in a world swirling with change. The political and ideological transformations that accompanied the Age of Revolution and the break from Great Britain created a new understanding of citizenship and representative government. Simultaneously, a series of economic changes dramatically altered the workplace, ultimately propelling the new United States into the aggressive capitalism of the Jacksonian era. Multivolume collections of the writings of the country's leading revolutionaries stand as evidence of these profound transformations and especially of the political innovations they stimulated. The essays and letters of Hamilton and Adams, Jefferson and Madison, have enabled historians to trace policy development and important ideological shifts. Scholars in the early twentieth century edited collections of the first stirrings of the trade union movement and of the labor conspiracy trials. These efforts, together with analyses of the workings of the marketplace, provided a preliminary understanding of the era's profound economic changes.

As important as these sources are, they tell only part of the story. While the papers of the founding fathers reveal the minds of the leaders, they are less informative about the rest of society. What about the tens of thousands of citizens who voted for them, who carried out their policies or objected to their plans, and who did the day-to-day work necessary for the growth of the new nation? The documents collected under the auspices of John R. Commons, valuable for an understanding of labor conflict and resolution, do not reach into other aspects of work experiences both inside and outside the workshop, including family relations, housing, religion, recreation, and fraternity. Recent historians, writers of the "new social history," have attempted to fill this gap by exploring the lives of ordinary, heretofore anonymous, working men and women. This collection is part of that effort; its goal is to bring attention to how this dual revolution touched the lives and aspirations of "ordinary" Americans. Specifically, this book presents documents that illuminate the work experiences of common New Yorkers—apprentices, journeymen, master craftsmen, mariners, African Americans, and women—and, in so doing, it reveals the portentous impact, political and economic, of the new republican universe.

The documents in this book are selected from a wide and varied body of material. We have spent most of the last two decades culling repositories for information on the social and labor history of New York and have chosen material that reflects a broad and representative spectrum of work experiences. Although many of the documents were located during our own research, we have also utilized the growing literature on the social history of New York and the early republic. This book reprints important documents on the early trade union movement, but many of the selections reflect a broader concept of labor history.

The documents in each chapter explore the impact of the revolution on New York's laborers. In some the connection is explicit, with direct references to the American Revolution and republicanism. In others it is implicit but can be discerned through an understanding of the setting and individuals. Whenever possible we have included autobiographical accounts, in which the workers speak for themselves. These sagas and the other documents offer fleeting but revealing glimpses of the homes, the shops, and the streets of early national New York, disclosing both triumph and despair. We were most successful in finding autobiographical material from groups of traditional interest to historians, such as masters and journeymen, and less successful in the newer areas of African-American and women's history. Perhaps future historians will fill some of the gaps that remain.

Like any primary document, each selection in this book must be approached carefully. In providing a general introduction for each chapter and more specific commentary for documents, along with annotation, we have aimed to assist the reader in a textual analysis. But there are many different ways to "read" any given document. We, the editors, may see a text in one way, the reader in another. The exciting part of making documents like these available to a large audience is that we all get the chance to see for ourselves a very special and important section of American society in the early years of the republic, and we can begin to appreciate how these men and women, as well as the more renowned founding fathers, were the keepers of the revolution.

This project has been assisted by many historians and archivists including Carl Prince, Graham Hodges, Jan Lewis, Daniel Cohen, Jane Pomeroy, Kathyrn Luhrs, Thomas Dunnings, Deborah Waters, Paul Pearson, Wendy Shadwell, Idilio Gracia-Peña, and Kenneth Cobb. Alfred F. Young, the dean of American artisan studies, gave this work a careful and most helpful reading, and his suggestions are deeply appreciated. In addition, Nick Salvatore, Roger Haydon, and Joanne Hindman tendered important assistance and advice. We thank the following institutions for support during the preparation of this book: University of Oklahoma, Center for the History of Freedom at Washington University, South Street Seaport Museum, New York University, and Florida International University.

The following libraries and archives deserve special acknowledgment: the New-York Historical Society, the New York Public Library, the Municipal Archives and Records Center of the City of New York, the Museum of the City of New York, and the Winterthur Museum and Library. Paul Gilje received release time and financial support from a Southwest Bell Summer Research Fellowship at the University of Oklahoma, a Senior Faculty Summer Research Fellowship at the University of Oklahoma, a Center for the History of Freedom Fellowship at Washington University, and from the Research Council and the College of Arts and Sciences at the University of Oklahoma. Barbara Million and Amy Forwoodson provided valuable secretarial support. Howard Rock received financial and technical support from the College of Arts and Sciences of Florida International University. Elena Maubrey and Sharon Johnson were invaluable in moving this work along.

We want to single out the support of our families. Paul Gilje is especially in debt to his parents, Arne and Wladja Gilje, and regrets his father did not live to see his own name in print. Howard Rock is delighted that his father and stepmother, Manuel and Beatrice Mitchell Rock, strong supporters of his work, are able to see the completion of this volume, and he trusts that whatever good it brings will reflect the love and encouragement of his mother, the late Lenore Rock. Our children, Erik Gilje, Karin Gilje, David Rock, and Daniel Rock, may not have directly aided our efforts—not that they lacked for questions about the computer—but then, they have yet to complete their indentures. Finally we each have a tremendous sense of gratitude to the mainstays of our respective lives, to whom we dedicate this book, Ann Elisabeth Gilje and Ellen Bernstein Rock.

PAUL A. GILJE
HOWARD B. ROCK

Norman, Oklahoma
and Miami, Florida

A NOTE ON ABBREVIATIONS AND ACKNOWLEDGMENTS

The documents and illustrations in this book come from a number of sources, to which we here acknowledge our gratitude. We have abbreviated the more common sources for space considerations, and these abbreviations appear with the illustration or document:

BA   Boston Athenaeum
MCNY   Museum of the City of New York
MMNY   Metropolitan Museum of New York
NYHS   New-York Historical Society
NYPL   New York Public Library
NYCMA   New York City Municipal Archives

Figures 49, 51, 54, 57, 66, and 68 are used courtesy of the American Tract Society, Boston Athenaeum. Figures 14, 24, 27, 31, 41, 45, 47, 60, and 65 are used courtesy of the Museum of the City of New York. Figures 2, 4, 7, 17, 40, and 46 are used courtesy of the Metropolitan Museum of New York, The Edward Arnold Collection of New York Prints, Maps and Ephemera, Bequest of Edward W. C. Arnold, 1954. Figure 39 is used courtesy of the Mystic Seaport Museum, Inc., all rights reserved. Figures 1, 5, 23, 32, 33, and 35 are used courtesy of the New-York Historical Society; Figures 11, 19, 36, 55, 56, and 62 are used courtesy of the New-York Historical Society, Samuel Wood and Sons, *Engravings Used by, or Available to, the Wood*

Publishing Firm to Illustrate Their Books (New York: Samuel Wood & Sons, 1820). Figures 3 and 43 are used courtesy of the I. N. Phelps Stokes Collection, Miriam and Ira D. Wallach Division of Art, Prints and Photographs, The New York Public Library, Astor, Lenox and Tilden Foundations. Figure 15 is used courtesy of the Society of Shipwrights and Caulkers Records, Rare Books and Manuscripts Division, The New York Public Library, Astor, Lenox and Tilden Foundations. Figure 37 is used courtesy of the Print Collection, Miriam and Ira D. Wallach Division of Art, Prints and Photographs, The New York Public Library, Astor, Lenox and Tilden Foundations. Figures 9, 13, 16, 18, 20, 21, 22, 38, 42, 44, 48, 58, 59, 61, and 67 are used courtesy of the Alexander Anderson Scrapbooks, Print Collection, Miriam and Ira D. Wallach Division of Art, Prints and Photographs, The New York Public Library, Astor, Lenox and Tilden Foundations.

Selections from the Alexander Anderson diary are reprinted with permission from the Rare Book and Manuscript Library, Columbia University. Selections from Stephen Allen's memoirs and the Reverend Henry Chase's diary are reprinted with permission from the New-York Historical Society. Selections from "The Minutes of the Union Society of Shipwrights and Caulkers" are reprinted courtesy of the Society of Shipwrights and Caulkers, Rare Books and Manuscripts Division, The New York Public Library, Astor, Lenox and Tilden Foundations. The following documents are reprinted with permission from the Municipal Archives, Department of Records and Information Services, City of New York: "Rights, Liberties & Privalages," petition of cartmen; "Guilty of Some Irregularities," depositions of John Dawson et al.; "A Torrent of Clamarous Abuse," petition of Philetic Havens 'et al.; "These Disagreeable Screamings," petitions of Adam Marshall and chimney sweeps; "Admitting Very Disorderly Persons," *People v. William Brooks*; "They Must Not Suffer the Man to Be Taken Away," *People v. John Dyos*; "Everything in Her Power to Extricate Him from His Difficulties," petitions of Elizabeth Kline and David Hay; and "Where White & Black Persons of Evil Fame Resort," *People v. Catherine Akens*.

All spelling in the documents is presented as it appears in the original source.

Keepers of the Revolution

INTRODUCTION

The American Revolution affected all New Yorkers. Yet the impact of changes initiated by resistance to imperial regulation in the 1760s and 1770s varied for the different groups encompassed by the documents in this book. Some entered the vortex of politics and war; others remained on the periphery. Artisans, apprentices, mariners, and blacks protested the Stamp and Townshend duties and demonstrated against the presence of British soldiers in a series of confrontations that culminated in the 1770 riot known as the Battle of Golden Hill. In 1774 many of the same types of people made up the crowd at New York's tea party. Men and women together joined to boycott British goods. Living through a revolution and experiencing the ensuing social and economic change indelibly altered sectors of the community that had been largely quiescent before the war.

The effect of the changes wrought by resistance was most obvious among New York artisans.[1] Besides taking an active role in the street

1. The terms "artisan," "mechanic," craftsman" and "tradesman" originally had different meanings. By 1800, however, they were used interchangeably, and that practice will be followed in this book. The principal determinant of artisan standing was the ownership of professional skills and tools. Traditionally, these skills or "mysteries" would be learned during apprenticeship, improved during the period of journeyman (wage-earning) standing, and then perfected by the time a mechanic became a master craftsman possessing his own business. See Howard B. Rock, *Artisans of the New*

politics of the day, craftsmen seized the opportunity during the disintegration of royal control to organize a separate, independent, and radical Committee of Mechanics that assumed some quasi-governmental functions and led the city's revolutionary movement. These mechanics took Thomas Paine's message to heart and insisted on independence months before more conservative New Yorkers were ready to act. Many of these workers subsequently joined the militia or the Continental Army; some became privateers. After 1783 they were determined that their enhanced role in government would continue. They demanded that the central place the artisan occupied in a republican society be recognized, maintained, and rewarded, and that the sacrifices of the tradesmen who composed the heart and soul of America's revered armed forces be eternally marked in the collective social memory.[2]

From their revolutionary experience, tradesmen shaped a distinctive "artisan republicanism," based upon longstanding republican traditions adapted to the new nation. To artisans, republicanism meant that society was best governed by those who were most critical to its well-being: the producers. They idealized the small, independently owned craft shop in the same manner that Jefferson idealized the independent yeoman. Artisans viewed the workshop as a place of harmony where masters and journeymen cooperatively provided the goods vital to the new nation's economic welfare. No conflict between employer and employee need exist within the shop; journey-

---

Republic: The Tradesmen of New York City in the Age of Jefferson (New York, 1979), pp. 4–14; Sean Wilentz, Chants Democratic: New York City and the Rise of the American Working Class, 1788–1850 (New York, 1984), pp. 24–34.

2. For an introduction to the literature of the participation of the urban New York labor force in the American Revolution, see Philip S. Foner, Labor and the American Revolution (Westport, Conn., 1976); Roger J. Champagne, "Liberty Boys and Mechanics of New York City, 1764–1774," Labor History, 8 (1967), 115–135; Champagne, Alexander McDougall and the American Revolution in New York (Schenectady, N.Y., 1975), pp. 27–66; Lee R. Boyer, "Lobster Backs, Liberty Boys, and Laborers in the Streets: New York's Golden Hill and Nassau Street Riots," New-York Historical Society Quarterly, 57 (1973), 281–307; Staughton Lynd, "The Mechanics in New York Politics, 1774–1788," Labor History, 5 (1964), 225–246; Bruce Bliven, Jr., Under the Guns: New York: 1775–1776 (New York, 1972); Bernard Mason, The Road to Independence: The Revolutionary Movement in New York, 1773–1777 (Lexington, Mass., 1966); Graham Russell Hodges, New York City Cartmen, 1667–1850 (New York, 1986), chap. 5; Paul A. Gilje, The Road to Mobocracy: Popular Disorder in New York City, 1763–1834 (Chapel Hill, N.C., 1987), pp. 37–68; Edward Countryman, A People in Revolution: The American Revolution and Political Society in New York, 1760–1790 (Baltimore, 1981).

man standing was only a temporary stop on the road to full proprietorship. Furthermore, they believed that the useful harmony of the workshop should serve as the model for the entire republic. Mechanics saw themselves as virtuous manufacturers, and hence the core of the commonwealth. They held politically suspect those who accumulated property without a productive trade, particularly mercantile speculators, bankers, and lawyers.[3]

Along with this commitment to the public good, republican artisans adhered to an individualist, Lockean outlook. The American Revolution ignited a spirit of expectant capitalism within the ranks of Jeffersonian partisans, including many in the artisan community. Craftsmen, already in the colonial era men of singular ambition, expected to expand their economic horizons further now that the fetters of British mercantilism were lifted and a strong American government in place. Indeed, much of their opposition to British measures had focused on the suppression of their right to participate fully in the market. The new republic held out the promise of an open accessible economy that would permit the meritorious—however humble their origins—to rise in the social order. American raw materials, combined with individual initiative and enterprise, would offer all hard-working farmers and artisans the opportunity to attain entrepreneurial independence and a better standard of living.[4] The civic humanism of Machiavelli's Florence and the individualism and contractual society of Locke went hand in hand as the end of deference and aristocracy brought forth a truly open marketplace.[5] Difficulties occurred, however, when the expectations that grew out of these ideas collided with the realities of a newly expanding economy.

3. Rock, *Artisans of the New Republic*, chaps. 1–5; Wilentz, *Chants Democratic*, chap. 1. Wilentz defines "artisan republicanism."

4. Joyce Oldham Appleby, *Capitalism and a New Social Order: The Republican Vision of the 1790s* (New York, 1984).

5. Among the important works for this discussion are J. G. A. Pocock, *The Machiavellian Moment: Florentine Political Thought and the Atlantic Republican Tradition* (Princeton, 1975); Pocock, "Virtue and Commerce in the Eighteenth Century," *Journal of Interdisciplinary History*, 3 (1972), 119–134; Lance Banning, *The Jeffersonian Persuasion: Evolution of a Party Ideology* (Ithaca, N.Y., 1978); Banning, "Jefferson Ideology Revisited: Liberal and Classical Ideas in the New American Republic," *William and Mary Quarterly*, 3d ser., 43 (1986), 3–19; Appleby, *Capitalism and a New Social Order*; Appleby, "Republicanism in Old and New Contexts," *William and Mary Quarterly*, 3d ser., 43 (1986), 20–34; Appleby, "The Social Origins of American Revolutionary Ideology," *Journal of American History*, 64 (1978), 935–958; Isaac Kramnick, "Republican Revisionism Revisited," *American Historical Review*, 87 (1982), 629–664.

4

The ambitions of American entrepreneurs grew far more rapidly and in different directions than most craftsmen could have anticipated. In New York City, the scope of this expansion can be seen in the six-fold increase in population between 1790 and 1830 (33,000 to 197,112). The value of taxable property and real estate rose even faster, with the latter reaching $95,000,000 by 1830.[6] Development on such a scale inevitably altered the world of the mechanic. The burgeoning marketplace, oriented to national and international trade, allowed artisan enterprises to extend well beyond the traditional family workshop. For successful masters this expansion meant new avenues to wealth. For journeymen, however, the picture was less bright. Larger capital requirements made it more difficult for them to become masters, especially in the expanding crafts of carpentry, masonry, shoemaking, tailoring, cabinetmaking, and printing. Too much money and too many business connections were needed to become independent. Furthermore, with the road to financial independence often obstructed, the social and economic distances between master and journeymen widened. Masters bought fine carriages and elegant brick homes; journeymen crowded into rented wooden structures with several other families. In their attempt to maximize profits and compete in expanding markets, masters cut wages and increased the available labor pool by employing cheap and lesser skilled hands.[7]

These developments ran counter to the journeymen's sense of self-worth and their place and role in society. How could the harmonious workshop of the independent artisan survive if fewer and fewer journeymen were able to reach the standing of independent proprietor? How could the free market extinguish aristocracy and guarantee a

6. For population figures see David T. Gilchrist, ed., *The Growth of the Seaport Cities, 1790–1825* (Charlottesville, Va., 1967), pp. 34–36; on real estate values see Elizabeth Blackmar, *Manhattan for Rent, 1785–1850* (Ithaca, N.Y., 1989), pp. 273–274. From 1789 to 1815 Edmund Willis has calculated for a sample ward (Fourth) a 741 percent increase in real property value ($577,000 to $4,851,700) and 1,208 percent increase in taxable personal property ($177,570 to $2,322,200). Edmund Philip Willis, "Social Origins of Political Leadership in New York City from the Revolution to 1815" (Ph.D. diss., University of California, Berkeley, 1967), pp. 113–118.
7. David J. Saposs, "Colonial and Federal Beginnings (to 1827)" in John R. Commons, et al., *History of Labour in the United States*, vol. 1 (New Haven, Conn., 1918), pp. 25–165; Rock, *Artisans*, pp. 237–294; Wilentz, *Chants Democratic*, pp. 23–48; Gilje, *Road to Mobocracy*, pp. 188–197, 253–264; W. J. Rorabaugh, *The Craft Apprentice: From Franklin to the Machine Age in America* (New York, 1986).

genuine republican society when the gap between the wealthy and the middling artisan classes increased and the influx of capital made economic independence and advancement less rather than more common?

The journeymen's confrontation with these obstacles to the fulfillment of their Revolutionary inheritance led to labor strife on a scale never before seen in New York. Many journeymen joined together to defend their wages, their jobs, and their identities. Before 1800 there were perhaps three or four strikes over these issues. Between 1800 and 1829 there were at least thirty.[8]

A strike manifesto by journeymen carpenters in 1809 revealed the republican spirit of these walkouts. In announcing their intention to desert their employers at the height of the building season, these articulate mechanics employed the words of the Declaration of Independence to assert that society owed its skilled craftsmen—who contributed so much to the commonwealth—a decent and secure living. Together with the "unalienable rights" of "life, liberty, and the pursuit of happiness," they argued that the "social compact" guaranteed "every class of society" the chance to "benefit in proportion to its usefulness." If a man fulfilled his duty to marry, bring up and educate a family, then society owed that man adequate compensation to achieve his goals.[9]

During the same period, and under the weight of the same combination of changes, sailors and waterfront workers also began to see themselves in a new light. They, too, had participated in street demonstrations during the 1760s and 1770s. The ten thousand bodies buried in the collective graves in Wallabout Bay attested to the sacrifices made by sailors held aboard prison hulks during the Revolutionary War. After 1783 many of those on the waterfront still may not have voted, but they remained active in street politics. In the early national period the American tar, or sailor, became an important symbol for the young United States, and a political rallying cry, representing some of the crosscurrents of republican ideology, was raised for "Free Trade and Sailors' Rights." Despite such slogans sailors remained vulnerable not only to the fickle and tempestuous elements at sea, but also to the depredations of pirates, warring nations, British press gangs, and the twisted discourse of diplomats. The commercial

8. Gilje, *Road to Mobocracy*, pp. 194–195.
9. *American Citizen*, April 10, 1809. See the Carpenters' strike manifesto in Chapter 2.

boom that sustained the American economy for most of the nation's first fifty years created great demand for waterfront labor. But merchants were loath to share their profits. Instead they reduced crews and pushed laborers as far as they dared. In reaction sailors and waterfront workers occasionally organized to strike for wages and to defend their sense of self-worth against the aggressive assault of market forces and a repressive labor system. By the 1820s and 1830s articulate spokesmen from among the ranks of sailors emerged to take republican rhetoric seriously. One such seaman, James Durand, decried the use of the lash aboard American naval vessels and declared that "such outrages on human nature ought not to be permitted by a government that boasts of liberty."[10] Samuel Leech, a tar who objected to autocratic control of a sailor's labor, proclaimed that "a man should be secured the rights of a citizen, as well on the planks as on the soil of his country."[11]

Revolutionary ideology, along with social and economic conditions, had a more complex and diffuse impact on youths and apprentices. When Thomas Paine attacked the king as a scion of a bastard, he also questioned all inherited hierarchies. The new egalitarianism that circulated freely in New York in the late eighteenth and early nineteenth centuries left many young men exhilarated and clamoring to attack even the hierarchy of the workshop. Impatient apprentices ran off before completing their time and increasingly refused to concede traditional deference to their elders. Economic and social changes encouraged this revolt against patriarchy. To cut costs and improve profits, masters hired apprentices by the day, half trained them, and used them as a semiskilled labor force. In the process, masters abdicated full responsibility for these young men after work hours. Freed from an overprotective paternalism, released to roam the city, and encouraged by the rough egalitarianism of the streets, apprentices in the 1810s and 1820s began to develop a special and rowdy youth cult of their own.[12]

10. James R. Durand, *James Durand: An Able Seaman of 1812* . . . , George S. Brooke, ed. (New Haven, Conn., 1926), pp. 18–19.
11. Samuel Leech, *Thirty Years from Home, or a Voice From the Main Deck* . . . (Boston, 1843), pp. 237–238.
12. Gilje, *Road to Mobocracy*, pp. 253–264; John R. Gillis, *Youth and History: Tradition and Change in European Age Relations, 1700–Present* (New York, 1974); Joseph F. Kett, *Rites of Passage: Adolescence in America, 1790 to the Present* (New York, 1977).

African Americans, too, experienced dramatic change in New York during the early days of the republic. The outbreak of the Revolutionary War provided an opportunity for blacks to take the initiative and obtain their freedom. Thousands of runaway slaves flocked to the British, who offered them their freedom. These blacks thus participated in what can be considered the most successful slave rebellion in American history.[13] The egalitarian logic implicit in republican ideology accelerated emancipation. Many New York slaveholders ultimately decided to manumit their slaves, rather than sustain a contradiction to their principles. After some resistance, and a good deal of reluctance about the future of free blacks, the state legislature passed a gradual emancipation law in 1799 that, with later revisions, brought freedom to all of the city's slaves by July 4, 1827.[14] In the meantime, as the number of slaves dwindled from 2,369 in 1790 to 518 in 1820 to 0 in 1827, the total number of African Americans in the city grew from 3,262 in 1790 to 13,976 in 1830.[15]

Although many of the city's African Americans at first retained a hope for greater and equal participation in a free society, ultimately New York law curtailed their political rights and blacks confronted reduced economic opportunity. In the face of these obstacles, and in part as a function of a self-confidence derived from the age of revolution, New York's blacks molded a community identity around "African" associations, churches, schools, and other institutions.[16]

The impact of revolutionary ideology, coupled with the effects of subsequent social and economic change, is most difficult to assess for women. Women lived through the same trials wrought by revolution

13. Graham Russell Hodges, "Black Revolt around New York Bay, 1775–1783," in *New York in the Age of the Constitution*, Paul A. Gilje and William Pencak, eds. (Rutherford, N.J., 1992).

14. Edgar J. McManus, *A History of Negro Slavery in New York* (Syracuse, N.Y., 1966), pp. 152–179; Leo H. Hirsch, Jr., "The Negro in New York, 1783 to 1865," *Journal of Negro History*, 16 (1931), 382–473; Gary B. Nash, "Forging Freedom: The Emancipation Experience in Northern Seaport Cities, 1775–1820," in *Slavery and Freedom in the Age of the American Revolution*, Ira Berlin and Ronald Hoffman, eds. (Charlottesville, Va., 1983), pp. 3–48.

15. Ira Rosenwaike, *Population History of New York City* (Syracuse, N.Y., 1972), pp. 18, 36.

16. Nash, "Forging Freedom," 3–48; Gilje, *Road to Mobocracy*, pp. 145–170; Shane White, "'We Dwell in Safety and Pursue Our Honest Callings': Free Blacks in New York City, 1783–1810," *Journal of American History*, 75 (1988), pp. 445–470.

and war that artisans, sailors, male youths, and blacks did. Indeed, women lost homes, were brutalized by armies, suffered absent husbands, sons, and fathers, and experienced food shortages. At times they participated in crowd actions, joined in boycotts of British goods, and cheered or jeered egalitarian rhetoric. The decline of deference and the challenges to patriarchy ought to have affected their status as it had other groups of laborers. Yet the evidence for great changes is mixed.

Some scholars argue that the revolution brought the household— the traditional workplace for women—from the private to the public sphere and that women, because of their wartime experience, gained greater control over their lives. Moreover, the republican emphasis on the development of a virtuous citizenry theoretically elevated the status of women. Mothers and wives became the special repositories of virtue and self-sacrifice, charged with the guardianship of the next generation of republican citizens (little boys) and the moral guidance of their husbands.[17]

The problem with this interpretation is that it is unclear how much of these republican values applied to the lives of New York's laboring women. For women on the top of society, or for those who aspired to the top, it was a reality. But what about an "Aunt Jenny" who danced to engraver Alexander Anderson's fiddle for a penny,[18] or the "hot corn girl" who sold her wares on the city's streets? For these women republican identity held no meaning. If anything, republican ideology may have left laboring women in a weaker position. Republicanism idealized the individual who was independent of the influence and control of others. Men were independent; laboring women were dependent and not to be trusted. At least one scholar has argued that republican ideas reinvigorated a misogyny that long had been a part of Anglo-American culture, and that after the American

17. Linda K. Kerber, *Women of the Republic: Intellect and Ideology in Revolutionary America* (Chapel Hill, N.C., 1980); Mary Beth Norton, *Liberty's Daughters: The Revolutionary Experience of American Women, 1750–1800* (Boston, 1980); Jacqueline S. Reiner, "Rearing the Republican Child: Attitudes and Practices in Post-Revolutionary Philadelphia," *William and Mary Quarterly*, 3d ser., 39 (1982), 150–163; Jan Lewis, "The Republican Wife: Virtue and Seduction in the Early Republic," ibid., 44 (1987), 689–721; Howard B. Rock, "A Woman's Place in Jeffersonian New York: The View from the *Independent Mechanic*," *New York History*, 63 (1982), 435–459.
18. See Alexander Anderson's diary in Chapter 1.

Revolution the image of woman as Eve—passionate and weak—in-tensified. According to Christine Stansell, this negative image of la-boring women as dependent and lacking "the moral status necessary for citizenship" permeated all levels of society, and, while these ideas on gender were never explicit, they were built into the culture.[19]

Ultimately, however, the same ideological, social, and economic forces that altered the world of artisans, sailors, youths, and blacks did affect the world of their mothers, sisters, and daughters. When journeymen found employment less regular, women had to search for work outside the household to augment family income. When a sailor left port, or any laborer temporarily or permanently left home, women had to eke out an existence somehow. Many women labored as domestics, others became hucksters, seamstresses, boardinghouse keepers, and storekeepers. A handful became artisans. Many more found themselves cast into the streets to fend for themselves, often depending on charity or resorting to prostitution.[20]

Although the possibility of earning an income outside the tradi-tional sphere created hardship for women, it also held out oppor-tunities. Single women—daughters of laborers—no longer had to live in a constant state of dependency. Like their male counterparts, young single women now had the option of turning to the streets, the dance halls, or the promenade on the Bowery to be independent, even if only for an evening. The breakdown of patriarchy, which was an indirect and unanticipated result of republican ideology, thus freed those women to develop a new identity. This same independence, however, carried with it serious risks. In this new youth culture young women eagerly engaged in different forms of sexual behavior with young men, sometimes but not always including sexual intercourse, in an effort to gain both personal pleasure and tangible rewards. Without the protective umbrella of the family or the neighborhood, many women were left vulnerable to exploitation by male counter-parts. The flirtatious girl on the streets of New York, described by the Society for the Prevention of Juvenile Delinquency, was a product of the new world that emerged in the aftermath of the American Revo-lution in the same manner as the rowdy male apprentice on New

19. Christine Stansell, *City of Women: Sex and Class in New York, 1789–1860*, (New York, 1986), pp. 20–30.
20. Ibid.

Figure 1. New York was a thriving seaport guided by its merchant elite. In this part of Francis Guy's famous painting, merchants can be seen inspecting their wares or talking of prices and trade conditions as other workers labor to move the goods. Francis Guy, *Tontine Coffee House,* 1797, section, oil, NYHS

Year's, the striking sailor or journeyman, or the emancipated black was.[21]

The political and ideological transformations that accompanied and flowed from the American Revolution and the economic growth of the early republic fed off and encouraged one another. The rise of equality fostered economic growth by releasing individuals from the bonds of hierarchy and deference, encouraging the pursuit of wealth and the exploitation that it entailed. Likewise, the new egalitarian economic and social world created the conditions that enabled the political ideal of equality to thrive. In few places did this dialectic between politics and ideology on the one hand, and economy and society on the other, occur with such rapidity and openness as in New York City. In portraying the world of working men and women, therefore, it is essential to visualize the settings that formed the backdrop for these great changes. During the momentous years between 1760 and 1830, as New York City underwent the transformation from a provincial port to the largest metropolis in the new republic, armies came and left, population shifted, new people moved in, and the city began its relentless march up Manhattan Island.

Although it was an important outpost of the British empire, New York, with 15,000 inhabitants, was less significant in 1760 than either Philadelphia or Boston in both population and shipping tonnage. Its economy was dominated by the sea, which surrounded the city on three sides, and most New Yorkers earned their living in one way or the other from shipping: as merchants, artisans, day laborers, dock workers, or sailors. Wealth during the eighteenth century had become increasingly stratified, and merchants dominated politics and the economy.

During the 1760s and early 1770s, population and trade continued to grow, despite the upheavals created by the imperial crisis. Then came war and independence. In the spring and summer of 1776 many people abandoned the city as the Continental Army arrived to defend New York, and, after several American military reverses, the British army occupied the city. Devastating fires ensued, destroying whole sections of New York. The British army turned public buildings and churches into barracks, stables, and prisons. Large numbers of soldiers

21. Ibid.

and sailors passed in and out of the city. As the war continued, flee-
ing loyalists from all over North America swarmed into the city, and
its population began to grow again. The loyalists remained until November 25, 1783, when the last British troops withdrew. Once again
the city was left half empty, as many of the loyalists departed for
Canada, the West Indies, or Great Britain. Indeed, with its vacant
houses, burned-out ruins that had never been rebuilt, and a shrunken
population, New York became the shell of a city.[22]

New Yorkers, however, were a resilient lot, even in the late eighteenth century. An expansion began and continued unabated, despite
the city losing its role as the capital of both state and nation. Business opportunities and trade drew old revolutionaries and many new-
comers to the port.[23] Because the staggering demographic growth
placed a tremendous strain on real estate and housing, the city
quickly encroached upon the farm- and meadowland that bordered it
on both the East and Hudson rivers. Public and private projects also
extended the city by filling in shoreline along the two rivers, as well
as swamps and ponds like the infamous Collect just north of the present City Hall (built in 1811). Some of the new buildings were fancy
brick structures, such as the homes of many of the elite which dotted
that grand avenue New Yorkers called Broadway. Closer to the waterfront, and over the old Collect, wooden buildings predominated. In
the most crowded sections, where even the cellars were used for lodging, houses were crammed up next to each other, alleys cut narrow
and shadowy paths to larger thoroughfares, and tenements became
the homes of the poor. By the late 1820s this sprawling metropolis
covered nearly a third of Manhattan.

Construction and renovation also marked the older sections of the
city. As one commentator explained in 1828: "A few years, and

22. Thomas Jefferson Wertenbaker, *Father Knickerbocker Rebels: New York City during the Revolution* (New York, 1948); Oscar Theodore Barck, Jr., *New York City during
the War for Independence: With Special Reference to the Period of British Occupation* (New
York, 1931).

23. Sidney I. Pomerantz, *New York, An American City, 1783–1803: A Study of
Urban Life,* 2d ed. (Port Washington, N.Y., 1965); E. Wilder Spaulding, *New York in
the Critical Period, 1783–1789* (New York, 1932); Thomas C. Cochran, *New York in
the Confederation: An Economic Study* (New York, 1932); Michael Kammen, "'The
Promised Sunshine of the Future,' Reflections on Economic Growth and Social
Change in Post-Revolutionary New York," in *New Opportunities in a New Nation: The
Development of New York after the Revolution,* Manfred Jonas and Robert V. Wells, eds.
(Schenectady, N.Y., 1982), pp. 109–143.

sometimes only a few months effect such revolutions that the citizen would scarcely be able to identify places with which he was well acquainted. The rage for alteration, for pulling down and building up, for enlarging and embellishing, is eternally at work achieving wonders."[24] In this bustling environment where real estate was at a premium, there was little respect for older buildings and, as Timothy Dwight declared in the early 1800s, "New York almost everywhere wears the vivid appearance of an entirely new city."[25]

At any time of day or night the cry of "fire" struck a note of terror in all New Yorkers. Every blaze had the potential of spreading and causing great damage to property and lives. In December 1796 a big fire swept through a commercial district, destroying several stores and houses, wiping out $74,000 in buildings and as much as one million dollars in stores and merchandise.[26] Stoves and fireplaces for heating contained special dangers in starting fires in the cold weather: In 1818 a conflagration consumed Richard Yeo's tanning shop on Van-dewater Street, quickly engulfed nearby carpenter shops, and then went on to destroy rental housing on both Skinner and Vandewater streets.[27] The poor suffered the most difficult losses in these blazes since they lived closest to the margin. In 1829 a fire in an alley running from Cross to Augustus Street destroyed a cluster of twenty small wooden houses and damaged many others. The impoverished residents—between two and five families occupied each building— lost all of their possessions and were left homeless.[28]

The fires that occasionally punctuated the lives of New Yorkers were only a small part of the complex of sights, sounds, and smells that assaulted everyone on the city streets. Open-air vendors called out to advertise their wares, which ranged from hot corn to oysters. Whenever a butcher got an exceptionally fine cut of beef or a number of sheep, he paraded through the principal avenues—Broadway, the Bowery, Greenwich and Canal streets—preceded by a band of music

24. *Statesman*, June 25, 1828.
25. Timothy Dwight, *Travels in New England and New York*, vol. 3, Barbara Miller Solomon, ed. (Cambridge, Mass., 1969; orig. pub. New Haven, Conn., 1822), p. 330.
26. *New York Journal*, December 13, 1796. See also Augustine E. Costello, *Our Firemen: A History of the New York Fire Department, Volunteer and Paid* (New York, 1887).
27. *National Advocate*, December 7, 1818.
28. *New York Gazette*, April 20, 1829.

Figure 2. An 1813 scene on Water Street near the docks. At the right is a boot maker's sho
with the traditional sign. Behind the gate is a boardinghouse, possibly owned by Daniel Davi
where single journeymen and apprentices commonly lived. Next to that, with the cloth
hanging on display, is a tailor's store, probably of Elizabeth Davis. Adjoining her store is
grocery where food and drink were readily available. In the foreground is the dog killer
work. Artist William P. Chappel was born in New York to Huguenot parents and earned h
living as a tinsmith. He painted this and other such scenes in New York late in his lif
perhaps in the 1870s, from memory. William P. Chappel, *The Dog Killer and Cart, Water St*
oil on cardboard, MMNY

and followed by other butchers from his market in their aprons and
shirt sleeves. Stopping in front of select houses, the butcher allowed
customers to choose the cut they wanted.[29] Less amusing were the
cartmen who violated the sensibilities of the more genteel with their
curses. These truckers picked their way through crowds and debris,
and, if there was an opening in the traffic, raced along at breakneck

29. Charles H. Haswell, *Reminiscences of an Octogenerian of the City of New York
(1816–1860)* (New York, 1896), p. 29.

speed (contrary to corporation ordinances). Apprentices who should have been at work harassed passersby, bumping into the men, rudely blackguarding women, and flippantly squirting tobacco juice on ladies' skirts.[30] Bawdy prostitutes, as one Police Office resolution stated, openly "perambulate[d] Broadway, and other principal streets of the city, making a public exhibition of their persons, and a public pronouncement of their course of life."[31] On a corner a street politician might harangue an audience temporarily drawn from the groceries and taverns nearby. Or the speaker might be some thunder-and-lightening evangelical such as "the well-known eccentric Johnny Edwards," who led an outdoor revival in the city park in 1810, and who for years afterward rode across town in his scale-beam cart to Essex Street Market, where, "getting on his favorite rock, he would entertain his hearers by his singular and pointed remarks."[32] In this crowded and charged atmosphere, with a mix of politics, people, and opinions, arguments broke out continually. Sometimes the shouting and pushing resulted from high-minded discussion. More often the cause was petty and practical, such as two shopkeepers fighting about the overflow of goods and merchandise on the sidewalk, obstructing the easy access of pedestrians.[33]

In addition to all these characters, dogs and pigs also roamed the streets, scavenging among the refuse and garbage there. In 1811, during a citywide effort to bring the canine population under control, dog catchers snatched over two thousand dogs off the streets, executing and burying them in the fields north of the city.[34] Hogs, however, were a more serious problem. They groveled and snorted about, were far more obstreperous, clogged and dug ruts in the thoroughfares, and occasionally attacked people. This "swinish multitude," as one wit termed them, caused a heated political controversy in the early decades of the 1800s. The city fathers wanted to drive the pigs from the streets, while the poor, who saw their swine as an important source of

30. *National Advocate*, September 14, 1815; *New York Evening Post*, February 28, 1818.

31. *New York Evening Post*, September 27, 1820.

32. Thomas F. De Voe, *The Marketbook: Containing a Historical Account of the Public Markets in New York, Boston, Philadelphia, and Brooklyn . . .* , vol. 1 (New York, 1862), p. 480. See also Gilje, *Road to Mobocracy*, pp. 211–214, 219.

33. For merchandise in the streets see *New York Journal*, December 31, 1790. For rowdiness in New York see Gilje, *Road to Mobocracy*, pp. 235–264.

34. Gilje, *Road to Mobocracy*, pp. 224–227.

Figure 3. Animals, and particularly hogs, roamed the streets of New York at will. Although a nuisance and a serious danger to pedestrians, they were necessary for ridding the streets of garbage and as a source of food for the poor during the winter. Baroness Hyde de Neuville, *Looking South from Chambers Street,* 1808, detail. NYPL

income and protein, insisted on their right to let these animals run free in the city.[35]

Of course, dogs and pigs did serve a useful purpose; they helped to clean streets that were notoriously dirty. In 1821 one complainant noted that the city contained "scarcely a street, particularly a wide one, but exhibits heaps of mud and dirt of the most offensive kind, raked up in the middle." This mixture of animal excrement, garbage,

---

35. Ibid., pp. 224–232; for the "swinish multitude," see the *New York Evening Post,* October 10, 1816. See also Howard B. Rock, ed., *The New York City Artisan, 1789–1825: A Documentary History* (Albany, N.Y., 1989), pp. 41–44; and Rock, "A Delicate Balance: The Mechanics and the City in the Age of Jefferson," *New-York Historical Society Quarterly,* 63 (1979), 101–111.

and mud—commonly called "corporation pudding" in reference to the city government—was both odious and odorous, and proved a danger "to persons passing in a carriage" at night.[36] Some streets, like Canal Street, had an open sewer running the length of it, and the resulting stench, blamed on the distilleries in the area, was difficult to bear.[37] To help ease the congestion and protect the sensitivities of almost every New Yorker, privies were cleaned out at night by "necessary tub men," mostly blacks, who then sold their collections as fertilizer. During the summer months, when New Yorkers slept with their windows open, the stench was so bad from these "night carts" passing by that residents complained of being awakened by the smell.[38]

This filth, which was distasteful enough, had an important impact on an often overlooked aspect of everyday life—the supply of clean drinking water. In the eighteenth century the most noted water supply was the tea water pump located near the northeast corner of Orange and Chatham streets. As the city expanded, wells were dug and town pumps placed at almost every corner. Starting in the 1790s the Manhattan Company piped water from its own well into the houses of the well-to-do in the lower part of the city. But as the dirt, excrement, and other refuse percolated down to the water table, well water became increasingly tainted. Carters carried hogsheads around the city and sold water at a penny a gallon, but since this water, too, was often polluted, and as urban growth made distribution around the city more problematic, this system also became unacceptable. Not until the 1830s and 1840s, with the opening of an aqueduct from upstate, were working New Yorkers provided with a palatable and healthy water supply.[39]

During the early nineteenth century distinctive neighborhoods that retained their special characteristics for decades emerged. Pearl Street, for example, became the mercantile center of the city, its broad byway lined with stores carrying the finest imported and domestic dry goods. Most of the rich lived in the lower part of the city.

36. *New York Evening Post*, April 3, 1821; Haswell, *Reminiscences of New York*, p. 168.
37. *New York Evening Post*, July 23, 1821.
38. Ibid., June 18, 1821.
39. J. Hampden Dougherty, "The Years of Municipal Vigor, 1837–1847," in *The Memorial History of the City of New-York: From its First Settlement to the Year 1852*, vol. 3, James Grant Wilson, ed. (New York, 1893), pp. 393–406.

Figure 4. Water in New York was often of poor quality. The well known Tea Water pump on the north side of Chatham Street offered good water that was sold by peddlers like the one pictured here. Notice the typical outer ward homes with back yards for animals. Numerous families would live in such homes. William P. Chappel, *Old Tea Water Pump and Cart,* detail, oil on cardboard, MMNY

Affluent artisans resided in the first and third wards between Broadway and the Hudson River. North of this area, centered around Church and Chapel streets was a poorer neighborhood where the homes of humbler mechanics interspersed with bawdy houses. Over the old Collect was the sixth ward, where the city's least desirable housing was built. By the 1820s, poor workers, Irish immigrants, and blacks filled that neighborhood. The heart of this ward and the most infamous section of the city was Five Points, the intersection of Cross, Orange, and Anthony streets. In this neighborhood "unblushing indecency—haggard poverty—bloated vice and beastly drunken-

ness" predominated.[40] Nine houses in a triangular block that comprised one of the five points contained eight groceries and one base-
ment porter house, as well as four lodgings "of a worse character" in
the second stories. Inside the "garrets and cellars" of these ramshackle
dwellings, one observer noted, lived "the vilest rabble, black &
white, mixt together." On Cross and Anthony streets over half the
houses included either a grog shop or grocery.[41] Visiting this area,
with its "rum holes," prostitutes, and gangs, became a dangerous yet
adventuresome expedition. In the second and fourth wards to the
east, artisanal neighborhoods intermingled with rougher waterfront
areas, especially along Catherine Street and, in the seventh ward, at
Corlear's Hook.[42]

Workers often sought amusement in both the more questionable
neighborhoods and in drinking establishments closer to home. Those
same brothels and bars that repulsed many middle-class moralists,
who viewed these dens of vice as "cancer like," acted as a magnet
that drew workers to them.[43] Many laboring New Yorkers gravitated
toward the Five Points, Bancker and Henry streets, or Corlear's
Hook, or they congregated in the myriad groceries and grog shops in
their own neighborhoods. These local taverns had an important function as purveyors of gossip and group identity. Grocers often advanced loans and lines of credit to neighbors and customers, which
helped to cushion the most serious effects of difficult times. The groceries also offered a moment of fellowship and mirth that was very
important to New Yorkers.[44]

The working class had other sources of amusement besides drinking. The streets themselves were arenas of excitement, given the
crowds, the noise, and the varied people and scenes that constantly
glided by. Everyone knew where and when the local cock fight would
take place. Occasionally butchers held bull baitings, though officials
frowned upon this activity and had all but stopped it by 1820.[45] Theaters were also important gathering places for the working class. In the

40. *Statesman*, March 27, 1829.
41. *New York Evening Post*, August 21, 1829.
42. Gilje, *Road to Mobocracy*, pp. 87–90, 127–128, 160–161, 239–241, 260–261.
43. *New York Evening Post*, August 21, 1829.
44. Rock, *Artisans of the New Republic*, pp. 296–298; Wilentz, *Chants Democratic*,
pp. 53–54.
45. De Voe, *The Market Book*, p. 389; *New York Evening Post*, July 30, 1807, and
September 7, 1821; *Commercial Advertiser*, July 6 and 21, 1801; *American Citizen*, July
1, 1808.

opening decade of the nineteenth century rowdies would fill the upper tiers and, as the actors struggled through their lines, entertain themselves by throwing fruit, nuts, and anything else at the stage and those who sat below. During the 1820s the working class got its own theater, the Lafayette Circus, that had shorter pieces, dancing girls, and horseback riding.[46] On Sundays the open areas on the northern rim of the city, like Washington Parade Ground and Lispenard Meadows, filled with boys and young men who played ball and other games in violation of sabbath observance laws.[47]

Despite the ribaldry, working-class culture did not exclude religion. Many industrious New Yorkers attended church, avoided the amusements described above, and lived upright lives.[48] In 1811 there were fifty-five churches in the city; by 1821, seventy-one. Many catered to artisans and workers.[49] "Johnny Edwards," a scale-beam maker, ran his own church in his Broome Street residence. Upholsterer Amos Broad set up his evangelical operation on Rose Street, but his ministrations were so bizarre that he repeatedly incurred the wrath of mobs during the 1800s. Most religious workers were more serious and attended regularly organized services.[50]

New York working-class culture had its own calendar that moved to the rhythm of the seasons. The happiest of times for New York workers began about the middle of March. New construction then commenced in earnest, and wages rose to their highest levels. The warmer weather brought more people out into the street. Young boys flew kites, adults scurried off to work, and the city, shaking off the winter frost, came humming back to life. April saw added excitement as politicians drummed up support for the city corporation elections. The highlight of the next month was May 1, when, for reasons attributed to old Dutch traditions, leases expired throughout the city, and it seemed almost all New Yorkers packed their belongings into a cart and moved. This peculiar practice created great uproar and confusion and was one more piece of evidence of spiraling real estate

46. Gilje, Road to Mobocracy, pp. 246–253.
47. New York Evening Post, April 21, 1807; June 23, 1815, March 25 and December 22, 1828.
48. Rock, Artisans of the New Republic, pp. 304–312; Wilentz, Chants Democratic, pp. 77–87.
49. Dwight, Travels, 3:315–316.
50. Gilje, Road to Mobocracy, pp. 206–220.

costs. New Yorkers felt compelled to move since their landlords tried to squeeze every cent they could from resident tenants, and received better offers from those seeking housing.[51] June was the most pleasant month, during which New Yorkers prepared for the fireworks, parades, and public ceremonies that occurred on the Fourth of July.[52]

As the sweltering heat of the summer began to build in July and August, fears intensified over the possibility of another bout with yellow fever. In some years New York escaped that scourge, but beginning in 1790 repeated visitation of the "bilious fever" decimated the city. The more affluent escaped to cooler and healthier climes on the northern end of Manhattan or in the surrounding countryside. Poor residents, especially those in the hardest-hit waterfront districts, remained to cope with the epidemic as best they could. Business ground to a halt as the death toll mounted. In 1799 the *Argus* reported that within a few months "a city with an abundant population, and an extensive trade, transformed into a deserted one, and exhibiting the complete contrast of its former appearance."[53] The worst years for yellow fever were 1795, 1798, 1799, 1803, 1819, and 1822. In 1795 as many as 525 died, and in 1799, 1,524, most of whom were poor working New Yorkers.[54] The fever disappeared soon after the first freeze, but then jobs became scarce and wages were lowered.

The cold season, with its shorter working day, brought hardship that was only temporarily relieved by the November elections for national and state offices, the anniversary of the British evacuation on November 25, and the celebration of Christmas and the new year. January and February were probably the most difficult months. Scanty resources were nearly consumed. In January 1797, for example, "Six Hundred Journeymen Mechanics and Tradesmen now out of Employ" petitioned that "in consequence of the season, without work; and many of them, by reason of large families, in want of sufficient FIRE and FOOD," wished to serve the city as watchmen to be on the look-

51. *New York Journal*, April 29 and May 6, 1795; *New York Evening Post*, February 21, 1825.

52. *New York Evening Post*, June 23, 1815; June 21, 1816; June 22, 1829.

53. *Argus*, October 10, 1799.

54. John Duffy, *A History of Public Health in New York City*, vol. 1 (New York, 1968); James Hardie, *An Account of the Malignant Fever, Lately Prevalent in the City of New-York* (New York, 1799).

out for fires.[55] Only the warmer weather of March, and the renewal of the yearly cycle, could fully alleviate the difficulties of winter for New Yorkers.

Other conditions besides the seasons affected the work lives of New Yorkers. The great European wars that began with the French Revolution and lasted almost unabated until Napoleon's final defeat in 1815 provided many opportunities and some hazards. Merchants could make great profits as neutral traders in a world at war. New markets opened in Europe, the West Indies, Latin America, and, in an unrelated development, in the Pacific, bringing high employment to tradesmen connected to the shipping industry: shipbuilders, sailmakers, and even coopers. Sailors, as well, found work plentiful. But the vicissitudes of war also created problems; repeated war scares and ship seizures by both France and Britain meant that profits could quickly disappear.[56] Similarly, cycles of boom and bust affected employment patterns. Economic downturns, such as occurred during postwar adjustments and after the Panic of 1819, created hardships because of deflation, bank failures and inadequate currency.

During the good periods, however, the constant cacophony of the streets, the fetid odors, continual commotion, and persistent industry left many visitors breathless. Timothy Dwight observed that "the bustle in the streets, the perpetual activity of the carts, the noise and hurry at the docks which on three sides encircle the city; the sounds of saws, axes, and hammers at the shipyards; the continually repeated views of the numerous buildings rising in almost every part of it, and the multitude of workmen employed upon them, form as lively a specimen of the 'busy hum of populous cities,' as can be imagined."[57]

By 1830 New York City, like other great urban centers, was a maze of contradictions. The city was a teeming metropolis that stood on the brink of greatness. Its size, centrality, and economic power would soon outstrip all rivals. Everyone who visited Gotham commented on the hustle and bustle, the constant tearing down and building up, and the ever-present and vibrating activity.[58] By 1830 New York

55. *Argus*, January 14, 1797.
56. Robert Greenlaugh Albion, "New York Port in the New Republic, 1783–1793," *New York History*, 21 (1940), 388–403; Albion, *The Rise of the New York Port, 1815–1860* (New York, 1939); Gilchrist, ed., *The Growth of Seaport Cities*.
57. Dwight, *Travels*, 3:330.
58. See ibid., 3:329–330.

crafts, banks, and insurance companies had grown into major manufacturing and financial interests, joining the prominence of the city's
shipping industry. Immigrants streamed in, as New York became the
clearinghouse for new arrivals from Europe.[59]

Despite the enormous capital that either entered or was produced
in New York by its advancing economy, many problems and inequal-
ities remained.[60] Epidemics such as yellow fever persisted as an ever-
present fear, especially in the poorer waterfront district.[61] Hardships
caused by the pulse and rhythm of the seasons continued, creating
periodic adversity for many workers during the harsh winter months.[62]
Even during milder months, however, unskilled laborers, women who
had to make it on their own, new immigrants, and blacks engaged in
a seemingly endless struggle for survival. Some workers, largely the
most skilled journeyman craftsmen, in an effort to bring their case
into the political arena, organized a Workingman's party in 1828 and
1829, but by 1830 it was being absorbed by the political operatives of
the Jacksonian Democrats.[63] Consequently, few articulate spokesmen
remained to represent many of the city's workers. Yet students of
history in the twentieth century, recognizing the central place of
workers in America and examining sources such as those in this
book, can listen to these workers and gain an insight into their daily
rhythm of life, as well as their triumphs and defeats.

59. Robert Ernst, *Immigrant Life in New York City, 1825–1863* (New York, 1949);
Wilentz, *Chants Democratic*, pp. 107–142.

60. Edward Pessen, *Riches, Class, and Power Before the Civil War* (Lexington, Mass.,
1973).

61. [Samuel L. Mitchell], *Hints Towards Promoting the Health and Cleanliness of the
City of New-York* (New York, 1802).

62. Gilje, *Road to Mobocracy*, pp. 193–197.

63. Wilentz, *Chants Democratic*, pp. 145–216.

1

APPRENTICES AND YOUTHS:
Freedom, Ambition, and Tradition

During the revolutionary and early national periods, apprenticeship was an important component of New York's labor system. In the ideal apprenticeship, based upon European examples, a youth bound himself to a master craftsman through articles of indenture that stipulated mutual responsibilities. The master ordinarily promised to instruct the apprentice in his trade over a course of years, usually to age twenty-one, and in return the youth agreed to work diligently at the tasks the master required. This contract often included other assurances. The master usually undertook to teach the apprentice to read and write, provide food and housing, and protect and guide his moral welfare—in other words, to act as a surrogate father. At the completion of the indenture the apprentice-turned-journeyman was to be given a set of clothes and tools. At that point the youth would have gained enough training to start out on his own in the hope of one day setting up shop for himself. Because of the ever-present demand for labor in America, the reality of life as an apprentice did not always match the ideal. The story of America's best known apprentice, Benjamin Franklin, attests to the difficulties in sustaining this labor system even during the colonial period. Franklin broke his indenture to his brother in Boston to seek employment as a journeyman in other cities.

In the decades surrounding 1800, the ranks of apprentices expanded as the artisanal labor force grew in burgeoning urban centers like New York. But although apprenticeship remained the best way to learn a trade and gain independence, the system began to show greater strain in the aftermath of the American Revolution. Masters enlisted more and more apprentices, paid them a wage but only half-trained them, and used these boys as a cheap source of labor to drive down the wages of skilled journeymen. Masters also began to abdicate their responsibility for their apprentices during nonworking hours. These developments did not occur uniformly in all trades, but were extensive enough to transform the world of the apprentice.[1]

In the long run this commercialization of the workplace, which either preceded or operated in tandem with mechanization and indus-trialization, meant the end of the craft work structure and led to the economic decline of journeymen as skilled tradesmen. To the eight-een-year-old boy, who now had coins jingling in his pocket and an independence of action off the job, the situation did not look so bleak. For him, working at a wage less than a journeyman's was far preferable to laboring under an indenture that provided no salary. Unmarried, he could obtain cheap board and housing and spend his money on drink, theater, and carousing. Such economic freedom al-lowed him to participate in a new youth cult that in the early 1800s created increasing problems for the maintenance of public order.[2]

Traditionally, all boys between the ages of twelve and twenty-two were lumped together into the general category of youths. Under close supervision of parents, guardians, and masters, they were inte-grated into the labor system through apprenticeship and other forms of indenture as servants, farm laborers, or even seamen. Nonetheless, their position between childhood and adulthood in some ways re-mained nebulous. To help deal with this awkward ambiguity, youths were allowed moments of misrule on certain proscribed holidays.[3] In

1. W. J. Rorabaugh, *The Craft Apprentice: From Franklin to the Machine Age in America* (New York, 1986); David J. Saposs, "Colonial and Federal Beginnings (to 1827)," in John R. Commons, et al., *History of Labour in the United States*, 1 (New York, 1918), pp. 114–118; Howard B. Rock, *Artisans of the New Republic: The Trades-men of New York City in the Age of Jefferson* (New York, 1979), pp. 237–294.

2. Paul A. Gilje, *The Road to Mobocracy: Popular Disorder in New York City, 1763–1834* (Chapel Hill, N.C., 1987), pp. 253–264.

3. John R. Gillis, *Youth and History: Tradition and Change in European Age Relations, 1700–Present* (New York, 1974); and Joseph Kett, *Rites of Passage: Adolescence in America, 1790 to Present* (New York, 1977).

New York City during the colonial period those holidays fell upon New Year's Day and Guy Fawkes Day. During such festivities, and, indeed, on a day-to-day basis as well, the youth peer group was a crucial frame of reference.[4]

The new social and economic circumstances of the early nineteenth century made that peer group even more important. No longer closely tied to masters and guardians, these youths clung together in gangs that turned to rowdy behavior not just on special nights, but, as the record of William Otter's activities indicate (see below), on any evening they chose. The resulting disorder left masters dismayed, but, because of changes in the work structure, powerless.[5]

In an effort to control the uncontrollable, masters began to extol the virtues of the craftsmanship that their entrepreneurial activities were destroying. Rather than asserting the moral guidance that theoretically had been theirs once, they created schools, libraries, churches, and other institutions for apprentices. These efforts met with mixed success. Bound apprentices, like Franklin one hundred years earlier, ran away from indentures that they believed inhibited their economic and personal independence. The rise of unruly youth continued, despite the efforts of reformers.[6]

"Endeavoured . . . to Excel My Fellow Apprentices"
STEPHEN ALLEN, THE GOOD APPRENTICE

The Revolutionary War created both hardships and opportunities. Tory James Leonard used his connections with the occupying British forces in New York City to his best advantage in his sail loft. Privateers being fitted out to attack whig (patriot) shipping needed canvas, as did the commissary department to supply bread bags to the

4. Gilje, Road to Mobocracy, pp. 19–30, 253–260.
5. Ibid., pp. 253–264. See also Herbert Asbury, The Gangs of New York: An Informal History of the Underworld (New York, 1928); David R. Johnson, Policing the Urban Underworld: The Impact of Crime on the Development of the American Police, 1800–1887 (Philadelphia, 1979), pp. 29–30, 79–89; Bruce Laurie, "Fire Companies and Gangs in Southwark: The 1840s," in Allen F. Davis and Mark H. Haller, eds., The Peoples of Philadelphia: A History of Ethnic Groups and Lower Class Life, 1790–1940 (Philadelphia, 1973), pp. 71–87.
6. Robert S. Pickett, House of Refuge: Origins of Juvenile Reform in New York State, 1815–1857 (Syracuse, N.Y., 1969).

army. Leonard could thus well use the services of apprentice Stephen Allen. For his part, Allen was glad to learn a trade and to gain the protection from British press gangs which Leonard provided.

Beginning his apprenticeship about 1780 when he was twelve, Allen found life difficult. Living and working conditions were rough, and the loyalist attacks on his whig sympathies were not always easy to tolerate. In this reminiscence (from "The Memoirs of Stephen Allen," typescript, NYHS, pp. 44–50), Stephen Allen recalled those conditions, his poor education, and his experience in occupied New York. Ultimately, however, the Revolutionary War provided Allen with an extraordinary opportunity. When he was only fifteen, the evacuation of his tory master in 1783 cut him loose from his obligations and allowed him to embark upon his own career in sailmaking. After a shaky beginning that included tramping to Albany, Allen's considerable skill and ambition guided him to eventual success. The impact of living through the Revolution in occupied New York, however, remained a defining feature of his business and later political career.[7]

For some cause or other Mr. Leonard did not appear to think it necessary to have any of his apprentices bound by indenture. This may have arisen from the situation of the country, —the city being under a military and not a civil government, —and besides any one having influence with the men in power (which was the case with Mr. Leonard) could at all times enforce obedience by confinement or impressment for the men-of-war, at pleasure. There did not appear any disposition in the boys to leave the place, and for myself I can truly avow that such a thought never entered my mind; and had he continued in the city until I became of age I should have worked every day I was bound to work by the simple verbal agreement of my mother, which was that I should serve from the day I entered until I was twenty-one years of age.

The usage we received was by no means such as it should have been, as we were neither well clothed, well fed, nor well lodged. There were but three of us apprentices at that time, my brother, a lad named Joseph and myself. We all lodged in the garret of the house occupied by the family, each of us having his hammock and a pair of

7. For his later career, see the first document in Chapter 3.

blankets, which served as bed and covering. Mr. Leonard's circumstances were moderate, but the business he was engaged in for the government turning out profitable, he soon became comparatively easy in his finances and accordingly purchased a house in Beekman Street, rather more genteel and commodious than the one he then occupied. On his removal to his new establishment it was concluded by the family that there was no room for the boys, and they were therefore sent to the sail-loft to lodge. Our meals were taken at the house regularly, without much variation as to diet. Our breakfast and dinner were eaten in the cellar story of the house, which was partly underground and our supper was served up to us in the yard or in the street, as it suited us. For breakfast we uniformly had cocoa with bread, —for dinner a stew composed of potatoes, onions and coarse beef, and in order to save trouble to the servants a large pot of this mess was cooked at one time and what we did not eat at one meal was served up at the next. So that I have known a single cooking last for a week, which by continued warming up became bitter, being burnt over the fire and sour from age and fermentation. No complaints were made however, at least none within the hearing of the family, except by looks and gestures and they were little minded or attended to by any one.

For our supper we uniformly had dealt out to us two slices each of the round of baker's bread with butter, which was usually dealt out to us in the yard of the dwelling, and if it rained or snowed we retired to an open shed, intended as a roosting place for the fowls, and after receiving our allowance we marched in regular order to the sail-loft eating our bread and butter as we went through the streets. Here we passed an hour or two in idle conversation or in other pastime by no means profitable until the time arrived for retiring to rest.

As the war of the Revolution progressed, the business of our sail-loft increased and there was much more sail-making to be done than formerly. This induced Mr. Leonard to take more apprentices and our number now amounted to five in all.

One of the arbitrary methods pursued by the British in manning their ships of war while at this port, was by impressment. This was effected by sending out an officer of inferior grade such as Midshipman, with a number of sailors, who took in custody every man or boy they met, who had the least appearance of being a sailor either in looks or dress. This was a great annoyance to the citizens, particularly

Figure 5. Work in a sail loft as pieces of sail are stitched together. Certificate of Membership in the Society of Master Sail Makers of the City of New York, 1785, detail, NYHS

the poorer classes who were thus dragged from their families on board a man-of-war and, unless they had some friend of influence to apply for their release, they were compelled, perhaps for years, to be parted from their friends and families and serve as a common sailor on board these British dungeons.

The boys in our loft had frequently to encounter these English press gangs that were prowling about the city, both day and night. The dress we wore, composed of canvas trousers and short jacket, exposed us continually to molestation, and it several times happened that we were taken up and kept in confinement during the night, until Mr. Leonard came forward to claim us in the morning. . . .

I was about this time in my fourteenth year, and these outrages upon our liberty had a strong tendency to increase my predilections in favor of the cause in which my country was engaged. They had in fact increased with my years and the same principles and feelings were imbibed by my brother William. We were denounced therefore by the other boys as rebels. Nevertheless we adhered to our principles, and always expressed a degree of sorrow whenever an American vessel was brought into port as a prize with the thirteen stripes triumphantly displaced under the Cross of Old England.

At such times we had to bear the scoffs and jeers of those who held to the royal cause, but when news arrived of the capture or defeat of any of the British forces we retaliated by exulting in our turn, and we made no secret of our feelings on such occasions. . . .

My education was very limited, having left school before I was twelve years old. I could read and write indifferently, and had learned a few of the rules in arithmetic, but possessed no knowledge of grammar and was wretchedly difficient in my spelling. I was nevertheless very fond of reading, and would readily part with any of my possessions in order to obtain a book. . . . I had of my own property . . . , nearly all the school books that I had formerly used, consisting of a Testament, Dilworth's Spelling Book, Dilworth's School Masters Assistant and a number of small story-books, which had been presented to me while a child, or which I had purchased with my holiday money; and I continued to add to my stock whenever my means would admit such second hand books as fell in my way and as I was enabled to purchase cheap. My reading therefore was desultory, such as old plays, novels, songs, poetry and history, and not infrequently, books of a pernicious tendency. . . .

The boys of our loft were usually fitted out at a slop shop and permitted to receive annually a round-about [short] jacket of coarse cloth, trousers of the same description and a waistcoat.[8] Over this they wore their canvass trousers during the winter, and in summer the woolen trousers were thrown by. They were allowed a clean check shirt once a week, and during the winter a pair of woolen stockings. Their hats and neck handkerchiefs were generally bought by themselves, and their shoes they obtained by frequent solicitations from [to] their master, but seldom before they were literally barefoot.

[When Allen was about fourteen years old, his widowed mother remarried. With a home and husband to back her up, she intensified her complaints about the treatment of her sons by their employer.]

8. A "slop shop" sold ready-made and cheaper clothing.

The remonstrances of my mother, and perhaps the fear that we might leave his employ, induced Mr. Leonard to alter his conduct toward us entirely. We were now directed to go to a tailor and get measured for a suit of clothes. I was permitted to go to my mother's to sleep at night, while a small room was prepared at the house of Mr. Leonard for the accommodation of my brother. The next Sunday after this revolution in our affairs we appeared in a new suit of decent clothes, being the first we had received during our apprenticeship, and the last we did receive as after-events will show. From this time forward until the close of the Revolutionary War, when we were left to shift for ourselves, we were treated both by Mr. Leonard and his wife with much more kindness and attention then formerly, and I trust that we requited this usage by a faithful discharge of our duty as apprentices.

The disposition which [had] led me to conciliate my school fellows in our tasks or studies operated upon me in a much stronger degree while learning my trade or calling, and I endeavored therefore to excel my fellow apprentices, and did excel many of them both in the knowledge of my business and expertness in its execution. This was observed by Mr. Leonard and he would frequently tell his brothers (two of whom followed the same business) how much work I had turned off in a day. They in turn, when complaining to their boys about the small quantity of work performed, would proclaim me as an example to them, and thus the enmity of these lads was excited to my prejudice, when I had in no way intended or thought of offending them.

I was frequently designated by Mr. Leonard to assist him in cutting out sails, and by strict attention and turning the thing constantly in my mind, I laid hold of the art without any special instruction. The thing in itself is very simple when once understood, but it is a rare occurrence that boys are enable to see it without frequent explana-tions, and it is therefore the last business taught an apprentice. I had reason to presume that Mr. Leonard saw I had some knowledge of the method he pursued in working his rules, for without inquiring whether I understood the operation or not, he one day just as he was about commencing the working of a rule for cutting a sail was called off and handing me the measure desired me to cut it out. I accord-ingly went to work and did cut it out before his return, with the performance of which, after examining it, he was satisfied. . . .

News finally arrived that negotiations for a peace between Great

Britain and the United States had commenced at the city of Paris, in France. This was dreadful news for the loyalists in this city, and their countenances and expressions on the occasion betrayed the bitter and malignant passions working within them. But to the Whigs, many of whom had been compelled through poverty to continue in the city during the whole contest, it was glorious and consoling news, and in such measure as they dared they exulted in the prospect of peace, independence and a free government, the choice of a free people. For my part I knew little or nothing of the difference between a monarchy and a republic as governments, but the barbarous cruelties I had witnessed on the part of the English, inflicted on the American prisoners and others by the friends and abettors of royalty, led me to detest the very name of King George the Third and those who adhered to his cause and sanctioned his measures. I therefore felt as much gratified as any that we were to be freed from the sight of the disgusting red-coats in our streets, as the British soldiers were then termed by the Americans. . . .

The Leonards were among those who had made up their minds to leave the city, and preparatory thereto James Leonard made a voyage to Nova Scotia in order to ascertain the situation of the country and the prospects of business and trade in the event of a removal. On this occasion I was left in the care of his business, my brother William having obtained work in another sail-loft, and on his return he spoke in flattering terms of the attention I had paid to his interest during his absence. . . .

The time finally arrived for the departure of the family [the Leonards] and about the middle of October, 1783, they all set sail for their new abode where the greater part of them, after experiencing many hardships and privations laid their bones. . . .[9]

I was now about fifteen years old, and was turned loose upon the world to seek my fortune, with nothing to commence but a good constitution, and a scanty wardrobe. My brother William had concluded to occupy the sail-loft of Robert and David Leonard, and to enter into partnership with a young man named Augustus Wright, who had served his time with them; and he proposed to me, as the

9. The Leonards left approximately one month before the complete evacuation of the British from New York City on November 25, 1783.

best thing I could do under present circumstances, to work with them until I was enabled to better my situation. To this I assented upon their paying my board and allowing me small perquisites. Thus I continued more than a year, and until they were compelled for want of business to give up the loft and work as journeymen. My brother, however, could not brook the idea of descending from the position of master sail-maker to that of a journeyman, in the place of his nativity. He therefore packed up his all, after disposing of a part of his books to pay the expense of a passage, and forthwith proceeded to Philadelphia, the greatest commercial place in the Union, where he obtained steady and regular employment in the line of his business.

It was not many days after this occurrence before I also found employment in one of the sail-lofts in this city, but it was with some difficulty that my employers were enabled to continue me at work on account of the numerous threats of the journeymen, who went so far as to insist on my discharge, declaring it was the height of impropriety to employ a boy upon the same footing as themselves who were men and had served a full apprenticeship to the business, while I was far from being of age and had only worked there a few years at farthest. My experience at the work however, and the diligence with which I dispatched the business, over-came all the objections of these journeymen in the minds of those who had employed me, and as work was by no means abundant in those times and the hands to perform sufficiently plenty the grumblers found it [to] their interest to be silent and I accordingly continued to labor in this loft until there was none to perform or rather until the work to be done was only such as could be completed by the apprentices.

"A Spirit of Republican Festivity"
ALEXANDER ANDERSON, THE INQUIRING APPRENTICE

Alexander Anderson (1775–1872) was an exceptional person. As a craftsman he stood out as one of the foremost engravers of his age, and his engravings appeared in countless books and newspapers. Indeed, one biographer referred to him as the father of American wood engraving. The following selection from Anderson's diary, however, describes his youth before he became so renowned (Diary of Alexander Anderson, Rare Book and Manuscript Library, Columbia University). Anderson was fortunate to attend a good school where he developed a love of reading, especially the classics. Anderson never served a formal apprenticeship. As a teenager he taught himself engraving by reading an encyclopedia and using pieces of copper, a penny, and the back of a pocketknife. Later an obliging blacksmith made him some tools and he began engraving for newspaper offices. He learned more of the trade by "peeping into the shop windows of silversmiths when they were lettering spoons and other articles," and from copper-plate engraver Peter Maverick. (He marched with Maverick at the head of the carvers and engravers contingent in the 1788 procession celebrating the ratification of the Constitution.) He used the money that he earned to help support himself and to pay his way through medical school at Columbia College.

Anderson's diary entries indicate that he worked hard at his studies, while simultaneously carving a niche for himself as an engraver. Under the tutelage of Dr. Joseph Young, Anderson finished his medical studies in 1795. During the next few years he struggled to make ends meet as a practicing physician and part-time engraver. His most regular employment as a doctor came during yellow fever epidemics in 1795 and 1797. The epidemic reached his family in 1797, when most of them, including a young wife, died. Despondent, he abandoned his medical work and returned to his true calling as an artist and engraver, leaving an indelible mark on book illustrations.[10]

The year 1793 was busy for New York and for Anderson. The diary shows how Anderson integrated all the various components of his life—his engravings, his studies, and his social life. No sharp boundaries separated these different activities. On the July 4 holiday, for instance, Anderson worked on an engraving, attended a lecture at college, went on a family outing, and roamed the streets with one of his friends. Through Anderson's evangelical eyes we see the streets of New York, where a prostitute exposes her breasts to young male passersby, and where crowds form at political meetings to espouse one platform or another. The larger political world was not absent from Anderson's thoughts; support for the French Revolution and for Jeffersonian Republicanism appeared in his desire to see the French

10. Frederic M. Burr, *Life and Works of Alexander Anderson, M.D., the First American Wood Engraver* (New York, 1893), and Jane R. Pomeroy, "Alexander Anderson's Life and Engravings before 1800, with a Checklist of Publications Drawn from His Diary" *Proceedings of the American Antiquarian Society*, 100 (1990), 137–230.

warship *L'Embuscade* and in his excitement over the visit of the French ambassador, Citizen Genet. Yet this political world was dwarfed by the rhythm of work and life that emerges in the pages of Anderson's diary. Anderson tells us of the engravings he is working on, of his dealings with other craftsmen, and of his relationship with friends and relatives.

January

New York. Wall Street No. 31.

1st.   Rose at 5 O'Clock; sat down by the Fire with a Tub of water and began to scower the copper-plate—prepar'd it for Engraving by breakfast time & work'd at it till 10 O'clock, when I went to see a house in Maiden-lane, occupy'd by one Van Dyk, Upholsterer, which was on fire last night—afterwards to Trinity Church—heard Mr. [John] Bassett preach from—Ephes V. 15, 16.

At dinner a dispute arose occasion'd by my brother's asserting that a part of the Discourse was not according to Scripture—Engrav'd till 2 O'clock, when I went to the Doctor's,[11] —kindled a Fire in the shop, and read a little—At half after 4, went down town with medicines, after delivering which, came home & Engrav'd—about 6 Papa and I went and heard Mr. [John] Stanford lecture Psalm XXIII. 6— He deliver'd some reflections on Baptism, it being just 16 years since he submitted to that Ordinance and enter'd on his Ministry—came home, and went with Mama to Mrs. Bradford's,[12] went down in the kitchen—saw two children dance, after which the Ladies began and footed it to the scraping of the old Negro. I play'd [the violin] two or three tunes. Mrs. Bradford gave me a glass of wine and a Cake— came home and read the first numbers of the Evening Mercury.[13]

2nd.   Last night I got up and began to kindle a fire, when thinking it might be too early I went up to Papa's room and look'd at his watch, found it to be about half past 1, at which discovery I undress'd and

11. When Anderson identifies someone as the "Doctor," he is referring to his mentor, Dr. Thomas Young.

12. Probably the widow of William Bradford, who ran a boardinghouse, 33 Wall Street, next door to Anderson's father's house at 31 Wall Street. William Duncan, *The New-York Directory and Register for the Year 1792 [1793]* . . . (New York, 1793).

13. The *Evening Mercury* was a short-lived paper printed in January 1793 by Anderson's friend Louis Jones.

went to bed again. Rose in the morning about 6, as soon as 'twas light enough, engrav'd at Hicks's Compass Plate. In my way to the Doctor's, call'd upon Mr. Durell and got 16 [shillings] of him—spent some time in kindling a fire in the Shop; read in *Cullen's Practice*— At noon engrav'd—went to Mr. Parr's & paid his bill £1.4.6.

At 3, went to the College and attend'd Dr. Bailey's lecture (Bones of the Head). I gave him the Draught of the Excresence [medicine] which I finish'd today. After lecture came home and engrav'd. Stopp'd at Mr. Davis's and drank glass [of] wine and got cake.[14]

Evening—got a Quire of Paper from Mr. Durell, on account—of some of which I made this Journal. Mrs. Bradford and Miss B. Cummings[15] spent most of the Evening with us & entertain'd us with several songs, and danc'd, while my brother play'd on the violin. A little before 10, I attended Miss Cummings home, across the street—there lay some planks in the middle of the street, on which she observ'd "it was quite timbersome."

17th. . . . At noon took the Copper-plate to Hicks, he pointed out some Amendments which were necessary. I brought it home, having finish'd took it back again—he desir'd me to engrave a small Copper plate for him, and he would then settle for both. Before 3, went to Anatomical Lecture (on the Heart). As I was returning with two others, a Prostitute, gaily dress'd, appear'd at the window of a house opposite the Brick Meeting,[16] and display'd her Breast to our view, with a most artful smile, affording an idea of a scene often described. . . .

14. Hicks's Copper Plate was probably owned by Adrian B. Hicks, mathematical instrument maker (maker of compasses, scales, rulers, etc.), corner of Wall and Front Streets. William Durell was a printer, bookseller, and stationer on Queen Street. Duncan, *Directory*. *Cullen's Practice* was a Scottish medical textbook, often reprinted, including in New York. William Cullen, *First Lines of Practice of Physic . . .* (New York, 1793). Parr cannot be identified. The lecturer was Dr. Richard Bayley, professor of anatomy at Columbia College Medical School, and "Mr. Davis" was probably Richard Davis, a carver and gilder at the corner of Church and Vesey streets. Duncan, *Directory*.

15. A quire was a collection of twenty-four or twenty-five sheets of paper of the same size and quality. Miss Cummings probably lived at 26 Wall Street, across the street from Bradford and Anderson, at Cumming and Gaffing, tavern keepers. Duncan, *Directory*.

16. "Brick Meeting" refers to the Old Presbyterian Church that was across the street from Columbia College.

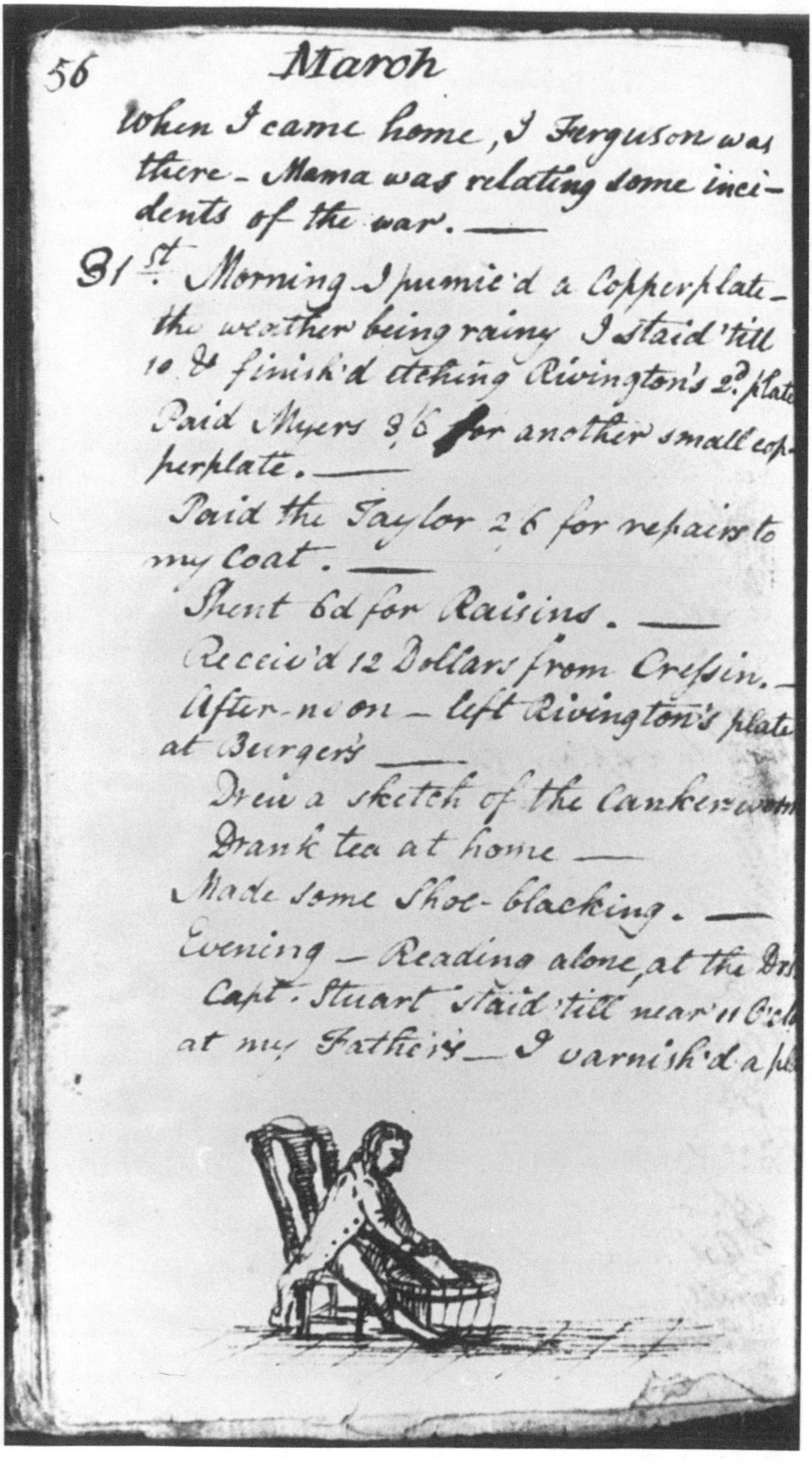

March

When I came home, I Ferguson was there — Mama was relating some incidents of the war. ——

31st Morning I pumic'd a Copperplate — the weather being rainy I staid 'till 10. & finish'd etching Rivington's 2d. plate Paid Myers 9/6 for another small copperplate. ——

Paid the Taylor 2/6 for repairs to my Coat. ——

Spent 6d for Raisins. ——

Receiv'd 12 Dollars from Cressin. ——

After-noon — left Rivington's plate at Burger's ——

Drew a sketch of the Cankerworm

Drank tea at home ——

Made some Shoe-blacking. ——

Evening — Reading alone, at the Dr[s]

Capt. Stuart staid 'till near 11 O'cl[c] at my Father's — I varnish'd a p[l]

Figure 6. Page with self-portrait of artist at work with copper plate. Diary of Alexander Anderson, courtesy of Rare Book and Manuscript Library, Columbia University

February
16th. Morning, after engraving, went to Jones's and made some little amendment to the Cut—from that to the Doctor's—Copy'd—read in Freneau's Poems—went to Mr. Bates's[17] to know about the Sleigh-ride—he was not in. At noon, Engrav'd till pretty late—Afternoon read anatomy and copy'd—it thaws considerably. . . .

March
17th. . . . I was sitting on the Stoop, enjoying the pleasantness of the weather, which lull'd me into an agreeable reverie, when the window-shutter was suddenly blown open and slapp'd my head against the wall so violently as almost stunn'd me, and made the tears run from my eyes. I was led to consider this as a miniature of Life; when we feel the most serene, and are pleasing ourselves with views of happiness, we are suddenly attack'd by some misfortune which rouses us from the pleasing reflection. —I am told that there is generally a calm before a hurricane. . . .
21st. Last night, about 11 O'clock, we were rous'd by an alarm of fire—I ran to the front windows and to my great astonishment saw a large flame arising near the new Coffee house, dress'd myself and ran out, join'd the ranks before our door, and handed full buckets for an hour, when the fire was nearly master'd, the ranks breaking up. I came home, and after drying my feet went to bed. This morning . . . I went to look at the remains of the fire. The upper parts of 3 houses next the Coffee house were consum'd, one of them occupy'd by Mr. West,[18] who was burnt out at the fire near the Fly market sometime ago. . . .
26. . . . Got home before 5 O'clock, made out to engrave a little, after tea provided myself with a pound of Raisins, and was preparing to go to the Theatre, my Brother surmounted his scruples and through the advice of his parents determin'd to accompany me. Papa gave us a dollar for tickets, which I bought at H. Gaine's.[19] The Doors of the Play-house were open'd before we arriv'd, and of course we did not get the front seat, though we had a very good view from

17. Louis Jones was a printer at 24 Smith Street. Duncan, *Directory*. Philip Freneau was an ardent Jeffersonian Republican. Mr. Bates cannot be identified.

18. Mr. West cannot be identified.

19. Hugh Gaines was a printer, bookseller, and stationer at 25 Hanover Square. He sold theater tickets in his office. Duncan, *Directory*.

where we sat. The Comedy was the *Fashionable Lover*, which I think afforded a very good moral. The Farce—*No Song no Supper*, a musical piece, replete with humor and vivacity. We return'd at a pretty late hour (between 11 and 12, I imagine). Mama was sitting up for us.

April

20th. This morning, finish'd the letter on the plate. Sent Mr. Debow 3d. At noon call'd at Burger's[20] and got a proof of the Copper-plate; after making some amendments took it to Durell's—he was well satisfied with it, said he was sorry he could not let me have some money at present. I undertook to execute one of the Fancy pieces for Josephus (representing the Massacre of the Jews at Damascus) came home and began to prepare for it, went & got a Rule made for 6d. Made a frame to contain the Plate whilst etching. . . .

21st. Sunday. This day concluded my 18th year.

> He who has help'd me hitherto
> Can help me all my journey thro'.

In the Forenoon at Church. Mr. Lemming preach'd from Matt. XVI. 27. A Deacon was ordain'd—Raw and cold. At noon read in Josephus—After-noon—at the Doctor's—read a Sermon preach'd on the death of Mr. Wesley, and an account of his death.[21] Carried some medicine in the Bowery—got a little sprinkled with the rain in returning home—Evening went and heard Mr. Stanford Lecture. Psalm CVII. 30.

May

30th. . . . We had a laughable scene at the Shop. I was playing on the violin, when Aunt Jenny (as they call her) came in asking for a penny. I play'd Yankee-doodle and asked her to dance, in expectation of getting her away, but was surprised to see this poor creature, who is almost bent double with age, begin to hobble about the room to the no small entertainment of the rest of the Family, who assem-

---

20. Garret Debow, boot and shoemaker, 17 Nassau Street, and John Burger, copper-plate printer, Barclay Street. Duncan, *Directory.*

21. Mr. Lemming cannot be identified. The selection was probably from *An Authentic Account of the Last Moments of that Great and Good Man, John Wesley, to Which Is Added a Sketch of His Character* (Leeds, 1791; often reprinted).

bled at the door—she kept on intimating that she expected a penny—I gave her one, which seem'd to inspire her with more animation, so that she accompanied the music with her voice, which set her in a very grotesque point of view. . . .

31st. At noon finish'd the 5th of J. Harrison's Cuts, and took it to him. Bought a pair of Pumps made in Canton in China, for 4 [shillings?]—began another cut. Read as usual. At tea time mended up a typemetal cut for J. Harrison—went to Tiebout's and got a piece of copper, weight lb. 3. 2 [oz].[22]

June

3rd. This morning, I spent in polishing the Copper-plate—fitted it for engraving.

In the afternoon, I went across the Fields[23] and saw two Balloons ascend; one a small one, and the other a pretty large one, about 36 feet in diameter—they were carried to the Northward, and after mounting nearly out of sight, afterward fell in the North [Hudson] River as I was told. . . .

11th. . . . Last night there was an affray at the Tontine Coffee-House between Whig & Tory, or, to modernize it, Aristocrat & Democrat.[24] At 11 O'clock went to the College hall and heard Dr. Smith deliver his Introductory Lecture to the Materio-Medica.[25] At noon, busy touching up the etching of my Plate. Afternoon, read etc.

July

4th. This being the 17th anniversary of American Independence, we were awak'd by the ringing of Bells and discharge of Cannon. I

22. John Harrison, printer, 3 Peck Slip, and Cornelius Tiebout, engraver, 24 Golden Hill Street. Duncan, *Directory.*

23. Located approximately where City Hall Park is today and northward.

24. The controversy was really between Federalists and Jeffersonian Republicans centering around the efforts of Citizen Edmund C. Genet, the ambassador from Revolutionary France, to embroil the United States in a war with Great Britain. Genet appealed to Americans to side with his republican France. Washington, however, refused this involvement and wanted to maintain strict neutrality. Anderson's "Aristocrats" would be the Federalists, the "Democrats" would be Jeffersonian Republicans. See Alfred F. Young, *The Democratic Republicans of New York: The Origins, 1763–1797* (Chapel Hill, N.C., 1967), pp. 349–365.

25. Dr. William P. Smith was professor of Materia Medica, Columbia College Medical School. Duncan, *Directory.*

work'd at wooden cuts 'till about 9, when I went to the Doctor's, got Nicholson's Philosophy from Durell at 24 [shillings?]—bought 6d worth of raisins—came downtown, fell in company with N. Burchell, look'd into the Old Presbyterian Meeting, where Mr. Miller was to deliver a discourse to some of the Republican Societies, but seeing it so full, we alter'd our course and walk'd on the Battery—had some discourse with Nat, on Printing chiefly—came home about 11 and got to work again. About 2 we (the whole Family) set off for Brannon's—my Brother & I took a different route from Papa & Mama, who arriv'd before us, we took possession of a pleasant summerhouse. I must confess that I was not much satisfied with passing my time in strolling about the Garden &c., 'till we were reliev'd by a seasonable dish of Coffee about 5—met B. Howe our old play-mate.[26] I took the Key and came off before the rest—paid for new sleeve buttons 1 [shilling]. Call'd at the Coppersmith's for new Plate, but he did not think proper to work today . . . came home—went to work till I could see no longer—play'd on the violin, went to the Doctor's, and took out some medicine. A slight shower came on—much eating, drinking, toasting, singing, noise and confusion in both the Coffee-houses—cannons fir'd and bells rung at particular hours of the day.

Cousin K. Carpenter and two of Mrs. Lockwood's Children, at our house in the evening—attended them home.[27]

A spirit of Republican festivity seems to have pervaded all ranks, the Children imitated their Superiors in the several testimonies of Joy, which have been greater than usual on this occasion.

August
3rd. . . . Copied for Dr. Smith, the address to Citizen Genet. At noon, cast some more of the cuts and began to engrave one.

Afternoon—W. Debow having procur'd a boat we row'd over to the L'Embuscade, where we staid till we had examined the whole Ship, from that we went on board her prize, a Portuguese Brig—staid

---

26. The book from Durell was probably William Nicholson (1753–1815), *An Intro-duction to Natural Philosophy* (London, 1782; often reprinted). Burchell and Miller cannot be identified. Brannon probably refers to Charles Brennyson, a tavernkeeper at 19 George Street. Duncan, *Directory*. B. Howe cannot be identified.

27. Neither Carpenter nor Mrs. Lockwood can be identified.

Figure 7. John Wesley Jarvis (1780–1840), *Portrait of Alexander Anderson (age thirty)*, oil, MMNY

here a few minutes and return'd about 5 O'clock, to the Doctor. Before dark, I finish'd Buel's cut, and a wooden one for Campbell— took the 3 cuts to Buel. . . .[28]

7th. Morning, began to work about half past 5. . . .

At 12 O'clock, the arrival of Citizen Genet was announced by the ringing of Bells. I went down to the Battery and saw him land under a discharge of Cannon. A procession was form'd and proceeded to the Coffee-house where the Address was presented to him by the Committee appointed for that purpose.[29] I was engag'd at my dinner which

28. W. Debow cannot be identified. The French naval vessel *L'Embuscade* arrived in New York port in mid-May 1793. Because the Jeffersonian Republicans supported the French Revolution, they held a grand reception in honor of the ship's victory in a naval duel with a British vessel off Sandy Hook. See Young, *Democratic Republicans*, pp. 351–360. John Buell was a printer at 28 Wall Street, and Samuel Campbell was a bookseller and stationer at 37 Hanover Square. Duncan, *Directory*.

29. The Frenchmen Genet created a great political uproar when he visited New York City to pursue policies to negate the neutrality of the United States. Ultimately

appear'd more interesting to me, during this part of the transaction. I finish'd one of Croswell's cuts.[30] At tea-time, went back to Peck Slip and bought a pail of Butter . . . which I emptied into a Tureen and brought home—Evening, play'd on the violin etc.

8th. . . . At 12, went to Broadway, opposite Trinity Church where a multitude had assembled, and heard an address deliver'd by Col. Troup on the advantages of a state of Neutrality—after which several resolves were pass'd, expressing their approbation of the President's conduct &c., amidst the general assent and shouts of the people— about 1 the meeting was dissolv'd.[31] I began the 2nd cut for Croswell. . . .

September

28th. . . . At dusk began to scower a plate. My Father being call'd upon to guard the wharves to prevent any boats from landing,* I offer'd to go in his place. At 8, I went to the Old Coffee House where our names being call'd over, a party of 12 of us were sent out at half past 9—stations were fix'd on the principal wharves of this ward, and I with 2 others patrol'd along the whole extent of them—being reliev'd a little before 12, we return'd to our place of rendezvous, where a Supper had been prepar'd, of which I partook to my sorrow, for it cost me 6 [pence?]. Altho' I did not arrive till the best of it was knock'd off. After this, we walk'd all round the first ward—in our way stopp'd at the Federal Hall and saw the stragglers which the watch had pick'd up. At half past 2, we were sent out again, and perform'd our duty as before—prevented several boats from landing. It was near five when I came home, and crept into bed.[32]

October

21st. I deliver'd the cut which I finish'd on Saturday. . . . As I was busy against the wall, a mulatto wench came up to me in a very

---

——*To prevent the introduction of Yellow Fever.

he was discredited and recalled. But he did not return to France; instead he married one of Governor George Clinton's daughters and settled in New York State. See Young, *Democratic Republicans*, pp. 354–362.

30. Croswell cannot be identified.

31. Robert Troup was a leading Federalist politician in New York and a political ally of Alexander Hamilton. Young, *Democratic Republicans*, pp. 134, 151.

32. The patrols were organized to prevent contact with ships and crews that were believed to be infected with yellow fever.

familiar manner, but finding I was not dispos'd to make free with her, begg'd my pardon, pretending she mistook me for some other person.

"Hard Work and Myself Had Had a Falling Out"
WILLIAM OTTER, THE WICKED APPRENTICE

If Alexander Anderson represented the model of what a good young man ought to be—honest, hard-working, studious, and religious—William Otter stood on the other side of the spectrum. He avoided strenuous work, drank, caroused, and fought. Otter's experience as a street tough who viewed a good night's ruckus as the epitome of happiness mirrored that of many apprentices in the early national period. Otter never became a fully skilled artisan; instead, he fled from his apprenticeship in New York to Pennsylvania, where, as "Big Bill the Plasterer," he took pride in his ability to plaster walls quickly and avoid jobs that demanded too much detailed work.

Born in England, he ran away from his Yorkshire home at the age of 11 to become a cabin boy in the Greenland fishery. After enduring a shipwreck on the return voyage, Otter was impressed into the British navy. Four years later, he escaped from British service and returned to his hometown to discover that his parents had emigrated to New York. Otter followed them there, arriving around 1805. The sixteen-year-old lad worked first as a servant, a position he had filled in the navy. He was quickly persuaded, however, that the best way to earn a living was by learning a trade. The selection from his autobiography included here describes the various negotiations between Otter, his father, and potential employers in finding Otter a craft (William Otter, Sr., *History of My Own Times: Or the Life and Adventures of William Otter, Sr.* [Emmitsburg, Md., 1835], 68–72, 84–85, 86, 99, 103–104, 106–107, 108). After trying his hand at shoemaking, venetian blind making, and carpentry, Bill settled on plastering.

Otter's *History of My Own Times* is a reminiscence that does not chronicle day-to-day activities as Anderson did in his diary. It focuses instead on those incidents that "Big Bill the Plaster" remembered best. We do not see Otter at work; we do see him rambling about the streets and drinking establishments of New York. We do see him avoiding night school, working independently, and absconding from his master. Apprentices like Bill Otter became an increasing problem

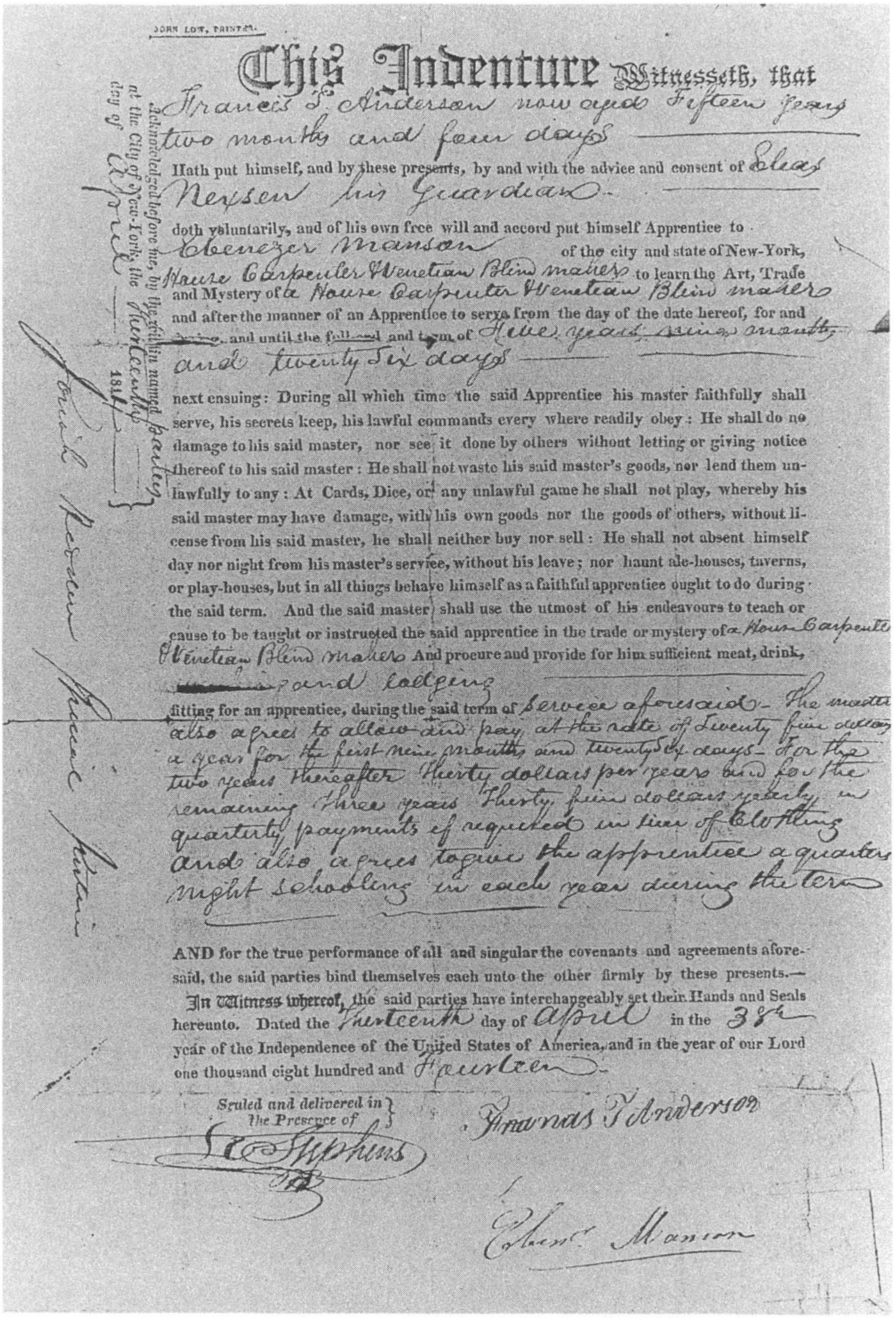

JOHN LOW, PRINTER.

This Indenture Witnesseth, that Francis T. Anderson now aged Fifteen years two months and four days Hath put himself, and by these presents, by and with the advice and consent of Elias Nexsen his Guardian doth voluntarily, and of his own free will and accord put himself Apprentice to Ebenezer Manson of the city and state of New-York, House Carpenter & Venetian Blind maker to learn the Art, Trade and Mystery of a House Carpenter & Venetian Blind maker and after the manner of an Apprentice to serve from the day of the date hereof, for and and until the full and term of Five years nine months and twenty six days next ensuing: During all which time the said Apprentice his master faithfully shall serve, his secrets keep, his lawful commands every where readily obey: He shall do no damage to his said master, nor see it done by others without letting or giving notice thereof to his said master: He shall not waste his said master's goods, nor lend them unlawfully to any: At Cards, Dice, or any unlawful game he shall not play, whereby his said master may have damage, with his own goods nor the goods of others, without license from his said master, he shall neither buy nor sell: He shall not absent himself day nor night from his master's service, without his leave; nor haunt ale-houses, taverns, or play-houses, but in all things behave himself as a faithful apprentice ought to do during the said term. And the said master shall use the utmost of his endeavours to teach or cause to be taught or instructed the said apprentice in the trade or mystery of a House Carpenter & Venetian Blind maker And procure and provide for him sufficient meat, drink, and lodging fitting for an apprentice, during the said term of Service aforesaid. The master also agrees to allow and pay at the rate of Twenty five dollars a year for the first nine months and twenty six days. For the two years thereafter Thirty dollars per year and for the remaining three years Thirty five dollars yearly in quarterly payments if required in lieu of Clothing and also agrees to give the apprentice a quarters night schooling in each year during the term

AND for the true performance of all and singular the covenants and agreements aforesaid, the said parties bind themselves each unto the other firmly by these presents.—

In Witness whereof, the said parties have interchangeably set their Hands and Seals hereunto. Dated the Thirteenth day of April in the 38th year of the Independence of the United States of America, and in the year of our Lord one thousand eight hundred and Fourteen.

Sealed and delivered in the Presence of

Francis T. Anderson

Stephens

Ebenr. Manson

Acknowledged before me, by the within named parties at the City of New-York, the Thirteenth day of April 1814

Elias Nexsen

Figure 8. This indenture of Francis Anderson to carpenter Ebenezer Manson, to last approximately six years, describes the standard demands of an apprentice-master agreement. It also requires Manson to pay thirty dollars per year in lieu of clothing and to give a "quarters night schooling" each year. Indenture of Francis Anderson to Ebenezer Manson, Carpenter, 1814, NYCMA for masters as they struggled to hire more young men to cut costs, as required in the emerging laissez-faire marketplace, and as they abdicated parental supervision, in accord with republican ideals of independence. The difficulty lay in the fact that youths like Bill Otter did not exhibit the virtues of hard work and discipline on their own, and seized upon the republican assault on authority to pursue their own anarchic ends.[33]

I went to market with my father every day, at length I found for myself a master by the name of John Paxton [a shoemaker], a resident in Water street in the city of New York, to him I went upon probation of a fortnight's duration, and staid with him a week all but three days, and then put out. From there I went home again, my father asked me how I liked the trade; to that enquiry I answered, that I did not like it at all, I had quit it; he asked me if I had told Mr. Paxton so; I told him I had; he asked me why I had quit; I told Mr. Paxton that it hurt me across my breast; my father asked me what are you going to learn now, I told him I did not know yet; I then walked about the city for two or three days.

I hunted for myself a master, in the meantime, and took a notion to learn the venetian blind making business, and found for myself a master in a man of the name of William Howard, who followed that business in Broadway, opposite the *park* he also took me on probation (as I had no notion to run a head of the wind) for two weeks; which is the established rule in the city, as to taking apprentices on probation. Mr. Howard put me at painting blinds; in that office I held out five days and found that the effects of the paint, on my part was intolerable; I told Mr. Howard I believed I would leave him, that I could not stand it, I would go home; he said, well you must know best yourself, I do not intend to persuade you against your own will, —and there, and in manner aforesaid, ended my second apprenticeship, and I put out home. When I came home my father was absent, my mother asked me how I liked my new trade; I told her I had quit; why, said she, William you learn your trades quick; I told her yes; and what are you going to do now, continued my mother; I told her I did not know. In the evening my father came home; my mother told

33. William Otter, Sr., *History of My Own Times: Or the Life and Adventures of William Otter, Sen., Comprising a Series of Events, and Musical Incidents Altogether Original* (Emmitsburg, Md., 1835).

him that I had learned another trade; he then asked me had I quit again; I told him yes; he asked me if I had told Mr. Howard, that I intended to quit; I told him I had; he then said that was right. He then asked me what I would join next, I told him I thought I would try to learn the carpenter business; well, said he, seek for yourself another master, I told him I would; accordingly I went in quest of a master and got one, by the name of Gausman, a Scotchman, in Broadway: he put me to sawing out boards all that week; on Sunday I went home; father asked how I come on, I told him very well, he said he was glad to hear it, hoping I would get myself bound the next week, I told him I would wait till next week was over before I got myself bound; I kept on sawing boards until Thursday; I told the foreman I believed I would quit it, that I had the back-ache and the work was too hard: and without any further ceremony I put out for home, and so ended my third apprenticeship. My father asked me how I came on at the carpenter's business; I told him I had quit it, he then gave me to understand that he entertained the thought that hard work and myself had had a falling out; I told him yes, that I did not like it much. He told me in good earnest to make up my mind and go to some trade and stick to it and learn it, as I was fooling away my time to no purpose, in the way I had been leaving trades; as bye the bye, I was master of none; and that after a while my name would become so notorious that I could not get a master, as he wished to see me do well; and if I got a master again to get myself bound straight-way. If I did not do that, I would never get a trade.

I then took a notion to learn the bricklaying and plastering busi-ness, and went to hunt a master in good earnest, and found one by the name of Kenneth King. I asked him if he would take a boy and learn him his trade; he asked if I was the boy, I told him yes, he then asked me my name and where I lived, which inquiries I answered; he told me to bring my father there the next day, I told him I would; the next day about two o'clock according to promise my father and myself called to see Mr. King. My father signified a wish to have me bound instanter as I had so many masters, and flew as often too; Mr. King told my father he had no apprehension about him; but that he could make a good boy out of me, as he had no less than eight boys at that time; my father told him if it suited, he would like to have me bound on the spot, to which Mr. King said he had no objections if I was agreed; I told him I was perfectly satisfied, and we went straight to a squire-shop [lawyer's office] and got myself bound for four years. The next morning I went to work in my new birth [berth], and worked on till Saturday evening; I asked permission of my master to go home and see my parents, he consented I might go provided I returned on Sunday evening; I told him I would; I went home, and father asked me how I come on, I told him very well; he asked if I liked my trade and my master, I told him I did; he said he was very glad to hear it, hoped that I would stay and learn my trade and make myself master of it. My mother said that she was glad that I had found a man and trade that I liked.

[Otter continued working as an apprentice for Mr. King for the next three years, during which time both of his parents died. Otter describes several of his and his friends' violent escapades, including a riot against Irish Catholics on Christmas Day, 1806, and the following incident.]

The next scrape I got myself into, long before my head was healed, and not exceeding four days after the mob in Irishtown, was at a dance at a Mr. Green's. Being a notorious dance-house, we went for the express purpose of raising a row and were gratified to our heart's content, for we had scarcely got into the house, until the crew of the English packet came in, and they scarcely had time to touch bottom, when we let them have it, and the way it went there was nobody's business only those whom it concerned; we had a battle-royal, and the first thing I knowed of myself I was in the hands of a watchman; as he was taking me on to the watch-house, he treated me uncourteously he had me by the collar, I told him I had occasion to obey a call of nature; he let go his hold by my collar, and as soon as he let go his hold, I put out, and the way I scampered off was just the right way, and he had no other than legbail [escape by fleeing] for my appearance. . . .

The holydays being over, I was put to night-school by my master, and I happened by some means or other to miss attending school as often as I happened to attend it. . . .

After the glories of the several sprees, as I was a very apt scholar in this kind of street etiquette; in the mean time I would attend night school by time, to keep up what may be termed a liberal attention to classic lore. What I forgot to learn one night, I'd be sure to learn the next. I attended night school for ten nights in regular succession.

[A few weeks later Otter and John Lane, an apprentice baker, determined to run away together to Philadelphia. To do so, Otter began to work independently at night to earn cash to finance his escape.]

The next week, me and another boy got a barber's shop to plaster, for which we got fourteen dollars, which we divided equally, so that I had seven dollars more to add to my stock to scamper upon; and while we were at the barber shop, a man living two doors from the shop, he had a partition to plaster; he asked us to come up to see it, and see what we would do it for. We went up and took a look at it, and told him we would do it for three dollars. He asked us, how much we would have, if we found the mortar. We asked him how many coats he wanted it to have; he said one would do it, we could make it smooth enough for papering. We told him, we would do it for six dollars, and do it well. He asked us when we could do it; as soon as we are done with the barber shop. We told him we would have to do it at night; he said he did not care, and in that week, it should be done, and accordingly we did the plastering. However, we used finesse with the barber, we made him make more stuff than he wanted; we bought it from him, and fixed the partition; he paid us the six dollars, we divided it, and by this time I had twenty dollars, for expenses on our contemplated journey. . . . [W]e came to the conclusion to hook it. We were to get our clothes ready, have another blow out by way of a clear up shower to our sprees, and then put out between two days. We accordingly put our clothes to a certain Mrs. Paxton, a widow, whose occupation was that of washwoman, to have them all ready for a go. We met our comrades one night to have the farewell spree at Mr. Drakes. . . . The boys began to dance, and danced for about an hour, and then we began to set things to rights; we broke every glass in the whole house, and cleared it of men, women, and children; and after that performance, we cleared ourselves from the premises. We scampered off to a grogshop, and there we took our farewell drink together; and the shaking of hands in the last farewell being over, Dick Turner was to take us over the North River in a pleasure boat, together with about a half dozen of choice spirits, to accompany us by way of escort. . . .

We then went to Dick Turner and the lads who were to go along with us over the North River, and found them at the wharf at their post like men; we got into the pleasure boat and we sailed across the river; John Lane and myself took our final adieu of the city of New-

York. We landed in safety on the Jersey shore, and went to the ferry-house; and made promise to write to one another to tell of our adventures; in our final exit, the city of New York lost two very fine boys, in John Lane and myself; however, I may be premature in my opinion, I will leave the reader to judge for himself.

"Awarding the Intelligent and Persevering Apprentice"
MASTERS ENCOURAGE THEIR DISCIPLES

Mechanics—skilled workers—thought of their work as crucial to the new republic. Their mastery of their craft would free the United States from dependence on imports from Europe. Apprenticeship, in this scheme of things, was vital to the preservation not only of a specific craft, but also to the independence of the nation. By 1825 many challenges faced craft production. In response, the city's artisans created the Mechanics Institute, an organization that sought to sustain mechanic culture in early national New York and thereby maintain the traditions of apprenticeship, the craft system, and artisan pride. In this effort, the group offered a prize to apprentices and advertised it in the following newspaper article (*Mechanics Gazette*, May 7, 1825).

MECHANICS—APPRENTICES.

We are requested by a very intelligent and public spirited mechanic, to call the attention of the mechanics, to the expediency of adopting measures to encourage mechanic arts and trades carried on in the city, by awarding premiums or medals to those apprentices, who shall on or before the 20th of June, present for exhibition, the best specimen of their (exclusive) work, in a manner somewhat similar to that practised last year at the Mechanics Institute on a limited scale, the articles to be exhibited in Mechanics Hall previous to the 4th of July, and the premiums and medals to be delivered on that day with suitable remarks best blending the practice of useful experiment with the celebration of American Independence. The proposition meets with out warmest wishes, and indeed we can imagine no plan better calculated to stimulate the young enterprise and ambition of our apprentices; more likely to add to the reputation and character of our city, and in effect, to benefit the master mechanics, than the one suggested: and in what more laudable, or more rational manner can we celebrate the anniversary of our National Independence than in awarding the intelligent and persevering apprentice the reward of merit for his attempts to render us independent of all foreign nations, by arriving at perfection in the mechanic arts, and thus rendering it unnecessary to resort to Europe for those articles, which, if duly encouraged, can be produced at home. The plan of last year was suggested by an individual, and was rather an attempt to ascertain how far it was in unison with public feelings and public opinion, and any expectation of great success; it was well received and highly applauded in all parts of the United States, and it extended itself far beyond the limits that had been originally imagined. The co-operation of many of our most respectable citizens was called into requisition, and pleased with the general design; they gave it their efficient and zealous support. The time was then too limited in many cases, to admit of that perfection in different specimens of work, that was desirable; but if commenced at this time, arrangements can be made that will gratify the ambition of the apprentices, and give the eclat to the celebration of the National Festival in this city, more enduring than any heretofore devised.

"Who Can Tell How Many Franklins May Be among You?"
THOMAS MERCEIN ON THE OPENING OF THE APPRENTICES' LIBRARY IN 1820

The following orations were delivered to mark the establishment of an apprentice's library in New York (Thomas Mercein, *An Address upon the Opening of the Apprentices' Library* [New York, 1820], pp. 6–9, 11–13, 19–22). The rhetoric of these talks is replete with hyperbole that reflected artisan republican expectations of the new nation: expanding vistas of opportunity opening in the new age of the common man. The first of the speeches, by master baker Thomas Mercein, waxes heavily about the possibility of a young Franklin residing among the city's apprentices. But even though the orator was upbeat, he did not disguise another purpose of the Apprentices' Library: to get youths off the streets and instill in them the proper "Franklin" values of hard work and correct behavior.

The apprentice's address, below, although tinged with the same patriotic language, was more pragmatic. In the end the apprentice avoided any claim to "higher walks of literature," asserting that all he aspired to was "the simple mental food, which imparts content to the mind and health of the morals." But, of course, artisan republicanism exalted such austere simplicity above the refinements of wealth.

On this day, the 25th of Nov. the APPRENTICES' LIBRARY of the city of New-York is to be opened; —we have chosen to perform this ceremony, on an anniversary consecrated by one of the most interesting events in the history of our National Freedom, and whose return is associated with recollections dear to every American bosom.[34] In 1820 we have thought proper to blend its commemoration, with circumstances calculated to exhibit the moral advancement of our metropolis, and to show the securities which we are planting around the fortress of Liberty, erected in the glorious and triumphant struggle of the Revolution.

The free institutions of the United States rest on public opinion; —while this is correct and enlightened, we have a perpetual guarantee for their prosperity and duration. A people will never submit to the subversion of their rights, nor will usurpers dare to invade them, while the great mass of the community are possessed of intelligence, and think and act for themselves. The general diffusion of light, both intellectual and moral, until its beams fall on every class of society, and cheer the retreat and asylum of the humble and obscure, shall prove an object of ardent devotion to the patriot, the philanthropist, and the Christian. As population increases and spreads, from the ocean to the mountains, from the great lakes to the wilds of the Mississippi, let the march of education, literature, and science, keep pace with the augmentation, adding new acquisition to the great mass of general information. Ignorance and Despotism have shown their kindred qualities, and their indissoluble connexion in every age—and Liberty has ever been most flourishing, when the faculties of a nation expanded with moral and intellectual energy. . . .

But the field is still wide, and the theatre of activity vast and boundless to our perceptions: as the City of New-York increases in

34. November 25 was an important holiday in early national New York City because it marked the anniversary of the evacuation of the British from the city in 1783.

population, the number of those engaged in the useful arts will greatly multiply. Perhaps among no class of citizens is it more important to cultivate elementary education with assiduity, than among the different denominations of mechanics' apprentices. In large cities, where their employment and intercourse with the rest of the community are extensive and multifarious, and contracts and responsibilities are constantly entered into and incurred; capacity and knowledge to understand rights and detect errors, are necessarily connected with their welfare and prosperity. The importance and respectability of the large and increasing class of citizens, to the well-being of society; the responsible situations to which they may be called; the representative and official capacities, which they may find it necessary to assume, in a government like ours, render the acquisition of intelligence a subject of additional interest and regard. . . .

No institution, whose expenses and establishment are confined to a similar compass, can be better calculated to impart lasting blessings than is the APPRENTICES' LIBRARY. While it will prove a source of rational and useful information, it will also prove a school of early ambition. Here may the young and ardent mind catch those incentives, which will endure through life, and direct every effort to the attainment of a high and laudable standing in society, —here will be caught those impressions, here will be gathered that early intelligence, here will be contracted those sound and commendable habits, that will mould the character, and elevate it to a standing, equally congenial to individual and general happiness. . . .

To you, *Apprentices*, I may speak in a different language [than students]. . . before you are some of the most exalted and illustrious examples of greatness, that have ever added worth and dignity to the human character. Franklin, and Rittenhouse, and Godfrey, and Fulton, emerged from the mechanical ranks, to a sphere of usefulness, fame, and honour; and to the latest ages of the world will be hailed as the benefactors of the human family. Who can tell how many Franklins may be among you? Who can tell how many Rittenhouses, how many Godfreys, how many Fultons may yet spring from the Institution this day opened! Your opportunities are great and liberal. The life of Franklin will tell you with what privations he struggled in early life; how his young and daring ambition ascended the rough and forbidding steps of knowledge, until he attained the summit of a celebrity where the sun of glory never sets; and yet Benjamin Franklin, in

Figure 9. The career of Benjamin Franklin was a source of pride and inspiration for many American craftsmen, and many artisan societies used his name in their title. This scene of the successful Franklin amid his apprentices typifies this ideal of republican opportunity, invoked by Thomas Mercein in his address to the city's apprentices. Alexander Anderson, *Scene from the Life of Franklin,* Anderson Scrapbooks, vol. 1, p. 81, NYPL

his younger days, deemed a single volume of the Spectator, obtained by accident, as a golden prize! You, young candidates for honourable distinction, can now repair to a Library, various, extensive, and inviting, and, on you the fault and reproach must rest, if your opportunities are not sedulously and judiciously employed. Cherish, I beseech you, a deep-rooted abhorrence of the alluring but fatal paths of vice and dissipation. . . . Industry, ardour, sobriety, and perseverance in your different pursuits, will lead to successful competition in the world: these will enable you to be useful in your generation, and in old age, to look back with delight on the bright season of your youthful days, when the foundation of your prosperity was securely laid.

Wealth, and the field of mechanical science, are before you. New combinations and new discoveries are constantly developed in the useful arts; and application, and the fervour of genius, may yet lead you to inventions valuable and important in the history of man. . . . Forget not that you live under a free government, whose honours and offices are equally open to all; and while you learn to appreciate its blessings, you may one day, like Franklin and Rittenhouse, be called on to put on the patriot's armour, and nobly and fearlessly to contend in defence of civil and religious freedom.

[A student from the Mechanic's School followed Mercein's oration with an address (not reprinted here) that celebrated the "land of liberty," "precepts of reason in the minds of their youth," and gratitude toward the institution's benefactors.]

Apprentice's Address
Ladies and Gentlemen,

I COME before you the diffident representative of that numerous class of SOCIETY, called *Apprentices*. We deem this an auspicious day. The institution of the APPRENTICES' LIBRARY, which you meet to solemnize, is to us the harbinger of light, the joyful precursor of moral illumination; and most fondly do we cherish the hope, that its benign rays will light up the way, to prove the happy guide to thousands of our numerous class.

It can hardly be expected that our restricted capacities should presently and adequately appreciate this acquisition; but we look with confidence to the period, when the Institution itself, cooperating with other aids, will enable us to perceive, and duly to estimate the full measure of the benevolence of its founders. Most of us, indeed, from the nature of our employment, are well aware of the difference between the rude, rough materials, on which we work, and the finished, useful furniture. None of us, perhaps, are ignorant of the superior worth and elegance of the refined and polished gold over the crude unsmelted ore; neither are we insensible to the symmetry and beauty of the finished statue, nor to the shapeless deformity of the unwrought block. Such, and similar knowledge, may be obtained by many apprentices from their daily occupations; but when we turn our eyes on the moral world, few, alas! very few of our number have any adequate perception of the immeasurable distance between the cultivated and the neglected human mind. This is the barrier we greatly fear: this darkness *may* impede the Institution's light; for the beauty and worth of intellectual endowments are scarcely more visible to the untutored, giddy mind, than the colours of the rainbow to the physically blind. . . .

To diffuse the blessings of the Library—to bring to this banquet of the mind—to this feast of reason, those apprentices who feel no appetite, who have no relish, may require patience and perseverance on the part of its Patrons, far surpassing the labour of its formation. But to these strong expressions of fear, permit me to add my still stronger and more pleasing expressions of confident hope, that the same kind of Providence which induced the enterprise, will not cease to foster and protect it. And that the same wisdom and benevolence which projected and formed the Institution, will consummate its usefulness. Indeed we will not, we cannot but cherish the hope, that most apprentices will require little more than mere initiation; that their young and yielding minds need but the introduction to intellectual exercises, and that habit will presently give to them pleasure and permanence.

The whole number of Apprentices dispersed throughout this City is believed to exceed eight thousand, and though our physical state may be comfortable, our trades or vocations never so eligible, yet a paternal care and circumspect watchfulness of our moral and intellectual education, are seldom compatible with an apprenticed condition. Will you not, then, kind Patrons, take us by the hand, and lead us to the board your bounty has so richly spread for us? You have not to go far;— We live in the midst of you; and we humbly trust, that such an act of genuine charity to the uneducated Apprentice is not unmannerly to solicit of a Christian neighbour. Nay more; to snatch from ruin even the perverse and self-destroying youth—to breathe persuasion in his ear—to guide him kindly to the fountains of knowledge— to point him to the paths of virtue and happiness, must thrill in harmony with the happiest vibrations of the benevolent heart. . . .

I beg this audience not to mistake me. We aim not at the higher walks of literature—we aspire not to the embellishments of refinement. Our lot of labour will ever stifle a hope so vain. The extent of our desires will be satisfied with the simple mental food, which imparts content to the mind and health of the morals.

Ladies and Gentlemen, my main purpose here was to give you thanks in behalf of the Apprentices, which I do most respectfully.

"A Little Wholesome Chastisement"
ASSAULT AND BATTERY ON JESSE FASH

The control of a master over an apprentice could lead to abuse. In such a case the apprentice did possess the legal recourse of taking his master to court. But as the short selection below suggests (from the *Independent Mechanic*, May 16, 1812), the chances of success were slim. In the early nineteenth century the modern sensitivity to corporal punishment had not yet developed. It was therefore entirely permissible to exert "a little *wholesome chastisement*" if the boy did not work hard enough or if he were impertinent and misbehaved.

LAW INTELLIGENCE.

Court of Sessions, Tuesday, 12th May—Present, his honor Dewitt Clinton, mayor, alderman Douglass, and alderman Morse. *The People vs Richard T. Lowery*—

Assault and Battery upon Jesse Fash.

The complainant was an apprentice of the defendant. He stated, that his master had whipped him excessively on his return from dinner, alledging as a reason, that he had not been steady at work during his absence. It appeared, however, from the difference, that the lad was a bad boy, and very negligent; that Mr. Lowery had found fault with him; and that he had grumbled, and used impertinent language, in consequence of which he had given him a little *wholesome chastisement*. The mayor informed the jury, that they had only to decide whether the defendant used an improper weapon; or if a legal one, then, whether he had carried his chastisement too far.— In either case, he told them, they ought to convict the defendant; but if they thought otherwise, it was their duty to acquit. *Not guilty*. J. W. Wyman, for defendant.

"No Community of Interest, . . .
No Community of Feeling"
"AN OLD APPRENTICE" LAMENTS MODERN TIMES

In the following articles from the *New York Observer* in October 1826 (October 7, 14, and 28, respectively), "An Old Apprentice" lamented the changes in the workplace that had, in his mind, all but done away with the system of apprenticeship. This crusty author claimed, particularly, that few masters now employed apprentices because they could not successfully bind them for long periods of time. He blamed Jeffersonian equality for loosing these young men in the free labor market with the attendant dire social consequences: idle youths and increasing crime. Equally worrisome was the impact of these changes on the workplace. Shoddy, tardy, and inefficient workmanship were all attributable to an undisciplined and untrained labor force.

"An Old Apprentice" was not wrong in seeing republicanism as a source of his complaints. The legacy of 1776 promised economic opportunity, and the country's youth were understandably eager to take advantage of this legacy in an expanding economy, even if it meant violating traditions. Moreover, the egalitarianism unleashed by the Revolution prompted impatience with the paternal control of masters.

The tendency of our laws, which give masters no control over their apprentices, or the manner in which these laws are enforced or abused, by affording to unruly apprentices inducements to complain of, and to mortify and perplex their masters, has induced the solution on the part of the most respectable master mechanics, not to take apprentices at all. It is a fact well known to many, that there are great numbers of poor and friendless boys in our streets, who are yet *honest*, and desirous to work, but who, in consequence of this state of disorganization, are unable to obtain the knowledge of a trade. These may be seen wandering about our docks, or lounging at the Intelligence Office, until their scanty funds are exhausted, when to avoid starvation, they resort to pilfering, and are at length brought to the House of Refuge or in some other place of confinement less favorable to the reformation of character.[35] I had occasion, recently, to look at the form of an indenture; and presuming that I should find several in the first shop I entered, I stepped into my tailors, when to my surprise I found that, although one of the largest establishments in our city, the proprietors had not a single apprentice. I then went to several

35. An intelligence office was an employment agency that found positions for those seeking work. The House of Refuge, established in the 1820s, was an institution for the reformation of juvenile delinquents.

other tailors, jewelers, watch-makers, printers, and bootmakers before I could succeed. In enquiring the cause, I found that they all agreed (with a single exception), in the reasons here assigned, viz. *the insufficiency of the existing laws to compel an apprentice to do his duty*, and the power given to an obstinant and exasperated boy, in case of even moderate punishment, to drag his masters before a court, exposing him to the degradation of unmerited punishment, or at least subjecting him to expense, loss of time and the mortifying sneers of the rest of the boys who thus learn that they may pursue the same course with impunity.

. . . That a master should not have the power of compelling to the performance of his duty, an obstinant boy, who has been of little or no use in the early part of his apprenticeship, and who, when he has half learned his trade, will *court* the breaking of his indentures that he may be employed elsewhere as a journeyman, is a monstrous extension of Mr. Jefferson's "free and equal" declaration. It is not only subversive of good order and government between masters and apprentices, but it is subversive also of these principles, in the exercise of which in their purity, we have the surest, indeed the *only* guarantee of the continuance of our boasted independence.

An Old Apprentice

It is generally admitted, that intemperance among mechanics, and among the boys employed by them, has alarmingly increased of late; and it is, I conceive, a natural consequence of the present loose system of taking boys. In the course of my inquiries I saw four or five boys, from ten to fourteen years of age, romping at their work; and upon asking, "Are not these boys apprenticed?" was answered, "Oh no! they are little journeymen; they are received upon the same footing, are paid their wages regularly, and know and feel that they are *freemen*; and of course soon discover it by their conduct. If one of them should dislike a word of reproof, he will call for his wages and quit me instantly; and there are employers enough who will receive them, and care nothing for their moral character, or their steadiness, or constancy at their work. . . ." [These employers] prefer that the boys *should not* be bound as in that case there is nothing binding upon *them*. If the boy is taken sick or is guilty of misconduct, he can be turned adrift upon the public or his friends, and no responsibility attached to the employer.

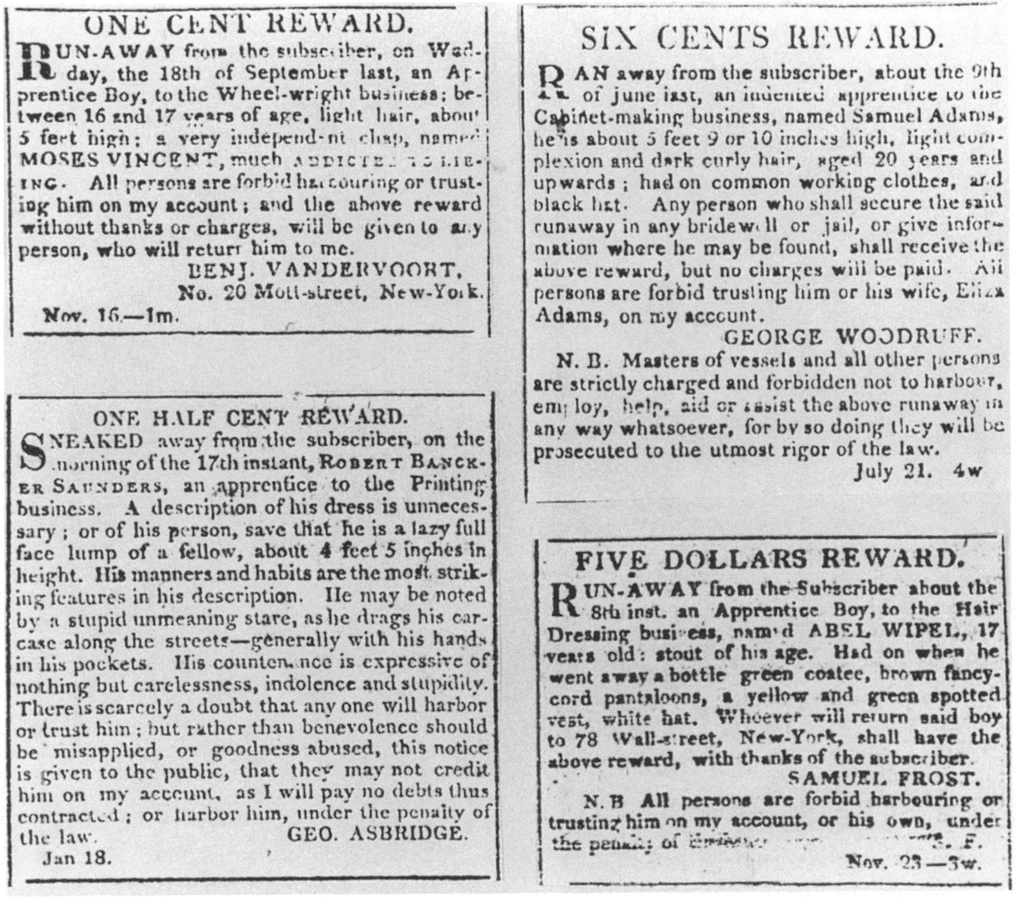

ONE CENT REWARD.

RUN-AWAY from the subscriber, on Wed-day, the 18th of September last, an Apprentice Boy, to the Wheel-wright business; between 16 and 17 years of age, light hair, about 5 feet high; a very independent chap, named MOSES VINCENT, much ADDICTED TO LIEING. All persons are forbid harbouring or trusting him on my account; and the above reward without thanks or charges, will be given to any person, who will return him to me.

BENJ. VANDERVOORT,
No. 20 Mott-street, New-York.

Nov. 16.—1m.

ONE HALF CENT REWARD.

SNEAKED away from the subscriber, on the morning of the 17th instant, ROBERT BAXCKER SAUNDERS, an apprentice to the Printing business. A description of his dress is unnecessary; or of his person, save that 'he is a lazy full face lump of a fellow, about 4 feet 5 inches in height. His manners and habits are the most striking features in his description. He may be noted by a stupid unmeaning stare, as he drags his carcase along the streets—generally with his hands in his pockets. His countenance is expressive of nothing but carelessness, indolence and stupidity. There is scarcely a doubt that any one will harbor or trust him; but rather than benevolence should be misapplied, this notice is given to the public, that they may not credit him on my account, as I will pay no debts thus contracted; or harbor him, under the penalty of the law.

GEO. ASBRIDGE.
Jan 18.

SIX CENTS REWARD.

RAN away from the subscriber, about the 9th of June last, an indented apprentice to the Cabinet-making business, named Samuel Adams, he is about 5 feet 9 or 10 inches high, light complexion and dark curly hair, aged 20 years and upwards; had on common working clothes, and black hat. Any person who shall secure the said runaway in any bridewell or jail, or give information where he may be found, shall receive the above reward, but no charges will be paid. All persons are forbid trusting him or his wife, Eliza Adams, on my account.

GEORGE WOODRUFF.

N. B. Masters of vessels and all other persons are strictly charged and forbidden not to harbour, employ, help, aid or assist the above runaway in any way whatsoever, for by so doing they will be prosecuted to the utmost rigor of the law.

July 21. 4w

FIVE DOLLARS REWARD.

RUN-AWAY from the Subscriber about the 8th inst. an Apprentice Boy, to the Hair Dressing business, named ABEL WIPEL, 17 years old; stout of his age. Had on when he went away a bottle green coatee, brown fancy-cord pantaloons, a yellow and green spotted vest, white hat. Whoever will return said boy to 78 Wall-street, New-York, shall have the above reward, with thanks of the subscriber.

SAMUEL FROST.

N. B. All persons are forbid harbouring or trusting him on my account, or his own, under the penalty of the law.

Nov. 23.—3w.

Figure 10. The growing opportunities for cash wages, the unwillingness of young men to endure masters' authority, and the republican spirit of independence led many apprentices to leave their masters before their indentures expired. A number of masters put ads in local newspapers, seeking the return of their apprentices, though many did so only in order to bring scorn upon these runaways. The master offering a five dollar reward was interested in regaining his fugitive apprentice. Runaway Apprentice Notices, 1811–1812 *Independent Mechanic*, 1811–1812

There is one important view of the subject, which this class of men seem entirely to have overlooked, viz. that they are contributing, by their practice, to form and to perpetuate the insubordinate characters of which they complain. Masters will tell you that their journeymen repeatedly leave them, with no word of explanation, for several days together; and it is proverbial that during the Spring races, troops of them invariably drop the paint brush or the saw, for the race-course; and the whole family is thus left in confusion till the races are past and the workmen are sobered. During last spring, I was hurrying to make some repairs for a tenant; three different mechanics undertook the job, and the workmen of each deserted for the race-course. Several of my friends experienced the same treatment.

Now, I ask, what is the cause of all these complaints? and why is a *punctual* mechanic so rare, as to induce the confession from one of the most worthy, "there is now no such thing as punctuality among them?" Is it not because the natural tie between master and apprentice, has been rent asunder? As there is now no community of interest, so there is no community of feeling between them. The master no longer lives among his apprentices, watches over their moral as well as mechanical improvement, accompanies them on Sunday to a place of public worship, counsels them when in trouble, keeps them and comforts them in sickness, and when he is able, gives them, with their good name, some assistance to begin the world for themselves.

An Old Apprentice

As I have before remarked, boys have *themselves* become the judges of the proper time to assume the character of journeymen; and it is lamentable, said my informant, to see men who profess to be respectable, countenance such a system. A stout boy lately applied to him for work, as a competent journeyman, and produced his credentials, viz. a certificate from a respectable mechanic, that the boy "*understood his business,* having worked for him *during the space of two years.*" Two *entire* years! to acquire a complete knowledge of an art and *mystery,* which in England is not learned short of seven years! Surely our mechanics deceive themselves, if they suppose that a plan which tends to reduce the perfection of their workmanship, and to degrade the moral character of boys, (the future mechanics of our city), can in the end be profitable.

An Old Apprentice

"Instruments of Deafening and Discordant Sound"
NEW YORK'S YOUTHS FORM THE
CALLITHUMPIAN PROCESSION

The American Revolution entailed an attack on patriarchy that released young people from close supervision and created the economic environment that provided a monetary base for youths to assert their independence. The result was a rowdy youth culture that threatened the order of the more respectable elements in society. Starting in the 1820s youth gangs became even more prevelant and their activities erupted into violence more frequently.

The Callithumpian processions of the 1820s represented an important variation of this trend in which New York apprentices and youths took the eighteenth-century tradition of misrule and applied it in an enlarged form as a general challenge to social authority. The word "Callithumpian" is an odd combination of Greek and Anglo-Saxon terms and literally means "beautiful thumping." Another term for the English custom of the "shiveree" or "charivari" (rough music), it consisted of banging on pots and pans, blowing penny horns, shouting and making other discordant noise, usually to molest some violator of local mores or customs. Somehow it was transferred across the Atlantic, the origins of this type of ritual being frequently obscured.

During the 1820s in New York City the Callithumpian procession was a celebration by young men on New Year's. In the eighteenth century, New Year's had been an important youth and plebeian holiday, celebrated by rowdiness, the knocking down of signs, turning over barrels, and similar pranks. The rest of New York tolerated this behavior on this special night largely because they saw it as a means by which youths might spend some of their extra energy. The assumption was that the damage would not be severe on New Year's Eve and that the young people, following long-standing traditions, would adhere to the normal rules of behavior the rest of the year. By the late 1820s those assumptions no longer applied. The result was a moment of disorder dominated by four thousand youths who proclaimed their democratic sovereignty of the streets and challenged any and all who might stand in their way.[36] The following documents, from *Gazette*, January 3 and 5, 1828, describe the youths' revelry.

36. Gilje, *Road to Mobocracy*, pp. 253–260.

"New Year's Amusements"

[*January 3*]

A few years ago a company, under some silly and unpronounceable name, was formed by a number of ill-bred boys, chimney sweeps, and other equally illustrious and aspiring persons, the object of which association was to assemble on New Year's eve and to perambulate the streets all night, disturbing the slumbers of the weary and the repose of the sick, by thumping upon tin kettles, sounding penny and other martial trumpets: in short by the aid of such harsh and discord-ant instruments of noise as could be collected together to furnish something more frightful to the ears than the confusion of Babel, or as horrific as the "weeping and wailing and knashing of teeth" in Tophet.

While all this was new, though it was certainly unpleasant, it was winked at and considered as a tolerable joke. But with every progres-sive year the *corps* has been increasing in noise and numbers, and to obstreperous discord they have at length added mischief and riot ren-dering any further toleration of the custom actually dangerous. Our police and watch department are, or ought to be, sufficiently strong to prevent such riotous procedures, and if they are not so, let them on these extraordinary occasions be doubled, or, if a resort must be had to extremities, let an armed force be called out.

In the Post of last evening we find the annexed account of the outrages Monday night, which will give a fair idea of the great height at which this evil has arrived.

Between eight and nine o'clock, a large crowd of people assembled in the Bowery with drums, tin kettles, rattles, horns, whistles, and a variety of other instruments of deafening and discordant sound. They began by pelting a public house in that street with balls of lime, flour, and other white substances, until they had changed its color from red to white. They then procured an enormous Pennsylvania [Conestoga] wagon, to which they attached a large rope several rods in length and harnessed themselves to it, took up their march down one of the cross streets to Broadway. In Hester Street they were set upon by a party of the watch, who having secured several of them were taking them off to the watch house. A rescue was called for by the mob; the watch were attacked, discomforted and forced to yield up the pris-oners, and the crowd resumed their march with more tumult than ever. Arrived at Chatham street they were reinforced by another throng equally numerous. The whole array now reached along Broadway from Chatham street to Courtland street. From Broadway they turned down Cedar street, and proceeded by the way of Pearl street to the Battery, making a great uproar as they went and demolishing the empty barrels and boxes left in the street. They reached the Battery between one and two in the morning when the crowd was estimated to be about four thousand strong. They endeavored to force the iron railing of the Battery in order to make way for the free ingress of the sovereign people, but were not able. They, therefore, contented themselves with throwing over a cart, and breaking some windows in one or two of the dwellings which look in front of the Battery. They then returned up Broadway until they came to the City Hotel. Here the sound of music, the strong light from the windows, and the gay head dresses seen passing before them, attracted their attention, and induced them to stop. The street became in a short time blocked up with an impenetrable crowd, and the hackney coaches conveying home the ladies and gentlemen, were obstructed and not suffered to pass. The inconvenience became so great, that a strong party of watchmen was collected with a view of taking into custody the leaders, and dispersing the rest. The mob prepared themselves for resistance; the long rope by which they dragged the huge Pennsylvania wagon was instantly cut into pieces of about three feet in length, and distributed among the leaders, and the watch were informed that five minutes were allowed to deliberate whether they would make way and allow them to proceed without molestation, or take the consequences of a different course. After a little consultation, the former alternative was adopted as the more prudent one, and the multitude passed noisily and triumphantly up Broadway. After this they visited different parts of the city, but the uproar gradually diminished towards morning.

[*January 5*]

In addition to what we gave yesterday in relation to the Callithumpian band we have been informed that the mob went to the African Church in Elizabeth [Street], between Pump and Hester streets, where the congregation were assembled, holding what is termed a "Watch Night." Here they demolished all the windows, broke the doors, seats, &c. and tied ropes to parts of the building in order to pull it down, but the ropes with which they drew the large wagon not being strong enough, they desisted, and poured their violence against the poor colored people, whom they pursued in all directions, beating them with sticks and pieces of rope. The poor preacher was obliged to make his escape through a back window, and after running a considerable distance, got clear of the mob, by turning into a narrow entry. Are such proceedings to be tolerated in the *city of New York?* Is not the Police of this city strong enough to put a stop to such disgraceful proceedings? If not, it is high time its strength and its numbers were increased. . . .

2

JOURNEYMEN
The Quest for Respectability

The risks and opportunities of the early republic's growing econ-omy touched all craftsmen, native and alien. This chapter opens with three accounts by immigrant journeymen who found themselves con-fronted with a hostile urban environment. Attracted to the city by the prospect of higher wages, they reacted to their travails differently. Grant Thorburn and John Doyle confronted adversity, applied a strong work ethic, and set themselves on the road to republican suc-cess. George Hart, however, was ultimately pushed, after a brief pe-riod of competence, to the periphery of society. He died in despair at the hands of an executioner.

These personal narratives allow us to view the human dimensions of both the immigrant's and journeyman's experience. Both were im-portant to early national New York. Thousands of workers from Eu-rope and rural America flocked to the city during the era of the new republic. These workers saw opportunity in many trades in one of the most dynamic labor markets in the United States. By the same token, their presence increased competition for jobs, helped to keep wages down, and ultimately undermined the bargaining position of most journeymen. Thus, the life stories of immigrant journeymen not only disclose the perils of leaving one's roots, friends, and way of life, they also attest to some of the fundamental economic changes transform-ing the world of New York City labor.

The impact of the expanding marketplace and capitalist innova-
tion was highly uneven. Many New York City trades such as black-
smithing and baking retained much of their eighteenth-century conduct of business, albeit in an expanded mode, operating as family
enterprises with only a few journeymen and apprentices. Within the
most significant artisan trades, however, profound changes took place
in production and employer-employee relationships. In these crafts,
the greater demand for goods, the absence of British mercantile
restrictions, improvements in communications, transportation and
business procedures, and available merchant capital provided mechanics with incentive to expand into national and international
markets. They expected increased profits from their entrepreneurship,
but they also found that success in a highly competitive economic
universe depended on the ability to organize efficient and cost-effec-
tive production within the workshop.[1]

In shoemaking, cabinetmaking, and tailoring, artisans sought expanded local and national markets as well as foreign, particularly
West Indian, outlets. Adventurous master shoemakers—sometimes
with mercantile assistance in procuring capital, credit, or markets—
bought leather wholesale and distributed it to journeymen who con-
verted the raw material to shoes. The master then sold this footwear,

1. No detailed study of market relationships of artisan trades in the port cities
exists. John R. Commons states that master shoemakers did their own retailing, including traveling to other ports, but David Saposs argues that merchant capitalists
were lending shoemakers and others considerable sums, doing much of the marketing
and often using the masters as foremen. Studies of Lynn, Massachusetts, for this
period reveal how commission merchants worked as both wholesalers and retailers to
some masters while acting only as creditors to others. John R. Commons et al., eds.,
A Documentary History of American Industrial Society 11 vols. (Cleveland, 1910–
1911), 3:34–39; David Saposs in John R. Commons et al., eds., *History of Labour in
the United States* (New Haven, Conn., 1918), 1:88–107; Paul Faler, *Mechanics and
Manufacturers in the Early Industrial Revolution* (Albany, 1981), chaps. 1–2; and Alan
Dawley, *Class and Community: The Industrial Revolution in Lynn* (Cambridge, Mass.,
1976), chaps. 1–2; Mary H. Blewett, *We Will Rise in Our Might: Workingwomen's
Voices from Nineteenth-Century New England* (Ithaca, N.Y., 1991). On general economic development see Thomas C. Cochran, "The Business Revolution," *American
Historical Review,* 79 (1974), 1449–1466; Cochran *Frontiers of Change: Early Indus-
trialism in America* (New York, 1981), chaps. 1–4, 6–8; Allan R. Pred, *Urban Growth
and the Circulation of Information: The United States System of Cities, 1790–1840* (Cambridge, Mass., 1973); David T. Gilchrist, ed., *The Growth of the Seaport Cities, 1790–
1815* (Charlottesville, Va., 1967), pp. 41, 56, 68–78, 113, 119, 199; Sidney I.
Pomerantz, *New York, An American City, 1783–1803: A Study of Urban Life* (New
York, 1938), pp. 149–166.

often of low quality, to slave-oriented markets in the South or West Indies or to the less wealthy of New York. In the manufacture of these shoes, skill was less important than cost and speed. Cabinet-making also found large national and international markets, particularly with the popularity of Windsor chairs, while tailoring saw a growing need for low-priced "slop" or ready-to-wear clothing.[2]

The building trades (masonry and carpentry), while not directly involved in export markets, were also affected by the expanding economy. Merchant investment in real estate and the erection of elaborate homes and countinghouses gave rise to a building boom. In constructing these sometimes complex dwellings, a new figure entered the business: the master builder. The duties of this middleman were to procure supplies, hire journeymen, and oversee construction—all at the lowest possible cost. Printing, too, became a more intricate business, with the development of elaborate and expensive machinery that allowed more efficient production. Under these conditions, a master was less likely to work alongside his journeymen; instead he spent his time overseeing shop operations and procuring accounts.[3]

Although masters working in these expanding trades did face the prospect of losing some of their independence and status to mercantile creditors by becoming foremen rather than proprietors, many did quite well in the new marketplace. The situation of the city's journeymen, particularly the 60 percent who worked in one of these six trades (shoemaking, tailoring, cabinetmaking, masonry, carpentry, and printing), was less bright. Working for set wages and hours, either based upon finished piecework or a daily salary, they eked out only a subsistence living. A sample drawn from the 1819 New York City jury lists reveals that only a small proportion (8.4 percent) of

2. Howard B. Rock, *Artisans of the New Republic: The Tradesmen of New York City in the Age of Jefferson* (New York, 1979), pp. 238, 258–259n; Charles F. Montgomery, *American Furniture: The Federal Period, 1788–1825* (New York, 1966), pp. 13–14; Wendell P. Garrett, "The Matter of Consumers' Tastes," in John D. Morse, ed., *Country Cabinetwork and Simple City Furniture* (Charlottesville, Va., 1969), pp. 205–233; Egal Feldman, "New York Men's Clothing Trade, 1800–1860," (Ph.D. diss., New York University, 1959), pp. 5–7, 35–37, 65–75, 143–158, 168.

3. Robert Christie, *Empire in Wood: A History of the Carpenters' Union* (Ithaca, N.Y., 1956), pp. 10–12; Pred, *Urban Growth*, p. 193; *New York Evening Post*, June 19, 1810; Rock, *Artisans of the New Republic*, pp. 239–240; Rollo G. Silver, *The American Printer, 1787–1825* (Charlottesville, Va., 1967), pp. 1–96; Richard P. Brief, "The Philadelphia Printer: A Study of an Eighteenth-Century Businessman," *Business History Review*, 40 (1968), 46.

journeymen owned even $150 worth of personal property, while most employers (72.4 percent) held at least that much. In addition, over one-fourth of the masters (25.5 percent) owned a house or store, as opposed to a small fraction of journeymen (2.1 percent). These disparities in wealth were compounded by the difficulties journeymen had in rising to independent standing. Wage earners outnumbered masters by almost four to one.[4]

The age difference between masters and journeymen in this sample averaged only four to seven years, with many craftsmen remaining dependent wage earners for their entire working lives. In the populous sixth ward, three-quarters of artisans less than fifty years old were still journeymen.[5] Consequently, journeymen faced an uncertain future. In all likelihood they would never become masters but would remain permanent wage earners, making subsistence salaries and struggling to stay clear of poverty.

Many journeymen established craft associations in reaction to these changes. These organizations acted as benevolent societies, collecting and distributing funds for the families of sick and deceased members, and they served as trade unions to ensure an adequate and secure compensation. One crucial area of conflict between masters and journeymen was control over the workplace. Urban journeymen struggled to prevent competition from new labor sources, such as immigrants, country craftsmen, and half-trained apprentices. These mechanics did not possess the fine craftsmanship of many of New York's veteran journeymen, but their abilities were suitable for the less refined work needed for large national and international markets. Employers liked them because they were willing to work for lower wages.[6]

To gain and to implement acceptable agreements, the journeymen

4. Rock, *Artisans of the New Republic*, pp. 265–268.
5. Ibid., pp. 267–268.
6. The decline of apprenticeship in the eighteenth century is traced by Ian M. G. Quimby, "Apprenticeship in Colonial Philadelphia," (M.A. thesis, University of Delaware, 1963); and Sharon V. Salinger, "Artisans, Journeymen, and the Transformation of Labor in Late Eighteenth-Century Philadelphia," *William and Mary Quarterly*, 3d ser., 40 (1983), 62–84. For the early national era, see W. J. Rorabaugh, *The Craft Apprentice* (New York, 1986). The origins of the migration of country mechanics to the city has been traced from New York City lists of the evening watch. Rock, *Artisans of the New Republic*, p. 243. On immigration, see Carol Groneman Pernicone, "The 'Bloody Ould Sixth': A Social Analysis of a New York City Working Class Community in the Mid-Nineteenth Century," (Ph.D. diss., University of Rochester, 1973), pp. 29–35; Pomerantz, *New York, An American City*, pp. 201–209.

societies resorted to collective action, including appeals to employers; communications with societies in other cities; the establishment of their own enterprises; appeals to the public; walkouts against individual masters; and general turnouts against all the masters in the city in a particular trade. In taking these actions, the journeymen often published appeals and manifestos declaring their motives. They did not see their hope for financial independence as entirely lost. Rather, they articulated, often eloquently, a high regard for their own abilities and standing in society. Aware of the great economic changes swirling around them, and infused with the republican ideology of the era, they feared a decline in their position as skilled workingmen earning a respectable living. They argued that in the spirit of the ideas of the American Revolution, industrious craftsmen should be treated with respect, given decent wages, and afforded financial security in old age or infirmity. These documents also reveal a sharp antagonism toward the master craftsmen, whom the journeymen portrayed as selfish and uncaring men bent on enriching themselves at the expense of their employees. By their actions these masters had broken the bonds that united mechanics as a producer class.

"One Bed, One Cup, One Knife and Fork, Table, and Chair, Is Enough"
THE LIFE OF GRANT THORBURN

Grant Thorburn was a Scottish immigrant who came to New York in 1794 at the age of twenty. A journeyman nailmaker, he had been briefly imprisoned in Scotland for reform activities and for his participation in a movement for constitutional change led by the London Corresponding Society. Even before leaving Europe, therefore, he had been affiliated with artisans inspired by the French and American revolutions.[7] Thorburn went on to live a prosperous life as a nailmaker, grocer, and ultimately a dealer in seeds. Although he knew

7. On the London Corresponding Society and the movement behind it, see E. P. Thompson, *The Making of the English Working Class* (London, 1964); and Albert Goodwin, *The Friends of Liberty: The English Democratic Movement in the Age of the French Revolution* (Cambridge, Mass., 1979). On the history of Jacobins emigres in America, of whom Thorburn was most untypical, see Richard Twomey, *Jacobins and Jeffersonians: Anglo-American Radicalism in the United States, 1790–1820* (New York, 1989).

little of American traditions, Thorburn's political education and commitment, his strong religious convictions, his practicality, and his willingness to work assisted him in overcoming serious economic and emotional setbacks, including the death of his wife, the loss of his trade to machinery, and insolvency.

His description of his first years in Gotham demonstrates the opportunities for journeymen to find employment in the prosperity of the 1790s as well as the perils of urban life. The driving ambition, the willingness to work long hours, the stubborn pride and loyalty are all part and parcel of the republican artisan tradition.

The following account from Thorburn's memoirs begins at his arrival in New York. Having no residence, funds, or work, he decided to stay on board ship a few more days (from Grant Thorburn, *Forty Years' Residence in America* [Boston, 1834], pp. 25–27, 32–37, 45–48, 54–58, 72–73).

While thus employed [eating dinner] a boat came alongside; in the boat was Dr. Kemp, one of the professors of Columbia College; James Anderson of Broadway; and George Cleland hardware-merchant, of Maiden Lane. When they came on deck, . . . Cleland asked if there were any nail-makers on board. I catched the word, and looking up, answered, I was one. He was a tall man, and looking down on me—who no doubt made a very small appearance, sitting flat on deck, with a bowl of potatoes nearly as high as my breast, he enquired, with a tone of surprise, "Can you make nails?" I answered quickly, "I would wager sixpence (all I had) I would make more nails, in one day, than any man in the country." The answer, manner, and speaker, set the company into a roar of laughter which ended by my receiving a card, to call at this store as soon as we got on shore. As an apology for the above boast I will only state, that a few weeks before I left home, in one day, from six A.M. to nine P.M. for a wager of sixpence, I made 3,320 nails. This was more by 400, as far as was ever heard of among the craft, to have been made by any man in the same time in Britain.

Next morning we sallied forth, with the important card in our hands, marked No. 33 Maiden Lane, to find George Cleland. At the head of the wharf we were stopped by a man, whose name, he told us, was Watkins. He inquired if there were any nail-makers on board; we said that was our trade, and informed him we were going to seek

33 Maiden Lane, where we expected to get employment. He advised us first to go and see his shop, and said he would give us employment, and pay us a penny a pound more for making nails than had ever been given before, as he was much in want, all his men having gone to sea about two weeks before at the raising of the embargo, when Mr. Jay sailed as ambassador for London.[8] We went and found places in his shop (situated in Batavia Lane) for twelve men to work, and only one man employed. He made us many tempting offers, which we partly agreed to accept; only, as we had first promised to see Cleland, we must give him a call. Our minds being so far made up to go to Watkin's, I thought it not worth while to go to Cleland's, but went back to the ship, and told my brother to go to Cleland's, to make good our promise. When he came back, however, and told me Mr. Cleland and his wife were Scotch folk, that we should have the shop to ourselves—and his shop was quite empty—that he said he would do all that Watkins had promised, and also told me he did not curse and swear as Watkins did, and, besides, added that they had no children, we concluded to go with him.

After-experience made us thank Providence, who had directed our choice, for they were Christian people, and treated us as if we had been their own children; and having the shop to ourselves, we were not exposed to bad company. We engaged board in a house which is still standing, No. 8, Dutch Street; Mr. Banker occupied the ground floor—he was a shoemaker; and David Brown, a journeyman carpenter, lived up stairs. His wife kept a few boarders, and they being Edinburgh folks, from national feelings we went to board with them. About sun down on the 17th, we brought our luggage from the ship to the said house; it consisted of a large chest, containing our clothes, a box of books, mattrass and blankets. I suppose, on the whole, we made rather a sorry appearance; for it was quite repugnant to our notions of Scottish economy to put on a Sunday coat on a week day; at any rate, our appearance, and the appearance of a cart stopping at the door loaded with moveables, drew out the wrath, tongue and body of Mr. Banker, to the street. He declared that our trash should not enter the house; that Brown hired the rooms above from him, and he should not bring any of his *dirty Irish* into his house, &c. Had

8. Chief Justice John Jay sailed to London in 1794, where he negotiated a treaty avoiding war over British impressment and seizure policies.

he called us lousy Scotch, I would have forgot it; but I could not swallow being called dirty Irish. However, after a parley we were permitted to deposit our bedding and luggage in the garret; but I thought it a very uncourteous welcome. . . .

[Within a month Thorburn and his brother moved nearer their workshop, taking rooms with a widow and her daughter on Liberty Street.]

On reflection I think the three months I resided at No. 100, Liberty Street, was the only period that I spent in America in what I may call boyish amusement. The school for the children belonging to the Society of Friends [Quakers] was kept in a small building, on the spot where the meeting-house now stands. Brown, afterwards General Brown, who bore a conspicuous part in what was termed the northern campaign (in 1812 or 1813), was at that time their teacher. The boys before school-hours assembled in our nail-shop,[9] where they used to warm themselves, and amuse away their spare time by feeding a young monkey that I had procured from a Portuguese vessel, and kept in the shop. They always brought nuts and apples enough to supply the wants of Jacko and his master too. By this means I formed an acquaintance with many of those young lads, who are now useful and respectable men of business in our city; . . .

About this time (October, 1794) they were putting the roof on the City Hotel—this is the first roof that was slated in America. When they came to put on the slates they were at a stand—slate-nails were not in the city, as they had never before been wanted; the American nail-makers had never made such a nail, for there was no demand for them; (there is an art in making the slate-nail, known only to those who have learned it). In this dilemma, they heard of my brother and I; the builder was a Scotchman, and knew we could make slate-nails. They applied to us, to know at how much per thousand we would make them; we promised to answer next day. In the mean time, my brother and I consulted on what we then thought the principles of equity and justice; we spoke of $1 per thousand, but concluded this was too much, and so fixed the price at 93 3/4 cents per thousand. I often since have smiled at our squeamish simplicity; had we charged

9. Cleland set up and financed their nail shop.

$2 per thousand it would not have been too much. It was a good day's work to make a thousand, and, when we had the trade and price in our hands, $2 per day was nothing extraordinary. However, my eye-teeth were not then cut; I found out since, that everyone has his price, and makes the best of any advantage that circumstances may put in his power.

[Thorburn and his brother moved again, and Grant fell passionately in love with Rebecca, his landlady's daughter and a seamstress, or "mantua maker."]

About this time, in the spring of 1796, my brother not being in good health, we hired a small store, having saved about one hundred dollars; we laid it out in hardware, and got fifty dollars worth more on credit, consisting of pins, needles, scissors, knives, &c. My brother was to attend the store, while I was to make nails to support us both. When I began to place our hundred and fifty dollars' worth of goods on the shelves, I found they would make a very poor appearance; and as I was just beginning to find out that appearances went a great way in this world, I procured a number of brick-bats and round sticks of wood; the wood I sawed in lengths, and covered it with ironmongers' paper, having one shaving-box or snuff-box attached to one end. These when laid on the shelves, occupied the space, and appeared to be six, twelve, or twenty-four boxes, just as the size may be; a brick-bat thus covered, having a knife and fork outside, looked as well on the shelf as two dozen real ones; so on with scissors, &c. &c., till the shelves were decently filled, and the store made a respectable appearance. I procured a glass case to stand on the counter, in which I kept four, six, or eight of a sort for retailing, and as they sold off I procured half-a-dozen more by wholesale; so I had no occasion to discompose my brick-bats nor wood blocks. . . . My brother got tired of attending store and went off to Philadelphia. I was now in great trouble; we were beginning to make some pennies by the store and did not like to give it up; neither did I like to give up my nail-making, for this was sure. So I resolved to push my courtship, calculating, that if I got married, I would have a shopkeeper of my own, but if not, to sell off and leave the city, for I could not live in New York and see her the wife of another; and in the mean time continued to keep both. For this end I arose at four o'clock, A.M., and made nails to eight; opened store at eight; staid in till twelve: thus getting scant four hours' sleep in the twenty-four. My nail-shop window opened into the yard of the house where I boarded, and where my girl lived. She used to come to the window; I helped her in, where she staid sewing or knitting till midnight; I working and courting, thus killing two birds with one stone.

Mrs. Lindsay, that mother of Israel in our church—wife of George Lindsay,[10] long a respectable stone cutter in this city, whom my wife had made her confidant, knowing we were engaged, proposed that we should get married at her house, as she said, to keep things quiet and prevent expense, knowing our stock was small. . . . As I always liked to save time this arrangement exactly met my ideas; I stuck to my hammer till the usual hour of seven o'clock, joined the company at eight, drank tea, was married, and got home before ten o'clock. The room we lived in was six feet by twelve; our furniture was a bed and bedstead, one pine table (value of fifty cents), three Windsor chairs, a soup-pot, tea-kettle, six cups and saucers, a griddle, frying-pan and brander. It was enough—it was all we wanted; we were all the world to one another. Now we have carpets to shake, brasses to scour, stairs to scrub; mahogany to polish, china to break, servants to scold; and what does it all amount to? For your own necessity, one bed, one cup, one knife and fork, table, and chair, is enough. . . .[11]

We went to housekeeping in a small wooden building, No. 22, Nassau street, having only a ground floor; this I partitioned off into a store, kitchen and bedroom, which also served for our parlor. Here we lived in peace and happiness—here, on the 22d of September, 1798, our only child was born. On that memorable day, sixty-three persons died of yellow fever in the city. On this occasion, and through the whole prevalence of that dreadful calamity, I have to record the preserving goodness and mercy of God. The fever com-

10. Lindsay was a master stone cutter, a Scotsman, and an elder in Thorburn's church.

11. In a later memoir Thorburn revealed that the marriage was rushed because of the jealousy of a rival suitor, Castelli, a wealthy merchant who lived nearby. Castelli became unstable and had to be watched twenty-four hours a day. According to Thorburn "he often exclaimed, had she only married a gentleman, he would have thought nothing of it; but to refuse him, and take a poor black nail-maker, was more than flesh and blood could bear." Castelli subsequently married the first eligible girl he met, with whom he had a daughter, and died. Grant Thorburn, *Fifty Years' Reminiscences of New-York* (New York, 1845), pp. 58–59.

menced about the middle of July, and on the 12th of August it seemed to rage with tenfold fury; the inhabitants began to fly, and in a few days the city seemed nearly forsaken.[12] We having no friends in the country to fly to, and not having money to support us there in idleness, concluded it was our duty to remain, and trust God with our lives and concerns. My employer, George Cleland, before he removed from town, laid in for me a stock of iron and coals; and told me to make and sell the nails if I was able, as all the hardware stores in the lower parts of the city were shut up. My chief employment now was to make and sell nails for coffins.[13]

All the hardware shops shut up, and I then had as much as I could do making nails for the coffin-makers. A carpenter residing in War-ren-Street employed the whole time while the fever prevailed in making coffins from the white-pine boards. He had a light hand-wagon, with four wheels, on which he placed his coffins, and sent forth his two little boys to sell around the streets, at four dollars each; stopping at intersections of the streets, they would sing out "Coffins! Coffins of all sizes!"[14]

The first alarm of the yellow fever was given on the 26th of July, 1798. By the 15th of August, fourteen cases were reported to have terminated fatally. By the 25th the excitement was terrible; the city was all commotion. Every vehicle, from the humble dungcart to the gilded carriage, was now in requisition, removing families, furniture, and goods—the old man of eighty with the stripling of one year, the lame, the halt, and the blind, all crowding the boats, the lanes and outlets from the city, fear quickening their pace, and the destroying angel at their heels. . . . About this time, many instances like the following, came under my notice: —A respectable shoemaker, living at the corner of Pine and Front Streets, removed with his wife and younger children. His son, about 21, and a confidential townsman of mine, and an old colored woman, requested permission to stay, as they said they were not afraid of the fever. In a few days all were

12. During yellow fever epidemics many merchants and men of wealth moved out of range of the fever's most dangerous areas. Very few artisans and unskilled laborers, who lived in the outer wards, were able to flee the city. See Rock, *Artisans of the New Republic*, p. 3.

13. Over three hundred died the week of August 12.

14. This paragraph is taken from Thorburn's later memoir, *Fifty Years' Reminiscences of New-York*, p. 70.

Figure 11. The scene of a coffin being carried through the streets was a common occurrence during yellow fever epidemics, and the sale of coffins was a profitable trade. *Coffin Carried by Bearers,* in Samuel Wood, *Proof Book* (New York, 1820), NYHS

taken sick. The journeyman was my townsman—I was intimate in the families. I procured a doctor and nurse, and gave what attention I could. On the 5th day, the son died. Early next morning I found the house locked up and the key gone—I made an entry though a low window—the nurse had fled, and took some of the small moveables by way of compensation. The black woman had rolled from her bed in the agonies of death, and was lying on the floor—being unable to lift her, I put a pillow under her head, covered her body with a sheet, and entered the next room where my friend lay, his eyes closing fast in the sleep of death: in two hours the woman died—I procured a hearse, and watched by my friend till 8 P.M., when he also died. . . .

Sabbath, 15th September. — All the Churches downtown, known by the name of *orthodox* and *reformed*, being shut up, the poor who could not fly, were very glad to pick what little crumbs of gospel they could find in the good old Church of the *Trinity* which was open every Sabbath. As the bell was tolling for afternoon service, Mr. J., and his wife, and myself and wife, (we had all been married within the year)

were walking among the tombs—as we turned the east corner [, . . .]
Mrs. J., who was a lively girl, turned her husband round, and exclaimed, (in a sort of playful manner,) "J., if I die of the fever you
must bury me there" (pointing to the spot). Next day she was reported; and on Friday, the 21st, we buried her there—and there you
may see her grave-stone until this day. . . . Very many fell a sacrifice
to the fever for want of proper attendance about this time, especially
among those who were left in charge of their master's houses. Relations, and sometimes acquaintances, would attend one another, but
many died unknown and unlamented. . . . Cats, and in some cases,
dogs, were thoughtlessly left, shut up to die a cruel death—the streets
also were swarming with famishing animals, whose piteous howlings
added much to the distress of the few inhabitants who were unable to
leave the city. In these times that tried the souls as well as the bodies
of men, I saw parents fly from their sick children, and children from
their parents, husbands from their wives; but never, except in one
solitary instance, did I see a woman desert her husband.

[Thorburn's wife died of consumption two years later, leaving him
alone with his child and work.]

Being thus left with a child two years and two months old, with
the care of a house and store, and thinking it more creditable and
wise to marry a wife than to hire a housekeeper, I again entered into
that state in 1801. Shortly after this, the introduction of cut-nails cut
me off from making a living by my hammer. I now kept a grocery,
and had a good run of customers: I still resided at No. 22, Nassau
Street.

On the east corner of Nassau and Liberty Streets, there lived the
venerable old gentleman, Mr. Isaac Van Hook, so well known as the
sexton of the New Dutch Church opposite his house, for nearly fifty
years. James Laing and William Smith, both cabinet-makers, and carrying on a respectable business, having in their employment ten to
twelve journeymen and apprentices; these men took a mad resolution, gave up the business, sold their stock, hired the corner house
over the head of poor old Van Hook, turned him and his tobacco-
pipes out of doors, and commenced the grocery business. Theirs being
a corner, took away the most of my customers; insomuch that I was
obliged to look round for some other mode to support my family.

[Thorburn began selling painted flower pots, then plants within pots, and ultimately he became a very successful seedsman. He was also a companion of Tom Paine in Paine's last lonely years, agreeing on politics but disagreeing over religion. His church, however, was less indulgent of this friendship with a notorious enemy of Christianity and expelled Thorburn from singing in church for three months for shaking hands with Paine.]

"A World of Trials, Troubles, and Vexations"
THE LIFE AND DEATH OF GEORGE HART

A journeyman's life in New York was never easy. Salaries were seldom much above a subsistence wage. Liquor was readily available, and, consequently, drinking and violence were common pitfalls for large numbers of artisans. In 1810, for instance, 1,300 groceries and 160 taverns had licenses to sell "strong drink."[15] The case of baker George Hart, executed for the murder of a girlfriend who angered him by taking some of his money, shows a journeyman who never achieved independent standing. His world and that of his employer, while not necessarily adversarial, had little in common. An encounter with a fellow worker left a mark on his life from which he never fully recovered. Certainly Hart was not typical, since most journeymen did not commit criminal acts. But his economic fall, his problems with drinking, and his propensity to violence were not very unusual among the city's unskilled and journeyman population.

Born in 1771 in Bowden, Scotland, Shire of Roxburgh, and raised by his blacksmith father, Hart was apprenticed to the baking trade. After working as a journeyman he opened his own shop in 1793. Forced to emigrate by the severe price inflation of flour caused by the French Revolutionary wars, he apparently lacked any partisan electoral affiliation or interest. He was an immigrant with little political education or awareness, looking only to survive. American revolu-

15. New York Evening Post, January 9, 1810; Report of the Committee of the Common Council, City Clerk Filed Papers, March 8, 1816, NYCMA; Rock, Artisans of the New Republic, pp. 296–298; Rock, The New York City Artisan, 1789–1825: A Documentary History (Albany, 1989), pp. 45–47. For an overview of alcoholism in the early republic see W. J. Rorabaugh, The Alcoholic Republic: An American Tradition (New York, 1979).

tionary traditions were foreign to him and he apparently never came under their influence. While this may or may not have been a contributing factor to his fall, attachment to republican values with an emphasis on virtue and hard work may have saved a number of journeymen from succumbing to poverty and other snares of an early nineteenth-century seaport. The document below, *Trial for Murder. Court of Oyer and Terminer . . . 1811. The People vs. George Hart, Murder* (n.p., n.d. [ca. 1812]), relates his last days.

I had entered into business for myself in the baking line, and had made considerable progress in my profession, had accumulated some property, and found myself in good circumstances, and so continued after I was married, until the commencement of the French revolution, which created so much trouble, and the high price of wheat, which was continually encreasing, caused me to give up all prospects of future success, and leave my native country in the summer of the year 1796. Having taken a farewell leave of my country, and leaving behind me one wife and one child, they not being willing to come with me. I sailed from Greenwich with about 50 other passengers on board the ship Polly, of Boston, capt. Cheeseman, bound to New-York. Among the passengers were my mother and sister; my father and brother having sailed before me had arrived and settled in New-York. We arrived here on the 7th of September, 1796, after a boisterous passage of near ten weeks.

Having landed once more on Terra Firma, I made an engagement with a Mr. William Ramage, a countryman of mine, who resided at the foot of Partition-street, to work with him at the baking business. I soon after quit Mr. Ramage's employ, and engaged with Mr. John Hyslop, in John-street, with whom I continued some time and afterwards worked with several other employers in this city.

About the commencement of the melancholy season of the year 1798, when pestilence and fever prevailed in the city, my wife and child arrived from Scotland, and about this time I lost my father and mother within 12 hours of each other, with the then prevailing epedemic or yellow fever. . . .

Previous to my leaving Mr. Hyslop's employ, an accurrence happened which caused considerable uneasiness in my own mind, as well as among my friends. The circumstance was this; a journeyman baker, of the name of Archibald McLaughlin came into the bakehouse, where I was peaceably at work; his language was of the most atrocious and provoking kind, which caused my passions to rise in a vehement manner. — When I seized him by the shoulders, or pushed him out or towards the door, he fell on his head on a flour barrel, which stood by the door, and was cut in a very severe manner. McLaughlin was at this time in a high state of intoxication, and was seldom ever sober either before or after this transaction. He, however, the next day obtained a warrant against me, when I was taken and procured the necessary security: we soon made the matter up and I was afterwards liberated from my bail.

[Though McLaughlin's head healed, he soon died of alcoholism. Fearing indictment, Hart fled to Baltimore, caught a severe cold, and returned to New York to find work.]

Being somewhat recovered, and having little money by me, I took a place in Rose-street, and went into partnership in the line of my profession with one Alexander Runey, who soon after contrived to deprive me of about seventy dollars, and left me to seek recompence as well I could.

Thus having been deprived of my little all, my next pursuits were that of a pedlar or a hawker of books; and should have done well in this kind of business, if I could have had controul of my own passions; but having to encounter such a series of misfortunes attendant on all my former transactions, my spirits failed me, and I began to give myself up to drinking, and could seldom keep sober a single day.

At this time, I went to live in East George-street in the upper part of a house occupied by a Mrs. Cooper, whose husband I understood was on board the Boston frigate; her appearance was that of a lewd woman, and in one of my drunken frolicks I treated her ill by calling her a w——e. This so much irritated her that she endeavored by all the means which lay in her power, to entrap and bring me into difficulty. In this business she soon succeeded. As artful as she was, she soon found a pliant tool, who by the by, was more subtle than herself, of the name of Bonner, who kept a store below: consultations were held between the two, to work my ruin if possible. The result was, that she applied to the Police Office, and swore that I had attempted to have connection with my little daughter then about eight years of age; with the help of Bonner, I was committed to Bridewell, stood my trial, justice was done, and I was liberated from confinement by an honorable acquittal. . . .

I then removed to Greenwich-street, where, not being able to pay my rent, my furniture was seized, and I, with my little family, went into the Alms-House; but not liking the confinement of this place, I left them there, and again assumed the occupation of a pedlar of books, &c. Now commenced the most awful part of a life already borne down by misfortunes almost too insupportable to bear up with, depressed in spirits and overwhelmed with grief, it was utterly impossible for me to keep aloof from the dram shop—so infatuated was I with this kind of way, that I began to lead a most dissipated life, and was scarcely sober a day or even an hour; oftentimes renting a room in one place, then in another, and frequently lodging in houses where I might have been a welcome guest, had I been so provident as to have laid up the means, which I could do were it not for my inordinate propensity for liquor. Left to myself—unhappy in my disposition—thinking of former prosperous days, and as often returning to my evil ways—taking copious draughts of a poisonous liquor, brings me now to an inglorious fate and untimely fate. The crime for which I must acknowledge, was one against the laws of God and my country, was committed on the 25th day of June last, on the body of one Mary Van Hansen; with this person I had but a slight acquaintance, only having known her since the month of April. When our connexion commenced, we lived in a cellar belonging to a Mr. Campbell, in Cheapside-street. The rent was 5s. per week. In order to ease my rent, I took in with me a man by the name of Thomas, a printer by profession, who was to pay half the rent. Thomas was out of employ and had engaged himself with others under the late Dog Act to destroy these animals.[16] Previous to my committing this most horrible deed, Thomas was idle; it being on Monday, and I having but few things in my basket to vend, I did not go out to sell anything, but went in pursuit of work with Thomas, and had the good luck to be employed to carry in 16 loads of wood for a Mrs. Campbell in Greenwich-street. This done we came home towards evening, when I

16. In 1811 city officials passed a more stringent dog ordinance and appointed a special dog collector, who then hired large numbers of men as day laborers to capture and execute dogs. At least two thousand dogs were captured and killed that year. Paul A. Gilje, *The Road to Mobocracy: Popular Disorder in New York City, 1763–1834* (Chapel Hill, N.C., 1987), pp. 224–227.

found a strange woman in the cellar, and asked her for Polly (meaning the unfortunate woman whom I murdered) and was answered that she had not seen her. I then went to several places in pursuit of her in vain. She not being in the habit of staying out, I arose in the morning at 5 o'clock, and found her sitting in the alley or gangway. I asked her what made her stay out; she made little or no reply, and went into the cellar. I left her and went to an adjacent store, drank freely, returned, and thought it too early to go out with my basket to purchase books &c. as I intended with the little money I had, and therefore, laid down and slept till about 7, on waking up, found no person in the cellar but myself and her laying alongside of me. When I arose, on feeling my pockets, found my money gone, and accused her of purloining it from me, she denied having taken it; but knowing that she had frequently plundered me, my passions were raised to a great height. I seized a billet of wood and beat her; the result is well known; her DEATH ensued, and to expiate my offence, I this day leave a world, and with it a world of trials, troubles, and vexations. . . .

And now taking a last and final adieu of all earthly things, I hope that the sins of a father may not be cast up as a reproach to the unoffending widow, and my dear and innocent children.

GEORGE HART

City Prison, January 2, 1812

"Speaking to the Judge as Familiarly as If He Were a Common Mechanic"
LETTER OF JOHN DOYLE TO HIS WIFE, 1818

Ireland was the source of many artisan immigrants. John Doyle, from Kilkenny, was the son of Edmund Doyle who was active in radical politics in Great Britain as a member of the United Irishmen. The elder Doyle, a member of the rebels in County Wexford in 1798, had his home gutted, his furniture burned in the street, and his family scattered among different relatives. Edmund eventually found his way to Philadelphia. John, who left his pregnant wife, Fanny, in Ireland, joined his father after the War of 1812. John eventually became a well-known bookseller in New York, keeping a store on Broadway until 1852.[17]

The following letter from John to Fanny (who would follow the next year) discloses an enterprising and adaptable journeyman printer who overcame discouragement and dishonest practices, and who was willing to change occupations with hardly a second thought ("Letter of John Doyle to His Wife, Fanny, January 25, 1818," *Journal of the American Irish Historical Society*, 12 [1913], 201–202, 204). His comments on the immigrant experience are most revealing. Equally enlightening are his observations on the republican manner in which Americans viewed themselves and foreign governments. Even with his wry observations of American notions, however, his final thoughts constitute an affirmation of republicanism.

We were safely landed in Philadelphia on the 7th of October and I had not so much as would pay my passage in a boat to take me ashore. My distress and confusion for the want of three or four pence was very great, and such was the jealousy and miserableness of the passengers that there was not one who would lend another even that sum. I, however, contrived to get over, and God is my witness that at that moment, I would as soon the ground would open and swallow me up. It was not long till I made out my father, whom I instantly knew, and no one could describe our feelings when I made myself known to him, and received his embraces, after an absence of seventeen years. The old man was quite distracted about me. He done nothing that entire day but bring me about to his friends. Their manner of receiving me was quite amusing; one would say you are welcome, sir, from the old country; another, you are welcome to this free country—you are welcome to this land of liberty. Pray sir, are you not happy to have escaped from the tyranny of the old country? When you would deny the tyranny and give the preference to home, they would look amazed and say, "What sir, would you not rather live in a free country than in slavery?" In short they imagine here that we can not act or speak in Ireland but as the authorities please. Their ignorance and presumption are disgusting, their manners worse. As to politeness and good nature, they are totally unknown and though

17. See Richard C. O'Connor, "John T. Doyle," *Journal of the American Irish Historical Society*, 11 (1912), 141–142.

they all pretend to be well acquainted with the affairs of Europe they are entirely ignorant of all transactions there, or at the best know them imperfectly. If my father's love could do me any good I did not want for it, for it amounted to jealousy. The morning after landing I went to work to the printing and to my great surprise I found that my hand was very little out. There is an immensity of printing done in America, still it is not as good as other businesses, and I think a journeyman printer's wages might be averaged at 7 1/2 dollars a week all the year round. In New York it may not be so much as they are often out of work. The bookbinding may be put upon a footing with the printing; they execute work here remarkably well. I worked in Philadelphia for four and one-half weeks and saved £6, that is counting four dollars to the pound. . . . I wrote to poor Lewis who gave me the most pressing invitation to come to New York where I now am, and where I every day experience from them some fresh kindness. My father put every obstacle he could in my way to prevent my going to New York but when he found that all he could do would not change my mind and that his entreaties to stay with him were in vain, he parted with me drowned in tears to such a pitch that he was unable to speak and since my arrival here he is every week writing to me to go back. I found the printing and bookbinding overpowered with hands in New York. I remained idle for twelve days in consequence; when finding there was many out of employment like myself I determined to turn myself to something else, seeing that there was nothing to be got from idleness. The trifle that I had saved was going from me fast. I drove about accordingly and was engaged by a bookseller to hawk maps for him at 7 dollars a week. This I done much to his satisfaction but when the town was well supplied he discharged me and instead of paying me my entire bill he stopped 9 dollars for maps which he said I made him no return for. I had to look for justice but was defeated for want of a person to prove my account. I lost the 9 dollars which I reckon to be 45 shillings. However, I got such an insight into the manners and customs of the natives whilst going among them with the maps as served me extremely. I now had about 60 dollars of my own saved, above every expense. These I laid out in the purchase of pictures on New Year's Day, which I sell ever since. I am doing astonishingly well, thanks be to God and was able on the 26th of this month to make a deposit of 100 dollars in the bank of the United States. Thus you see, my dearest Fanny, God has at length done something for us; every penny of it is my own hard earnings and I am now convinced that it is only by deserving his blessing that we can hope or expect to merit His favors; *apropos*, I must inform you that I made a solemn promise to God while at sea that if it was His goodness to spare my life till I get ashore, I would make a hearty confession of my sins, which I thank Him for having granted me time and grace to perform, and this I mention, my love, because I know that it will be a source of pleasure to you; though living happy in the midst of my brother's family whom you know that I always loved and being as yet very successful in dealing in the pictures and indeed I may say in everything I have taken in hand since I came to America, I feel, particularly in the evenings, when I return home, a lonesomeness and lowness of spirits which oppress me almost to fainting. Oh my dearest Fanny if I could but convince you now that I am so many thousand miles from you of how insipid and distressing society and particularly women is to me, you would pity me of all creatures and fly to fill up that vacancy in my mind and spirits which my absence from you occasions. . . .

As yet it's only natural I should feel lonesome in this country, ninety-nine out of every hundred who come to it are at first disappointed. They need never expect to realize the high expectations they have of it. Still it's a fine country and a much better place for a poor man than Ireland. It's a money-making country too, and much as they grumble at first after a while they never think of leaving it, though they could get a passage home every day for a trifle if they wished it. I have seen a great many of the Kilkenny people here, and they are all in good health except James Maxwell with whom the climate does not seem to agree. It gives me great courage to find that I have now more to the good and made more of my short time than most of them who are here two or three years. The fact is some of them earn a good deal, but they indulge too much in drink.

A man who can make a living at home has no business to come to the United States. . . . One thing I think is certain that if the emigrants knew before hand what they have to suffer for about the first six months after leaving home in every respect they would never come here. However, an enterprising man, desirous of advancing himself in the world will despise everything for coming to this free country, where a man is allowed to thrive and flourish, without having a penny taken out of his pocket by government; no visits from tax gatherers, constables or soldiers, every one at liberty to act and speak as he likes, provided it does not hurt another, to slander and damn government, abuse public men in their office to their faces, wear your hat in court and smoke a cigar while speaking to the judge as familiarly as if he was a common mechanic, hundreds go unpunished for crimes for which they would surely be hung in Ireland; in fact, they are so tender of life in this country that a person should have a very great interest to get himself hanged for anything!

"None But Persons of Good Character"
THE CONSTITUTION OF THE NEW-YORK JOURNEYMEN SHIPWRIGHTS SOCIETY

The economy of New York depended on commerce. During the largely prosperous years of the early national era, the wharves were scenes of constant motion. Cartmen drove their wagons filled with supplies and wares; coopers constructed the barrels essential to trade; and the shipyards along the Hudson and East rivers resounded with the noise of shipwrights, riggers, and caulkers hammering and sawing as they labored in the construction of ships both large and small.[18]

The maritime trades comprised one of the major industries of the port cities. Mechanics in these trades worked in cooperative ventures under the guidance of a boatbuilder who would hire the needed shipwrights, riggers, and sailmakers. Many of these journeymen and masters moved from shipyard to shipyard, depending on which builders received contracts. A few craftsmen worked indoors, such as coopers in large workshops and sailmakers in lofts.

The journeymen in the maritime trades have left few records of walkouts against employers. They were deeply concerned, however, with the possible entry of lesser skilled employees into their trades, namely, mechanics who threatened to lower wages and degrade a respectable craft. Article 20 of the New-York Journeymen Ship-

18. The importance of the seaport may be seen from the effects of the trade embargo of 1808–1809. See John Lambert, *Travels through Canada and the United States, 1806–1808* (London, 1814), pp. 62–65; and George Daitsman, "Labor and the 'Welfare State' in Early New York," *Labor History*, 4 (1963), 248–256.

Figure 12. Shipwrights traveled from shipyard to shipyard, working for whatever contractor had positions available. Many occupied a position between journeyman and master craftsman. Edward Hazen, *Shipwright,* in *Book of Trades,* (1807), Courtesy of the Library of Congress

wrights Society's Constitution required members not to work with or have anything to do with any fellow member who might "intrude" in the craft and "underwork fully skilled and trained journeymen."

This constitution, typical of journeymen organizations, reveals a republican legacy (*Constitution of the New-York Journeymen Shipwrights Society* [New York, 1804]). The charter called for strict democratic procedures, including open elections, rules for order and decorum, and careful oversight of funds. Organizations like the New-York Journeymen Shipwrights Society served the role of benefit societies, with their funds carefully preserved for relief of distressed members or their families. They also provided a recreational outlet with symbols, rituals, and festivities. Finally, they attempted to regulate trade and preserve their independent economic standing.[19]

19. For a discussion and examples of other constitutions, see Rock, *Artisans of the New Republic,* pp. 272–274; and Rock, *The New York City Artisan,* pp. 199–205.

Figure 13. Alexander Anderson, *Caulkers Repairing a Boat in Dry Dock,* Anderson Scrapbooks, vol. 12, p. 6, NYPL

CONSTITUTION

ART. I. This Society shall be composed of Shipwrights and Caulkers residing in the city and county of New-York; and none but persons of good character shall be admitted.

ART. II. Every candidate for admission into this Society must be proposed and seconded by members at least one meeting previous to introduction. He is then to be balloted for, and if three-fourths of the ballots appear in his favour, he shall be declared duly elected. He shall then be notified to attend for initiation at the next monthly meeting; but if he does not apply for this purpose within three months, he shall forfeit his right of admission.

ART. III. The fee of initiation shall be as follows: For the first six months after the formation of the Society *one dollar*; for the next six months *two dollars*; for the next six months *three dollars*; and for the next six months, and to the end of four years, *four dollars*; after which period it shall be raised to *five dollars*.

ART. IV. Each member of this Society shall pay into the hands of the Treasurer *fifty cents* per month, until it shall be deemed expedient to adopt a greater or less sum. The first monthly due to be paid at the time of initiation.

ART. V. The office-bearers of this Society shall be a President, Vice-President, Secretary, Treasurer, a Standing Committee of five persons, and two Stewards; who shall severally be elected annually by ballot, on the first Thursday in January, and shall be installed at the ensuing monthly meeting. In the intermediate space between their election and instalment their predecessors in office shall arrange and close all their accounts, and deliver them to the officers elect. Every member absent at the time of election, except through sickness or out of the city, shall forfeit *fifty cents*.

ART. VI. The President shall preserve order in the Society: he shall state all reports, and take the sense of the Society upon all questions referred to their decision: he shall also sign all instruments and documents relative to, or on behalf of the Society.

ART. X. The Standing Committee shall inquire into the character of every candidate for admission into this Society. They shall also inquire into the circumstances of indigent and deceased members, so as to prevent imposition, and direct the relief afforded by the Society to proper objects. They shall likewise, in conjunction with the President, appropriate the funds in such manner as shall appear to them best calculated to promote the interest of the Society.

ART. XI. The Stewards shall duly attend at the place of meeting, and open the doors at the appointed time: they shall have charge of the lights, of the boxes, balls, &c. and shall attend at the door, in order that none but members, or persons to be initiated, have entrance: they shall keep lists of the names of the members, with their places of residence, and shall notify them of extra meetings.

ART. XII. The stated meetings of this Society shall be on the first Thursday in each month, an hour after sun-set, at such place as shall be agreed upon.

ART. XIII. Twenty members shall be necessary to form a quorum and proceed to business.

ART. XIV. When a member rises to speak, he shall address the President uncovered. One member only to speak at a time; and he shall not be interrupted unless it be to explain. If a speaker departs from his subject, the President shall call him to order.

ART. XV. Every motion shall be seconded before it is put. A major-

ity to prevail in all cases, except in such as may have relation to the Constitution. The President shall not vote unless on equal divisions.
ART. XVI. In order not to diminish the funds, no money shall be drawn out until after the expiration of one year from the organization of this Society.
ART. XVII. On the death of a member, the President shall cause the Stewards to invite the Society to attend the funeral. The Standing Committee shall inquire into the circumstances of the family of the deceased, and if they are found necessitous, shall report them as such to the Society.
ART. XVIII. At the meetings of this Society the members shall conduct themselves in a decent and orderly manner. Any member appearing intoxicated, or behaving disorderly, shall, for the first offence, be reprimanded by the President, and for the second shall be subject to such censure as the Society may direct.
ART. XX. Every member who shall countenance, instruct, or otherwise assist in their pursuits such persons as intrude on the regular business, and underwork the established wages of the members of this Society, shall in like manner be expelled.
ART. XXIII. No alteration shall be made in this Constitution unless by a concurrence of three-fourths of the members of the Society.
ART. XXIV. Any member contravening or acting in opposition to this Constitution shall be expelled [from] the Society.

MEMBERS

Jeremiah Dodge,
Blathwaite Bonham
[and forty-eight additional signatures]

"He Is Sorry for All That He Has Done"
MINUTES OF THE UNION SOCIETY OF SHIPWRIGHTS AND CAULKERS

The Union Society of Shipwrights and Caulkers does not use the word "journeymen" in either its title or constitution, and its membership may have been open to masters. By 1815 the shipbuilding business, like a number of mechanic trades, had so grown in complexity that only a few artisan entrepreneurs owned shipbuilding operations (including the waterfront property required). Consequently the difference in standing between masters and journeymen may have almost vanished, as nearly all shipwrights were wage earners working for the boatyard owners or their contractors. The concern of the members of the Union Society is well stated in its very first article. Rather than establishing offices and procedures as most such constitutions did, it proclaimed that the journeymen would only work for genuine and experienced shipbuilders. This stipulation was an attempt to keep out interlopers who might cut wages and bring in cheap labor, consequently degrading the profession and undercutting its customs and values. If the shipwrights had to remain wage earners, they intended to have a say as to whom they would accept as employers. The penalty for violation was expulsion and ostracism.

"Minutes of the Union Society of Shipwrights and Caulkers" (1815–1816, NYPL) outline patriotic and charitable activities and detail a case of enforcement of the society's bylaws against both an offending employer and members who worked for that man. Maintaining these regulations preserved the wage and the standing of the craftsman, both central to their place in the new American republic.

May 27, 1815
The minutes of the last meeting was read and approved. The following members was proposed and balloted for and duly elected: Abish Higgins, William Banton, Charles Gordon.
Afterwards
It was moved and seconded [that] the society furnish a Banner by subscription for the purpose of walking in procession of the fourth of July next. It was then moved and seconded that a general meeting of shipwrights and caulkers would be published in the Mercantile, two days; Gazetteer, two days; Columbia, two days—Friday and Saturday.

June 8, 1815
Thursday evening monthly meeting.
The society met at John Morris. The minutes of the last meeting was read and approved. No report from the standing committee. The select committee that was appointed by the society to wait on the different portrait painters of the city of New York for painting a Banner suitable for the union society of shipwrights and caulkers made

Figure 14. Shipyard workers with boats at different stages of construction. Certificate of Membership of the Union Society of Shipwrights and Caulkers, 1814, detail, MCNY

the following report: that they had waited on the most eminent portrait painters in the city to paint this Banner towit Mr. Tuffil, $65 Van der Pool, $90 Jarvis, the highest in the city Smith $100, Plum $80, Childs $80. But afterward considered that he [Childs] could paint the same for $70. The society then agreed unanimously that the said Mr. Childs should appoint the Banner afterwards proposed and balloted the following members, namely, Sanford, Manasseh Beckwith, Philip Doyer, John Dickey, William Williams, Joseph M. Beckwith. The Society then commenced balloting for a steward in the place of Peter Maalamar resigned, and William Martin was duly elected.

Sept. 14, 1815
    The society met at John Morris. Being in order the minutes of the last meeting was read and approved. On a monthly dues collected to the amount of $8. The standing committee reports that Daniel Read and Benjamin Basset members of the society went to work for Sea-

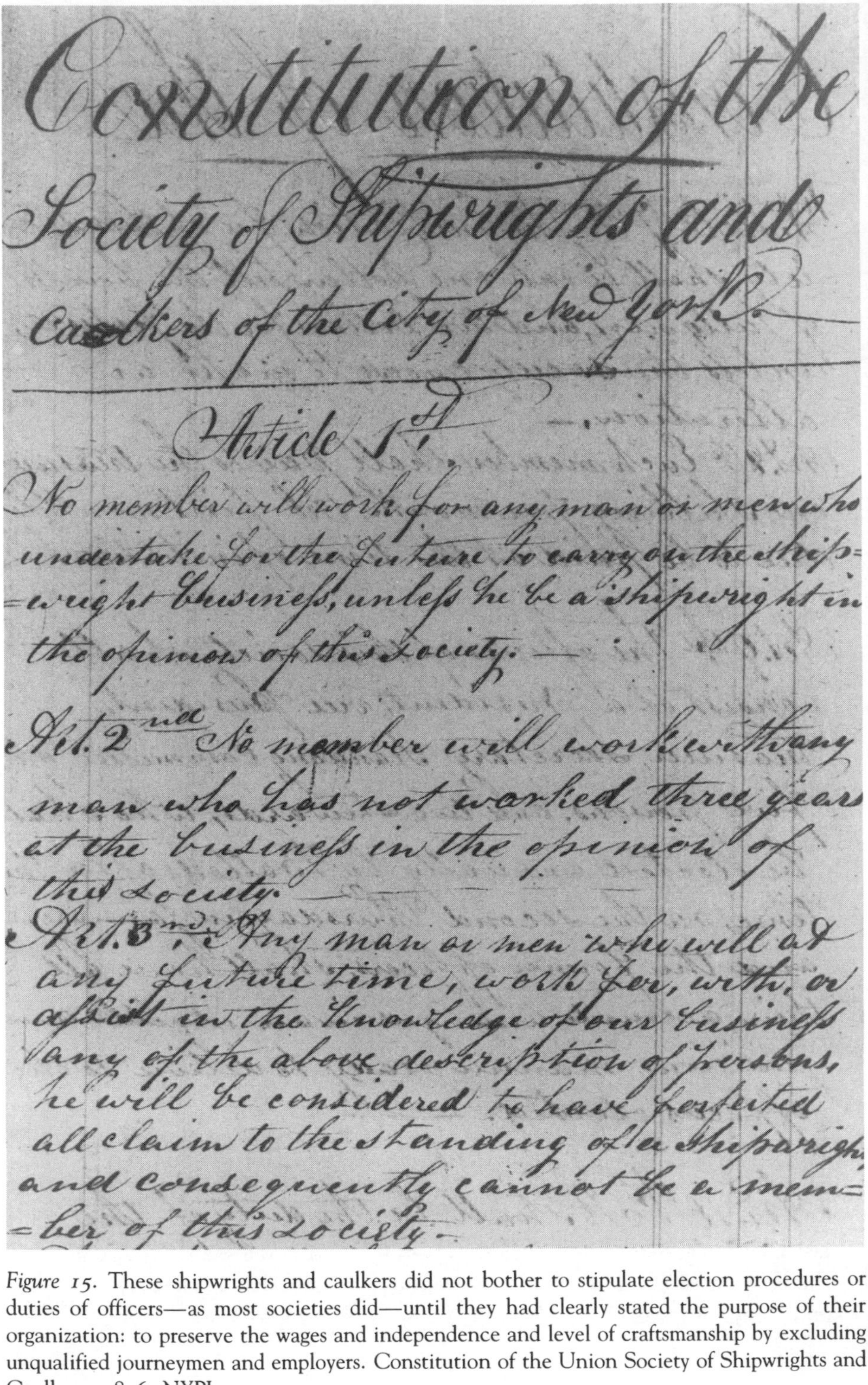
Constitution of the Society of Shipwrights and Caulkers of the City of New York.

Article 1st.

No member will work for any man or men who undertake for the future to carry on the ship=wright business, unless he be a shipwright in the opinion of this Society.—

Art. 2nd No member will work with any man who has not worked three years at the business in the opinion of this Society.—

Art. 3rd: Any man or men who will at any future time, work for, with, or assist in the knowledge of our business any of the above description of persons, he will be considered to have forfeited all claim to the standing of a Shipwright and consequently cannot be a mem=ber of this Society.

Figure 15. These shipwrights and caulkers did not bother to stipulate election procedures or duties of officers—as most societies did—until they had clearly stated the purpose of their organization: to preserve the wages and independence and level of craftsmanship by excluding unqualified journeymen and employers. Constitution of the Union Society of Shipwrights and Caulkers, 1816, NYPL man & Kingsland in opposition to the first article of the constitution when by the unanimous vote of the society they were expelled.

It was moved and seconded and was unanimously carried that a committee of three be appointed to appoint three brothers to draw up a plan of the certificates for the society and offer to them for approbation on the next monthly meeting when the following brothers were chosen: John Dodge, Abraham Devere, Peter Turner, John Buel, Reuben Hoyt.

Sept. 21, 1815

An extra meeting of the society met at John Morris. Being in order the minutes of the last meeting was read and approved. Monthly dues received to the amount of $10.

The standing committee reports that Mr. Kingsland had waited on the chairman of the committee and also the president of the society. [He would] know if he could bring sufficient vouchers that he had worked three years at the shipwright business whether or not the society would not work for him. If found so by the society that he had worked three years at the business they will go to work for Mr. Kingsland. The society then commenced balloting for candidates when the following member was unanimously elected, namely Reuben Miles.

Oct. 12, 1815

Being in order the minutes of the last meeting was read and approved. Monthly dues received to the amount of $12.06. The report of the second quarterly meeting by the treasurer and secretary was read and approved. The standing committee reports that Bennona Boss went to work for Seamond & Kingsland ignorantly and not knowing that he had violated the first article of the constitution. There was a motion made and seconded that he should be reinstated which was done by ballot and he was accepted unanimously. The chairman of the standing committee reports that Ichabod Avery went to work for Seamond & Kingsland and that he was acting in violation of the first article of the constitution. He says that he is sorry for all that he has done and hopes that the Society will forgive him. If so, he will come forward and pay his monthly dues. Several members waited on Mr. Ichabod Avery who was in the lower room and was in no way desirous to come up when the secretary requested: unanimously agreed that Ichabod Avery should be expelled from the society.

It was unanimously agreed to by the society that the certificates be laid over till the next extra meeting held on Monday next for subscription. Received by subscription the sum of $9 for the widow Mills; brothers appointed to carry the money, Donald Cutting, Abraham D. Mevine.

New York, Jan. 3, 1816

The society met at the house of John Morris. Being in order the minutes of the last meeting was read and approved. The society then commenced the proposition of candidates when the following was duly elected: Ichabod Avery was duly elected over again.

"Printing Shall Live and Freedom Reign"
SAMUEL WOODWORTH, JOURNEYMAN POET

Printing in early national New York carried with it a noble tradition. The most illustrious craftsman in the American Revolution, Benjamin Franklin, was a hero within the artisan community. Many societies, particularly but not exclusively in the printing trade, named themselves after him. Samuel Woodworth, a journeyman printer who became a well-known craftsman-poet, was also secretary of the New York Typographical Society. In his poetry Woodworth expressed the journeyman artisan's republican pride in American independence as well as the centrality of the trade of printing in the rise of freedom, reason, and science, and in the struggle against despotism and superstition. The following poem by Woodworth is reprinted from George A. Stevens, *New York Typographical Union Number Six* (Albany, 1912), p. 89.

Printing and Independence

When wrapp'd in folds of feudal gloom,
    Dark superstition awed the world,
Consign'd fair knowledge to the tomb
    And Error's sable flag unfurl'd;
Earth heard this mandate from the skies,
"Let there be light—great Art, arise!"

Fair Science wip'd her tears and smil'd,
  And Infant Genius plum'd his wing,
The Arts assemble round the child,
  And all the glowing chorus sing:
Rise, son of science, quick arise!
And lend thy light to darken'd eyes.

Our Art arose and man had light,
  The clouds of superstition fled,
The fiend of ignorance took his flight
  And Error hid his hateful head;
Whilst swell'd this chorus to the skies,
Our Art shall live and Freedom rise.

The goddess, who for ages past,
  Had wept beneath despotic might,
Her cankering fetters burst at last,
  And claim'd the charter of her right:
While men and seraphs join'd this strain—
"Printing shall live and Freedom reign."

Hail, Freedom! hail, celestial guest!
  O never from thy sons depart;
Thine be the empire of the West,
  Thy temple every freeman's heart;
The Art of Printing gave thee birth,
And brightens still thy reign on earth.

Arise, ye favor'd sons of light,
  Professors of our Heaven-born art,
And in the chorus all unite,
  While joy expands each throbbing heart;
"The Art of Printing shall endure,
And Independence be secure."

"To Render an Art Respectable"
THE NEW YORK TYPOGRAPHICAL SOCIETY'S APPEAL AGAINST HALFWAY JOURNEYMEN

Printing, one of the city's trades most strongly affected by economic growth, was a highly capital-intensive enterprise by the early nineteenth century. Printers could publish more and better books, newspapers, and stationery, but the presses required to do so were costly. The expense of the equipment, therefore, made it difficult for journeymen to go into business for themselves. As the journeymen printers lamented in an 1802 appeal to Congress, "the business of Printing being very expensive to establish, from the high price of materials, very few of those, who are obliged to resort to journey-work when they become free, ever have it in their power to realize a capital sufficient to commence business on their own account."[20]

Masters found themselves less and less on a familial relationship with their journeymen and apprentices, and more and more concerned with customer relations and capital expenditure. Cutting costs was a vital concern in this highly competitive business (New York had up to ten dailies), and if half-trained labor could be used in the printing business (and for a number of tasks it could), then they were willing to acquire the inexpensive services of apprentices with uncompleted indentures and laborers with limited abilities.

Nothing was as distressing to the journeymen as the employment of "half-way journeymen," those who had not completed a full apprenticeship and lacked the skills of trained craftsmen. Their employment denied journeymen the opportunity to achieve the respect and reward due one of the most hallowed of artisan professions. In 1811 the New York Typographical Society, an organization similar to that of the shipwrights, addressed this issue with an impassioned plea to the city's master printers, emphasizing two republican mainstays: economic security and respect (from George A. Stevens, *New York Typographical Union Number Six*, pp. 67–69).[21]

To the Master Printers of the City of New York:

Gentlemen: Viewing with deep concern the improper practices in many of the printing offices in this city, the journeymen composing the New York Typographical Society have appointed the undersigned a committee to address you on the subject and represent the many

20. Rollo Silver, "The Printers' Lobby: Model 1802," in Frederic Bowens, ed., *Virginia Studies in Bibliography* (1950–1951), 2:217–218.

21. For extensive discussions of New York's early typographical unions, see George A. Stevens, *New York Typographical Union Number Six* (Albany, N.Y., 1913); and George Barnett, "The Printers: A Study in Trade Unionism," *American Economic Association Quarterly*, 3d. ser., 10 (1909); and Rock, *The New York City Artisan*, pp. 201–205, 216–218.

Figure 16. Printers held their trade in high esteem because it brought culture and civilization to the vast body of mankind. Anderson engraved many scenes of printing presses and printers at work. Alexander Anderson, *Printing Shop,* Anderson Scrapbooks, vol. 1, p. 80, NYPL

evil effects they have on the art of printing in general and the demoralizing effects on the professors.

The practice of employing what is usually styled "half-way journeymen" in preference to those who have served their time, while it holds encouragement to boys to elope from their masters as soon as they acquire sufficient knowledge of the art to be enabled to earn their bread, is a great grievance to the journeymen and almost certain ruin to the boys themselves. Becoming masters of their own conduct at a period of life when they are incapable of governing their passions and propensities, they plunge headlong into every species of dissipation and are often debilitated by debauchery before they arrive at the age of manhood; and it also tends to an unnecessary multiplication of apprentices, inasmuch as the place of every boy who elopes from his master is usually supplied by another, while at the same time the runaway supplies after a manner the place of a regular journeyman and one who probably has a family dependent on his labor for support.

We also beg leave to call your attention to a practice as illiberal and unjust as the former and attended, perhaps, with evils of a more aggravated nature. We mean that of taking full-grown men (foreigners) as apprentices for some twelve or fifteen months, when they are to be turned into the situations of men who are masters of their business, which men are to be turned out of their places by miserable botches because they will work for what they can get. By these means numbers of excellent workmen who ought to be ornaments to the profession are driven by necessity to seek some other means of support.

When a parent puts out a child to learn an art it is with the pleasing idea that a knowledge of that art will enable him when he becomes a man to provide for himself a comfortable subsistence. Did he know that after laboring from his youth to manhood to acquire an art he would be compelled to abandon it and resort to some business to which he was totally unacquainted to enable him to live, he would certainly prefer that he should in the first instance seek a livelihood on the sea or by some other precarious calling than trust to the equally precarious success of a trade overstocked by its professors. Of the number that have completed their apprenticeship to the printing business within the last five years, but few have been enabled to hold a situation for any length of time, and it is an incontrovertible fact that nearly one-half that learned the trade are obliged to relinquish it and follow some other calling for support.

Under the direful influence of these unwarranted practices the professors of the noblest art with which the world is blessed have become birds of passage, seeking a livelihood from Georgia to Maine. It is owing to such practices that to acknowledge yourself a printer is to awaken suspicion and cause distrust. It is owing to such practices that the professors of this noble art are sinking in the estimation of the community. And it is owing to such practices, if persisted, that to see a book correctly printed will after a few years be received as a phenomenon.

To render an art respectable it is indispensably necessary that professors should be perfect masters of their calling, which can only be acquired by serving a proper apprenticeship. And in our art it is not always true that time will perfect the printer. Regard should always be paid to the capacity and requirements of a boy before he should be suffered to learn the art of printing; for it is too often the case that boys of little or no education are taken as apprentices, which the first services as devil frequently preclude the knowledge of, until they are bound, when the discovery is too late to be remedied. Owing to this deficiency they make the sorry printers; whereas, had they learned some trade which does not particularly require a good education they might have been perfect masters of it and better able to gain a livelihood.

These are evils, gentlemen, which we sorely feel, and which it is in your power to remedy, and we sincerely hope that this appeal to your justice and your humanity may meet with that consideration which its importance demands.

D. H. Reins, W. Burbidge, S. Johnston, Committee
July 13, 1811

"The Duties Which Society Owes to Individuals"
CARPENTERS' STRIKE MANIFESTO, 1810

The building trades employed the largest portion—two-fifths—of journeymen in the city, and they were essential to the growth and economy of this dynamic seaport. They were organized as early as the 1780s and resorted to walkouts as often as any trade. Their compensation took the form of a daily wage generally determined by negotiations between committees of masters and journeymen. Strikes occurred when negotiations failed or employers made unilateral decisions. These confrontations generally took place at the height of the building season and were directed against the master builders or contractors who, having received a contract from a customer, hired carpenters and masons to construct.

The following 1809 manifesto of the carpenters (in *American Citizen*, April 10, 1809) demonstrates how solidly journeymen had integrated republican values into their sense of what a worker's obligations were and what, in return for the fulfillment of these obligations, society owed to skilled workingmen. Many of the themes are similar to those of the printers in the previous document, but the words of this proud and militant body of craftsmen are far more assertive.[22]

22. On the carpenters see Christie, *Empire in Wood*; Rock, *Artisans of the New Republic*, pp. 249–253, 275–282; Rock, *The New York City Artisan*, pp. 230–238.

Figure 17. The increasing ratio between journeymen and masters is illustrated in this painti
of a master builder directing nine journeymen in the construction of a house in the tenth wa
at the city limits. In this figure the frame of the broadside of the house is being set.
constructing a house, a whole side was put together on the ground and then lifted in pla
with long poles. The other sides would then be lifted up, and beams, braces, and studdi
pinned and nailed in. Only then would the roof be put on. William P. Chappel, *House Rais
in Grand St/Between 3rd now Eldredge & Allen Sts.*, oil on cardboard, MMNY

To the Public

At a general meeting of the Journeymen House-Carpenters, convened at Harmony Hall on Tuesday, the 4th of April, it was unanimously resolved, that on mature consideration of their rights, and the
necessity of their situation, to work no longer than April the tenth
inst. [instant] for less than eleven shillings per day.

When one class of society find it necessary to act in any manner that concerns the general interest, justice to themselves and respect for the public require that the reasons of such actions should be assigned.

Among the unalienable rights of man are life, liberty, and the pursuit of happiness. By the social compact every class of society ought to be entitled to benefit in proportion to its usefulness, and the time and expence necessary to its qualification. Among the duties which individuals owe to society are single men to marry and married men to educate their children. Among the duties which society owe to individuals is to grant them compensation for service, sufficient not only for the current expences of livelihood, but to the formation of a fund for the support of that time of life when nature requires a cessation from labor. We will now revert to the particulars of our own situation, to show the justice and necessity of our demand. We have only to give a statement of our annual income and expences. The year is composed of 365 days, 52 of which are Sundays, which leaves 313 days of labour. Deducting from this amount those days of which custom and labor deprive us of pursuing our avocation, we will find that 300 is the aggregate amount of the days a mechanic can call his own for pursuing the means necessary to the support of himself and family. Calculating from the 10th of March to the 10th of November;

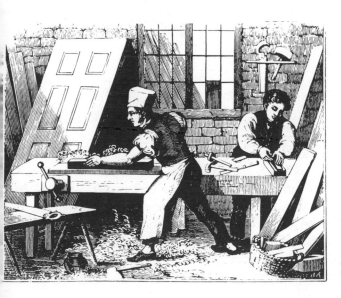

Figure 18. Carpenters worked both indoors and out, and this illustration shows the skill of those working inside. Alexander Anderson, *Indoor Carpenters*, Anderson Scrapbooks, vol. 1, p. 73, NYPL

which is two thirds of the year, (that is 200 days according to our calculation, at eleven shillings per day) the amount is $275.

From the 10th of November to the 10th of March, at 10sh.
per day, $125.
Total amount of our income is $400.

    The items of our expences will be:

House rent	$ 55
Fire wood	50
Victualling a family at the average of 50 cents per day	162 50
Our own wearing apparel	60
Expense of wear & loss of tools unavoidable in our branch	10
Contingent expences	20
Total amount of these items	$357 50
Balance	$ 42 50

Leaving for wife's cloathing, expences of family, sickness, and the cloathing and education of children, the sum of 42 dollars 50 cents. And now let us ask those that are fathers of families to judge what will be the amount of the surplus for the maintenance of old age?

ROBT. TOWNSEND Jun.
RICHARDSON RYAN
BENJ. HOGHLAND

Committee appointed by and on behalf of the Journeymen House-Carpenters.

"Most Tyrannical Violations of Private Right"
THE PROSECUTION OF THE JOURNEYMAN CORDWAINERS

Second only to the construction trades in the number of artisans employed, shoemaking, or cordwaining, was the artisan craft most profoundly affected by the new American marketplace. The trade became highly competitive, as all seaports contained considerable numbers of shoemakers trying to reach the expanding domestic and West Indies markets. Some towns, most notably Lynn, Massachusetts, specialized in the production of shoes. While local genteel clientele continued to purchase "bespoken" or made-to-order high quality shoes,

Figure 19. This caricature of carpenters relaxing and imbibing during work hours represents a traditional work culture yet present in New York that included many breaks in the day and a lack of work and time discipline. This behavior was becoming less and less frequent, however, as the demands of the marketplace for cheap labor and quantity production made employers more demanding in their work rules and supervision. Employees in turn needed similar discipline to struggle for higher wages. *L'Absent Carpenter*, in Samuel Wood, *Proof Book* (New York, 1820), NYHS

the bulk of production consisted of great quantities of "slop" footwear destined for both the retail and wholesale trade.

Shoemakers labored at home, sometimes with the aid of their families, or in a workshop. In either case the master furnished leather to the journeymen who made the shoes or boots and then returned them to the master, who then marketed them by himself or, more commonly, through mercantile connections. Masters labored in a difficult business; they struggled to produce shoes with adequate quality yet cheap enough to sell in the larger markets. Journeymen experienced even greater pressure. Without capital or connections with merchants, journeymen had limited chances for advancement, and as the profession moved toward quantity production, the market demand was for more work of less skill. Masters reduced price lists to a point where longer hours at a quicker pace were required to earn a reasonable salary.[23]

As a result, master shoemakers were among the most active and ambitious entrepreneurs, while journeymen emerged as militants seeking to retain the status of skilled and adequately compensated artisans. Consequently the trade experienced bitter labor unrest.[24]

In their conflicts with journeymen, the master shoemakers took the boldest and most potent step available to master craftsmen: criminal prosecution. English common law forbade journeymen from conspiring to raise prices and wages or to prevent other employees from obtaining employment because of nonmembership in the society. Broadly interpreted, such laws prevented almost any kind of trade association with objectives other than benevolence and recreation.[25]

The New York Journeyman Cordwainers Society was the best organized and strongest such association in the city, willing to use its collective power to protect its position even if it meant prolonged and contentious confrontation. The constitution of the Cordwainers Society compelled all employers to hire only society members. Journeymen new to New York and apprentices completing their indentures had to join within a month or face a considerable fine.

Following a successful indictment of Philadelphia shoemakers in 1805, the New York masters took the journeyman society to court. At issue was journeyman shoemaker Edward Whitess, who had been expelled and ostracized by the society for nonattendance and misconduct. After his expulsion, Whitess was dismissed by his employer, Aimes. Yet the society still took action against Aimes, forbidding its men to work for him after he refused to dismiss (along with Whitess)

---

23. Faler, *Mechanics and Manufacturers*; Dawley, *Class and Community*; Blewett, *We Will Rise in Our Might*; Blanche Hazard, *The Organization of the Boot and Shoe Industry in Massachusetts before 1875* (Cambridge, 1921); Dorothy Brady, in Gilchrist, ed., *The Growth of the Seaport Cities*, pp. 94–95; and Victor S. Clark, *History of Manufactures in the United States* (New York, 1929), 1:354–355, 443.

24. The "sweated" condition that would eventually squeeze masters and journeymen into nearly intolerable conditions after 1820 is discussed in Wilentz, *Chants Democratic*, chap. 3.

25. The place of the conspiracy cases in labor history is discussed in Marjorie S. Turner, *The Early American Conspiracy Cases, Their Place in Labor Law: A Reinterpretation* (San Diego, 1967); Leonard W. Levy, *The Law of the Commonwealth and Chief Justice Shaw* (Cambridge, Mass., 1957); and Twomey, *Jacobins and Jeffersonians*. See also Rock, *Artisans of the New Republic*, pp. 283–287, and *The New York City Artisan*, pp. 239–241, 247–249.

an apprentice also working in violation of its constitution. After the city's other masters came to Aimes's aid by surreptitiously filling his orders, the journeymen called a general walkout and the masters initiated their prosecution.

The indictment against the journeymen shoemakers charged that their association intended to "unlawfully and unjustly . . . extort great sums of money . . . with force of arms" and had conspired to deprive the expelled Whitess of his ability to earn a living. Basically, the case hinged upon the legality of the closed shop, which required employers to hire only members of the trade association.[26]

Despite their hard line against the journeymen, the masters saw themselves as protectors of their craft. Indeed, the masters held to a vision of social harmony typical of classical republicanism. From their perspective, journeymen organizations were divisive and selfish. Once a citizen had chosen his place in society, argued counsel and Jacobin emigre Thomas Emmet, each man was bound to perform his work as part of the public good. This outlook not only sustained an organic view of society, it also provided a patriotic justification for the masters to oppose militant journeymen societies.[27] The document below is from *People vs. Melvin*, in John R. Commons et al., eds., *A Documentary History of American Industrial Society*, 10 vols. (Cleveland, 1910–1911), 3:328–329, 377–399.

Suppose the bakers of this city were to combine not to bake a loaf of bread till some demands, as to the assize, were complied with; and that the butchers were at the same time to combine not to sell a pound of meat till some object of theirs should be gained, what would be the consequence? A misfortune worse than pestilence would instantly befall the city. And are we to be told, that not only the individuals of those classes of men, to whom, in the general distribution of employment, society has confided the care of providing for its most important wants, may singly abandon their duty; but that those classes *en masse*, without any intention of permanently relinquishing

---

26. *People vs. Melvin*, in John R. Commons et al., eds., *A Documentary History*, 3:252–256.

27. This justification is seen most clearly in the arguments of the 1809 conspiracy trial of New York's organized cordwainers. The transcript is reprinted as *People vs. Melvin* in Commons, *A Documentary History*, vol. 3; pertinent sections are reprinted in Rock, *The New York City Artisan*, pp. 201–203, 247–251.

or changing their occupations, but merely as a measure of extortion from the necessities of others, for private interest, may lawfully conspire together to inflict the most terrible calamities on the community; and this is called the mere exercise of individual rights, and the toleration of it is considered as sound political economy! But no. Individual rights are sufficiently secured by letting every man, according to his own will, follow his own pursuits, while public welfare forbids that combinations should be entered into for private benefit, by the persons concerned in any employment connected with the general welfare; in which combinations they would make common cause against the community at large; and in which the individual rights of those in the combining classes, who may wish to be industrious, are most grievously violated; because, if they were permitted to follow their pursuits, it would tend to relieve society from the extortions of the conspirators. These combinations are an infringement of that tacit compact which all classes reciprocally enter into, that when they have partitioned and distributed among them the different occupations conducive to general prosperity, they will pursue those occupations so as to contribute to the general happiness; and they are therefore at war with public policy. But when it is further considered that they are always accompanied with compulsory measures against those of the same class or trade, who would willingly pursue their occupation with industry and tranquility, they are most tyrannical violations of private right, and inevitably tend to the unjust impoverishment of multitudes, either of those against whom the confederacy is directed, or of those who are forced into it, or devoted by it, for exercising their own individual rights, and refusing to cooperate with the unlawful association. . . .

Mr. Griffin [co-counsel for the prosecution] then argued upon the evidence, and admitted that there had been no personal violence, no outrage or disorder, but asked if the coercive measures of the society were less cruel or oppressive for that reason. He made strong remarks upon the imperious and tyrannical edicts of the constitution and by-laws of the society, and asked whether it was possible for any workman to enjoy without molestation, the indisputable rights of peace, neutrality, and self-government, in his own private and particular concerns. A journeyman was neither free to refuse entering into the society, nor at liberty, having done so, to leave it, without incurring ruin or unmerited disgrace; and to the real impoverishment which he

Figure 20. By 1800 shoemaking had become a very competitive trade, with a growing number of journeymen working for a single master. Alexander Anderson, *Bootmakers Shop*, Anderson Scrapbooks, vol. 1, p. 73, NYPL

must undergo, and to the evils heaped upon all who befriend him; to all this was added, the opprobrious epithet of scab. If an individual master refused obedience to their laws, or fell under the displeasure of the society, a stroke was directed against him. And, though this stroke was not a corporal wound, it was a cruel and ruinous infliction, from which he could have no relief, unless the law provides one. He was proscribed without remorse, and outlawed without mercy.

If the master workmen in general happened to offend this society, a general cessation of labour amongst the members of their own body was decreed, to which obedience was rigorously enforced; however much the necessities of their families might require their work, idleness was enjoined upon them. They were commanded to do no manner of work; but it was a sabbath not of rest, but of vengeance, of desolation, and of suffering. Mr. Griffin urged then, a variety of other topics with great strength and effect, and concluded by what might be understood as a summary of his argument. He did not complain of the defendants for forming themselves into a society, but for compelling others to become members. He did not accuse them of having advanced the price of their own labour, but of conspiring to regulate, by measures of rigour and coercion, the wages and the will of others;

his charge against them was not that they chose and determined for what employers they would or would not work, but that they had exercised an aristocratic and tyrannical control over third persons, to whom they left neither free will nor choice; and that they employed, to effect this purpose, means of interference in their concerns to which it was impossible for the sufferers to oppose any resistance.

"Combining against Starvation"
THE DEFENSE OF THE JOURNEYMAN CORDWAINERS

William Sampson, also a noted emigre Jacobin attorney, argued eloquently in the journeymen's behalf that English common law, since it was not based on the equal rights of all citizens, was unsuitable as precedent in a truly republican country. Furthermore, he asserted, in a just society the shoemakers should have the same right to combine as men in other occupations. Pointing to the journeymen's economic plight, he argued that the journeymen deserved an equal opportunity to create leverage in the marketplace.

Recent studies claim that the journeyman shoemakers were hindered in their efforts to make their way in the marketplace because they accepted the republican ideal of the harmonious workshop long after economic conditions had separated both the interests and standing of the masters and journeymen.[28] The journeymen, however, were not mired in classical republicanism. Instead they wanted the right to compete on equal terms in the marketplace and the courtroom. For the most part journeymen were not at odds with the entrepreneurial ethos. Rather, it was the masters, ambitious entrepreneurs when trading in the marketplace, who turned to an increasingly obsolete vision of an organic society in their attempts to thwart the journeymen. The journeymen demanded only the right to combine freely in the marketplace in negotiations. They did not reject capitalism; they wanted the rules to allow them a fair opportunity to compete as organized labor.[29] The document below excerpts highlights from Sampson's

28. Wilentz, *Chants Democratic*, pp. 13–18; Twomey, *Jacobins and Jeffersonians*, chap. 6.
29. Rock, *The New York City Artisan*, pp. 249–250, 252–253.

speech in *People vs. Melvin*, in Commons et al., *A Documentary History*, 3: 279–280, 299–302.

Shall all others, except only the industrious mechanic, be allowed to meet and plot; merchants to determine their prices current, or settle the markets, politicians to electioneer, sportsmen for horseracing and games, ladies and gentlemen for balls, parties and bouquets; and yet those poor men be indicted for combining against starvation? I ask again, is this repugnant to the rights of man? If it be, is it not repugnant to our constitution? If it be repugnant to our constitution, is it law? And if it is not law, shall we be put to answer to it?

If it be said, they have wages enough, or too much already, I do not think any man a good witness to that point but one who has himself laboured. If either of the gentlemen opposed to us will take his station in the garret or cellar of one of these industrious men, get a leather apron and a strap, a last, a lap-stone and a hammer, and peg and stitch from five in the morning till eight in the evening, and feed and educate his family with what he so earns, then if he will come into court, and say upon his corporal oath that he was, during that probation, too much pampered or indulged, I will consider whether these men may not be extortioners. . . .

But to examine the substances of the charges in these respective counts more particularly. So far from having been anything illegal or immoral in the conspiracy or agreement to which these defendants were parties, the court will find that their confederacy, and the rules which they adopted, were not only legal but highly meritorious. Like most other societies of the same nature, the journeymen shoemakers' society is a charitable institution.

They raise a fund, which is sacred to the use of their helpless or unfortunate members, and to the relief of the widows and orphans of their departed brethren. Their by-laws are, each member shall contribute to this fund. And to induce every one to join the society, while by his labour he may make something to spare for their fund, they refuse to work with any one who is so wanting in charity as not to join them. And as a sanction to their laws, they have also declared that they will not work with any who shall break their by-laws, that is, who shall refuse to pay his dues, till he has paid a fine. Who will say that an association of this nature is illegal? What human laws can presume to punish acts, which, according to the laws of God are deserving of rewards even in heaven? or can it be said that the resolution not to work for a master who employed more than two apprentices, was unpraiseworthy? The masters were in the habit of crowding their shops with more apprentices than they could instruct. Two was thought as many as one man could do justice by. The journeymen shoemakers therefore determined to set their faces against the rapacity of the masters, and refused to work for those who were so unjust as to delude with the promise of instruction which it was impossible they could give. In England, the legislature has interfered on this point, and has by statute limited the number of apprentices which certain tradesmen may take.

It is to be observed, that neither of these counts charge that the design of the defendants was to raise their wages. And though it should be admitted that a conspiracy to raise their wages would subject the defendants to an indictment, yet I doubt if any authority can be found to support an indictment for charges like these. . . . The 4th count charges, that these defendants, intending to injure E[dmund]. W[hitess]. conspired, by wrongful and indirect means to impoverish him, and hinder him from following his trade, and that they did, in pursuance of their conspiracy, indirectly hinder him from following his trade. . . .

Now it may well have been that the defendants intended to injure the persons named in these counts, by indirect, yet by perfectly lawful means. If they had agreed that they would work better or cheaper than the persons named, this would have been an indirect, means of injuring them. If they had combined in the invention of some improvement of the cordwainer's art, which should have entitled them to a patent, this would have given the defendants a monopoly which could not fail of being an indirect means of injuring all who were not sharers in it. If they agreed to increase the number of master workmen in our city by inducing those who are now settled elsewhere to take their abode with us; or, if the defendants had agreed that they would no longer work as journeymen, but establish themselves as masters. All these would have been indirect means of impoverishing and injuring other persons engaged in the trade. But will it be said that indirect means like these would be unlawful means? I am sure it will not. It follows, then, that the defendants are not charged by either of these counts, with a conspiracy to do an unlawful act.

"Out of Our Power"
THE NEW YORK TYPOGRAPHICAL SOCIETY RESPONDS TO THE CORDWAINERS' TRIAL

Recognizing both the importance of this trial to the ability of journeyman associations to prevail in the marketplace as well as the cost of employing one of New York's most skilled attorneys, the cordwainers appealed to sister societies for assistance, declaring their "determination to . . . carry it from court to court into the Court of Errors." When this appeal reached the Typographical Society, it caused a considerable dilemma for the printers. While sympathetic to the shoemakers' plight, this organization was ultimately unable and perhaps unwilling to take the risk of directly supporting the shoemakers in their court battle. The request was first referred to a general meeting where a motion of support, after initial passage, was rescinded out of concern "as to the legality of the proceedings of the Cordwainers' Society."[30] The issue was then referred to a special committee of three. The report of that committee, which follows (reprinted in George Barnett, "The Printers: A Study in Trade Unionism," *American Economic Association Quarterly*, 3d ser., 10 [1909], 358), brings into question—given the lack of legal standing that journeyman associations had—the ability or willingness of journeymen of different crafts to cooperate in defense of common interests.

Board of Directors, *March 31, 1810*:
The Committee appointed to obtain information respecting the suit now pending between the Journeymen Cordwainers and their employers made the following report:
The grounds of the prosecution against the Cordwainers' Society by the Master Shoemakers appears to be in the letter of the law an unlawful combination for the purpose of raising and establishing wages; that is the head and front of the bill of indictment, though it contains several charges of trifling consequence some of which are false and groundless—that relative to apprentices particularly having not the least degree of truth attached to it. The President informed your committee that their cause would be brought on for trial the ensuing week and should judgment be given against them there, the

30. Barnett, "The Printers," 357.

determination is to carry it from court to court into the Court of Errors should judgment be given in each against them. Your committee did not feel themselves authorized by the powers vested in them to offer any arrangement in support of their cause but have left it to the management of the society. After some debate, a motion was made and carried that a committee of one should be appointed to answer the communications from the Cordwainers' Society—expressing the good wishes of this Board for the success of their cause and stating that from the recent exhaustion of our funds in assisting our own members who had stood out for wages, it was totally out of our power (at present) to render them the assistance required.

"The Well Known Liberality of the Citizens"
JOURNEYMAN SHOEMAKERS OPEN A STORE

Journeyman shoemakers deserted their masters nearly as often as did the masons and carpenters. Although most such confrontations went unreported, some of the most bitter and protracted reached the newspapers—usually when journeymen placed an ad appealing for public support. Their arguments commonly dealt with the greed and unfairness of the masters and their right to a decent wage. But it is significant that they also professed faith in a "discerning" public. Such a body, critical to the survival and preservation of republican society, could not but support the journeymen's cause.

During an extended walkout, journeymen mechanics occasionally opened their own shops and sold directly to the public. The document below announces the opening of one such establishment (in *New York Evening Post*, February 4, 1815). Along with the tailors and cabinetmakers, the boot and shoemakers resorted to this means of raising income and putting increased pressure on their employers. It was a difficult undertaking and seldom succeeded. James Melvin and John Morehouse, the proprietors of this store, were well-known leaders of the journeymen's society: Melvin had been indicted in the 1809 prosecution. The two shoemakers launched this endeavor with faith in both their own ability and the "liberality of the citizens of New York."

TAKE NOTICE

The publick are respectfully informed, that owing to the differences existing between the journeymen boot and shoe makers and their employers occasioned by an ungenerous attempt on the part of the employers, to reduce the journeymen's wages at this inclement season of the year, when they had good reason to believe their necessaries should compel them to submit to whatever reduction of prices the employers might think proper to offer—considering such treatment too harsh to be borne, the journeymen have been induced to open a shop, where the public may be supplied at a few hours notice with gentlemen's boots and shoes of every description. The above articles shall be manufactured with the very best of materials; and as it is an association of the journeymen the public will really see that they have it fully in their power to furnish all articles in the above line at the first rate workmanship, which they promise faithfully to perform—and they trust that the well known liberality of the citizens of New York will not be backward in support of an establishment which has for its object to do justice to the laboring mechanic and honestly to serve the publick. Application to be made at the store, No. 32 Maiden-Lane. The business will be conducted under the firm of MELVIN and MOREHOUSE.

"The Justice and Utility of the Republican Cause"
JOURNEYMEN AND POLITICS

In the 1790s artisans frequently voted Federalist. However, the Democratic-Republican party, with its attack on deference, emphasis on the equality of all citizens, and willingness to put artisans on the ballot and defend their economic interests, captured a large majority of the mechanic vote by 1800.[31] Most journeymen craftsmen believed that this party promised them the respect and position due them as urban yeomen and patriotic citizens. Since many Democratic-Republicans were masters as well as journeymen, labor relations seldom entered politics.

In 1801, however, Republicans accused the Federalists of stalling

31. For a discussion of artisan involvement in partisan politics see Rock, *Artisans of the New Republic*, chaps. 1–5; and Wilentz, *Chants Democratic*, chap. 2.

on legislation that would limit shoe production in the state prison located in New York City. Master shoemakers knew this issue was important to their journeymen, who feared that the cheaper price of prison manufacturing would cost them jobs and lead to a reduction of wages. The Federalists countered Republican charges by attempting to drive a wedge between the Republican masters and journeymen shoemakers. The Federalist "Brutus" in the *Commercial Advertiser* (April 20, 1801) presented an interesting argument that represented some of the mixture of the social and political crosscurrents of the age. "Brutus" relied on his faith in traditional social relationships by suggesting that the Federalists in the state senate might pater-nalistically respond to the shoemakers' request concerning production in the state prison, if, by implication, the shoemakers deferentially supported the Federalists in the election. Simultaneously, Brutus at-tacked the master shoemakers involved in Republican politics for their efforts to intimidate journeymen in the workshop and deprive them of their rights as American citizens. Indeed, by declaring that the masters' efforts sought to reduce journeymen to the status of a "hired negro wench," "Brutus" offered a trenchant social commentary about the self- identity of journeymen as "independent" citizens and about the prevalent views on race and gender.

The Republicans responded (in *American Citizen*, April 24, 1801) that the shoemakers were not influenced by any such men; instead, as truly "independent" citizens they made their decisions on the basis of principle. From this perspective the Federalists were only trying to hide the real issue: their support of aristocracy, monarchy, and tyr-anny. Only by shunning Federalist guile could mechanics avoid vas-salage and enjoy the fruits of their labor and industry.

Federalist Appeal to the Shoemakers
To the JOURNEYMEN SHOE-MAKERS
Friends and Fellow Citizens,
    Since I wrote the letter to you . . . I am told you had a meeting last Friday night, and that it was agreed between a good many that they would *stick together* till they obtained relief, and that the meeting was turned into a political meeting and they voted to support the democratic ticket. But do you not see by what I have already said and stand ready to prove, that this is not the way even to obtain relief? How will you ever get the bill [limiting prison shoe production]

through the Senate? Let me ask you that. Besides, how do you know
that the federalists are not perfectly willing to grant you all the relief
you want, or can reasonably ask for? Tis they who have got a majority
in the Senate. Had you not better than at least try them? But I
believe, nay I know that all this is mostly owing to a few particular
men among you, and I also know their names. There is first of all
Mills and Vanderbilt, and then comes M'Cready and little Bunn.
Now *journeymen shoe makers*, for it is to you I am here speaking, I
must tell you a little about Mr. Mills and Mr. Vanderbilt, for as to
M'Cready and little Bunn, I hope really you don't let them have a
great deal of influence *over* you.

A number of years ago, when every article of produce was constantly raising, and the price of labor among mechanics in general
raising too, the journeymen shoemakers, not finding their wages to
raise in proportion to the rest of the mechanics, turned out almost to
a man, to see if they could not make their Bausses do something for
them. What does a number of the master workmen do, but get together, three of them, viz. *Philip Arcularius* (who is on the Republican ticket, and who was then in partnership with his brother in the
tanning business,) *Philip Arcularius, John Mills* your chairman, and
Abraham Bloodgood,[32] the tanner, these three drew up a writing and
carried it around to all the *master tanners* to sign, which writing was
an agreement that they would not on account or for any sum of
money whatever, sell one ounce of leather to any journeyman shoemaker in the City of New-York, till they had given up these attempts
to have their wages raised. This is the first thing I have to tell you
about this *Bause Mills* you think so much of.

I shall now tell you something more about his friendship to you,
him and another *Bause* along with him. This story is not a great
while ago.

John Mills, Oliver Vanderbilt, and a few more that now have so

32. These men were all prominent Democratic-Republicans. John Mills, master
shoemaker, was appointed state prison inspector in 1804. Philip Arcularius (1747–
1825), appointed prison inspector in 1805, served as assistant alderman from 1797 to
1800 and as state assemblyman from 1798 to 1799, 1801 to 1802, and in 1805.
Abraham Bloodgood (1767–1837) served as assistant alderman in 1805 and 1808. By
1815 both Arcularius and Bloodgood were worth over $20,000, high for artisans but
below that of the mercantile class. See Edmund P. Willis, "Social Origins of Political
Leadership in New York City from the Revolution to 1815" (Ph.D. diss., University
of California, Berkeley, 1967), appendix; *American Citizen*, April 21, 1807.

much influence with you, a little while since, took it into their heads that they would have better regulations among the journeymen, so what do they do, but propose to have an agreement in writing drawn up and signed by every *Bause* in the city of New-York, that none of them would hereforth employ any journeyman shoemaker, *till the journeyman had first got a regular discharge from the Bause he had worked with last.* —You see, fellow citizens, without my telling you, what a rascally proposal this was; it would just have put the journeymen shoemakers upon the same footing with a hired negro wench, that must have a recommendation before she can get a place. And I need not add, they would then have settled the price of your wages at just what they pleased. . . . Don't you know that *Mills* and *Vanderbilt* and *M'Cready* and *little Bunn,* have always belonged to the party of the democrats, and have always made it a constant practice, long before the State-prison was ever thought of, to run about at elections and bring up people to the polls to vote for the democratic ticket? And ought this not to make you suspect their design when they tell you, that you will obtain redress from that party? But what redress do they wish you? Go into the shop of *Mills* or *Vanderbilt,* and I'll be bound for it, you'll find ten pair of shoes made in Jersey and the other states, which they have bought up, where there is one made in their own shops by their own journeymen. And as to the other cause of griev-ance, that the making so many shoes in the state prison is a disgrace to the trade, if you want this grievance lop't off, you must come to the Federalists for it, the others *cannot* help you; and I say they do not mean to help you if they could. . . .

BRUTUS

[Democratic-Republican Reply]

TO THE
JOURNEYMEN SHOE-MAKERS
OF NEW-YORK

Fellow Citizens,—

We have been lately addressed by a person signing himself *Brutus*— As one of the craft I think it my duty in my own behalf, as well as for the honour of the body, to make some reply to this renowned Roman— Sir, you suppose, and take it for granted, that we are influenced by Mr. John Mills, Mr. Vanderbelt, and a few more. No, Sir, we are capable of thinking and acting for ourselves— As to the persons your invenomed darts are pointed at, they are persons of respectability, and highly esteemed, not only by the Journeymen Shoe-Makers in particular, but their fellow citizens in general. This Brutus is one of the tricks of your party, to sully the character of individuals who oppose the measures they adopt. But know ye that we act from principle; we act from conviction of the justice and utility of the Republican cause; we contend with you not about men but principles; we conceive the measures of the federal party have had for their objects, the suppression of liberty and the promotion of tyranny. If not, why this Sedition Law, and why this Alien Law?[33] Why all this contempt of the terms liberty and equality? 'Twas years past, the man attached to the principles of '76 was looked upon as Jacobin or a Devil— Nor was it uncommon being in *polite* and higher *circles* to hear it said that a Kingly government was certainly the best— And how was it that this principle was so popular? I will tell you Mr. Brutus— It was thought probable as things were going that we might have a renovation of government, —and who were more likely to obtain the height of nobility but the wealthy and good Federalist? True, our government or its administrators are changed, and we hope to keep them whom we have helped to put there— We hope to see from them a revival of philanthropy and liberty, and a spirit of conciliation— As to the affair of the bill of last session, I consider that foreign to the present question. The present contest is Republicanism against anti-Republicanism and I hope there is not a Shoe-Maker in this city but will support the former. Your hopes have been directed to the Federalist party; and it is said they will make your trade better. — No, they will not, nor any sub-servant to a foreign nation. But for my part, I prefer poverty and equal laws, to riches and vassalage. But thank God, you can get a comfortable living by your present industry, and so you will continue to do where you are not oppressed by high taxes, the unavoidable effects of a standing army.

33. The sedition acts of 1798 were Federalist measures taken to curtail vitriolic partisan attacks on the Adams administration. Under its provisions, individuals or publishers speaking against the government or its officials could be prosecuted and jailed. The alien acts, passed for partisan reasons, made it more difficult for immigrants to become citizens (and vote against the Federalists). Some of the alien acts were also intended to control citizens of nations at war with the United States.

You can now live like Princes, when compared to men of your occupation, under a Kingly government. Then support Republicanism—then will you still enjoy the fruits of your industry under the guidance of benign Providence—in hopes that we shall sit under our own Vine and our own Fig-tree, and none to make us afraid. I am theirs affectionately,

A SHOE-MAKER.

3

MASTER CRAFTSMEN:

Competence, Independence, and Leadership

Like the journeymen, masters working in the vital and burgeoning marketplace faced new economic horizons. Given the need for large capital investment and market connections, some masters had no choice but to surrender a portion of their independence and status to mercantile creditors by becoming foremen rather than proprietors. Others, however, able to secure capital and possessing marketing skills, did quite well, achieving considerable financial gain and opportunity. Master craftsmen typically held between $2,000 and $5,000 in assets, a comfortable sum, though not equal to those of many merchants and attorneys.[1]

The master craftsmen saw themselves as the protectors of their trades, believing that they alone had the knowledge and foresight to set the proper compensation for work and to outline the limits of permissible employee conduct. As noted in Chapter 2, the masters formed their own associations, coerced suppliers of raw materials, locked out employees, hired strikebreakers and, when pressed, pros-

1. The most successful tradesmen amassed considerable fortunes, such as baker Thomas Mercein ($2,600 in 1808; $11,000 in 1815), potter Clarkson Crolius ($8,300 in 1808; $22,400 in 1815), and glazier Jacob Sherred ($120,000 in 1815). Edmund P. Willis, "Social Origins and Political Leadership in New York City from the Revolution to 1815," (Ph.D. diss., University of California, Berkeley, 1967), pp. 123, 130, appendix.

ecuted recalcitrant journeymen. They saw their role as guardians, however, as being far broader than adversaries in labor relations. They maintained that through a combination of ambition, skill, discipline, and good management, they could advance the mechanic trades toward greater profits and productivity. They believed that it was up to them to protect the professions against the dangerous inroads threatened by monopoly in the form of factory production—an event becoming all too common in England—and to fend off unfair or unwanted regulation. They believed their duty extended as well to lobbying Congress for tariff protection. Finally, the masters assumed the heavy responsibility of reminding both the mechanic community and society as a whole of the central place that artisans occupied in the founding and maintenance of freedom and republicanism in America.[2]

"By Industry and Strict Attention to Business"
THE AUTOBIOGRAPHY OF STEPHEN ALLEN

As noted in Chapter 1, Stephen Allen began his career as a poor apprentice in a tory sail loft during the Revolution. He went on to become a prominent sail maker, an eminent politician, and, finally, mayor of the City of New York. The section below of his autobiography ("The Memoirs of Stephen Allen," typescript, NYHS, pp. 44–50) describes his rise to fortune, beginning with his short stint as a journeyman during the postwar depression of the 1780s. Through self-described "diligence and high quality of work," Allen persevered in seeking intermittent work until he finding steady employment with Thomas Hillson. He subsequently persuaded his master to take him in as a partner. This step in his career allowed young Allen to wed his sixteen-year-old sweetheart. Then, finding his associate's business habits too lax, Allen forced him out of the partnership.[3] With Franklinlike discipline and help from the commercial boom generated by

---

2. On masters' sense of paternal responsibility, see Howard B. Rock, *Artisans of the New Republic: The Tradesmen of New York City in the Age of Jefferson* (New York, 1979), chaps. 6, 9; and Sean Wilentz, *Chants Democratic: New York City and the Rise of the American Working Class, 1790–1850* (New York, 1984), chap. 1.

3. On partnerships see Rock, *Artisans of the New Republic*, p. 157.

the Napoleonic Wars, he succeeded. His words portray the ambition, drive, and perseverance of many young artisans and describe some of the opportunities that awaited the most skilled and industrious after the Revolution. His experience during the war and his pride in American republicanism were constant throughout his life.

[*1786*]

This was the darkest and most discouraging period of my life, for there was so little mercantile business carried on that sail-making was almost at a stand-still, and it was with much difficulty that a single days work could be obtained. I had my full share of employ, small as it was, as I used due diligence in looking for it, and enjoined upon myself the duty when out of work of visiting every sail-loft in the city daily, and would frequently by this means obtain half a days work in one, and sometimes two or three days work in another, so I have often worked, during the period alluded to, in three or four different lofts in a week; and what added to the embarrassment of the times was the poverty of the employers, for after I performed the labor there were but two or three of the master sail-makers who had the ability to pay. And it often happened that I had as much labor to perform in collecting my small earnings, as I had in earning them.

The next year business was much better, and I obtained a situation in a sail-loft belonging to Thomas Hillson. . . . There were then a number of the Friends[4] who owned shipping, and Hillson being the only one in the city at that period connected with the society, and who carried on the business of sail-making, he obtained the whole of their work, and consequently was enabled to keep two or three hands constantly employed. He therefore engaged Augustus Wright and myself by the year, at low wages, and boarded us at his house, but we were compelled to lodge in the sail-loft. . . .

We continued to work as journeymen in this loft until the year 1787, when Hillson concluded to take a partner in his business and finally proposed the matter to and offered me the situation. . . . On the 1st of May, 1788, we commenced our partnership under the firm of Hillson and Allen. About the same period Augustus Wright who for so many years had been my shop-mate, received a similar offer of partnership from a sail-maker of the name of Cone, which he ac-

4. Allen makes frequent reference to "the Friends," or Quakers.

cepted also, and they commenced business on the same date that we did. . . .

The adoption of the new Constitution, as it was called, was opposed by some of our most respectable citizens. The reasons assigned for this opposition were the local advantages possessed by this state over others in a commercial point of view, —that our true interest was to continue independent and instead of sending our large revenue to the United States Treasury, that we ought to use it for our own advantage and improvement. These reasons had their influence with many, but for myself the measure of a federal government had my decided approbation, because it appeared to me that in the event of war or internal commotion under the old confederacy, we should be disjointed and divided, but that in union we should be strong and able to meet any shock which might occur, and what we lost in revenue would be fully made up to us by the extension of our commerce and business concerns.[5]

For some time previous to the period alluded to I had been acquainted with a young woman, the daughter of Widow Marschalk, at whose house I spent many of my leisure evenings. A union between us had been agreed upon and we were only waiting for some favorable circumstances to occur in order to consummate our mutual wishes. The most important was the arrangement I had entered into with Hillson to commence business as a master workman, which would enable me, as I believed, to provide for a family with decency. No sooner was our partnership agreed upon, therefore, than I proposed our marriage forthwith, and being assented to by the parties, it was effected on the 17th day of May, 1788, when I was not quite 21 years of age and my wife not quite 17!! I was now commencing a new era in life and not only felt the necessity but turned my whole attention to the object of increasing my ability to provide for a family, and my exertions did not go unrewarded as the sequel will show. . . .

5. Alfred F. Young argues that New York mechanics were almost all in favor of the Constitution. See Alfred F. Young, *The Democratic-Republicans of New York: The Origins, 1763–1797* (Chapel Hill, N.C., 1967), pp. 100–102. For an interpretation that questions journeymen's allegiance, see Paul A. Gilje, "The Common People and the Constitution: Popular Culture in Late Eighteenth-Century New York City," in Gilje and William Pencak, eds., *New York in the Age of the Constitution* (Rutherford, N.J., 1992).

I commenced the world as a man of family, as I before observed, in May, 1788. My means were small indeed, inasmuch as my whole fortune consisted of my wardrobe which was pretty scantily supplied, and ten pounds currency, equal to twenty-five dollars, which I had by great economy in my expenditures saved from my earnings as a journeyman in order to pay the expenses of our wedding and to commence housekeeping. We took rooms for the first year in a house at the upper end of Pearl Street, belonging to a Mr. Arden, who occupied a part of the same building, with his family. . . . The principal furniture of our rooms belonged to Mrs. Marschalk, my wife's mother. . . .

I now attended to the business of my sail-loft with redoubled assiduity and industry while my partner Hillson spent a large portion of his time in walking the docks, as he said in pursuit of business. My acquaintance with the customers of our establishment was very limited, particularly at the commencement of our partnership and during the first and second year of its continuance, inasmuch as they were principally such as had employed Hillson previous to our connection, and the collecting of the money with other outdoor business, being mostly performed by him, it was seldom that an opportunity offered for me to become acquainted with them, and I had therefore no choice but to be contented with matters as they were conducted, which threw upon me all the labor of the establishment, together with the keeping of the books and accounts. Remonstrances had no other effect than to irritate and promote altercation, and I found that instead of amendment matters grew worse. . . . Finding that no change in his conduct was likely to be effected, I told him that I would dissolve our partnership, be the consequences what they might. To this threat he paid no attention whatever and I therefore stated to the person of whom we rented the sail-loft, the situation of our concern, and my reasons for the determination I had formed of dissolving my connection with Hillson, and then left it at his option, either to continue me as his tenant or to rent the place to Hillson. He preferred that I should continue in the loft, which was of some importance, as we generally did as much work for the landlord as would pay the rent. I accordingly informed Hillson of the arrangement, and at the same time tendered him a part of the loft for any work he might have, until he could provide himself with another.

This partnership therefore, which had existed for nearly four years was finally dissolved on the first day of December, 1797, and I commenced business on my own account.

My prospects were not very flattering, for a large portion of our customers in the shipping business were the particular friends of Hillson, drawn to him by his Quaker connections and those among the boatmen and coasters who were also attached to him on account of his constant association with them on all occasions. He had acquired also a great name with the Long Island people for cutting a handsome sail, many of whom were our employers. With a full view of all these advantages on his side and disadvantages on my own, I did not suffer myself to despair of being enabled by industry and strict attention to business to make a living, for I had long before this come to the determination of using the utmost economy in all my concerns, in order to keep myself from obligations of every sort, and to lay by something in case of misfortune, or accident to myself or family. . . .

The first year I was in business after the dissolution of copartnership with Hillson, my profits were quite small and did not pay expenses. I made the most of the work, however, which came to me by working early and late, so long as there was anything to be done, and hiring as few journeymen as possible; and I prided myself upon being able to say that no person who employed me was ever disappointed, for the work was always done at the time promised. . . .

It has been the uniform custom of those following the business of sail-making to obtain the materials such as sail duck, bolt-rope, twine, thimbles, marlin and lines, from the ship chandlers, giving them the retail profit on those articles, which it had always appeared to me belonged to the manufacturers of the sails; and I had determined whenever my means would permit to furnish these articles myself. I commenced therefore, about this time to purchase a portion of the articles alluded to from the importer, in such quantities as my means would admit, and prudence appeared to warrant, and charged them in my bills at the prices fixed upon them by the ship chandlers. My second purchase of real estate was a house (lot) in Oak Street, upon which I shortly commenced the building of a more roomy and convenient house, than the one I then occupied. My means would not permit me to completely finish this before occupying it, and I only finished therefore as many rooms as were necessary for the family, always keeping in mind the maxim I had set out with, *not to be in debt, if possible to avoid it.*

In order that I might ascertain whether I was gaining anything by my business, and how much, I had adopted the practice, (and which ought to be followed by all who wish and expect to gain a fortune) of annually examining my affairs by taking an inventory of stock on hand and debts due, as also the debts I owed, by which means I was able to see how I had thrived for the year. Thus I found that on the 1st of January, 1796, after having been in business about eight years, I was worth at least four thousand dollars more than when I commenced. I now determined to commence the purchase of small lots of sail duck, for which purpose I attended sales at auction where I frequently made advantageous cost purchases that netted me a large profit. I also purchased small lots at private sale when opportunity offered but only from those who had sufficient confidence in my integrity and punctuality in payment, and who were willing to sell without receiving a note at hand for the amount, for so fearful was I that a demand might be made for the payment on a day when through some unforseen disappointment I might not be able to meet it, that I preferred the loss of profit on a purchase to the loss of my credit. . . .

The Revolution in France which commenced in 1793[6] and the belligerent state of all Europe had called into action the whole commercial resources of our country, and every kind of business flourished, but particularly the business I was following. And, as I had started with the determination of gaining by honorable means a competent support for myself and family, whenever business was given me to do I exerted every nerve to perform it by the time required, in order that no disappointments might be experienced by my employers, and that at the same time, by quick despatch my profits might be augmented. Year after year, during the fall and winter months, which was always the most busy season, have I labored at least fourteen hours out of the twenty-four. My practice was, in order to save time, to take breakfast before daylight and with a lantern containing a light, proceed to the sail-loft with the apprentices, there kindle our fire, and commence our work, perhaps an hour before the journeymen would arrive (as

6. Although the French Revolution began in 1789, its effect did not take hold on American commerce until the French war with England that commenced in 1793. Allen probably used this year for that reason.

they worked only by the day) which in winter was 7 o'clock. . . .
And at night we worked by candle light till 9 o'clock, and sometimes
later, according as we were pressed for time, to complete the business
engaged to be done; but I never worked on a Sunday, preferring the
most unremitted and hardest labor through the week to the violation
of the Sabbath.

"Forge Me Strong, Finish Me Neat, I Soon Shall Moor a Federal Fleet"
MECHANICS AND THE GRAND FEDERAL PROCESSION

On July 23, 1788, New York was host to a spectacular procession
in honor of the United States Constitution. Cities in other states had
had parades following their convention's ratification, but New Yorkers held their parade before their state convention committed itself to
the Constitution. Federalist leaders had prepared the procession hoping for ratification by July 4. When the convention dragged on well
into July, the Federalists decided to put pressure on their oppponents
with a public demonstration of support. The idea was to inaugurate
the new form of government with a public ritual that would mark
social unity and a common commitment to the ship of state—represented in the parade by a large model frigate.

New York's mechanics were highly visible in the grand procession,
forming the bulk of seven of the parade's ten divisions. Their high
profile, however, was not the intention of the cavalcade's organizers.
The Federalist leadership, adorned in elaborate costumes, feathers,
and insignia of rank, intended the procession not only as a political
statement, but as an affirmation of their own social vision. The
places of privilege in the parade had been reserved for members of the
city's political elite. Yet despite these efforts, the master craftsmen
stole the day by displaying their particular work experience in their
banners and paraphernalia. The selection below (*Independent Journal*,
August 2 and 6, 1788) describes the appearance of three of the many
trades in the parade. Integrated into this demonstration of symbols
were representations of the masters' assertion of a unity of interest
within their trade, a celebration of their craft, and a political message
in support of the Constitution based in the belief that the new form
of government would expand markets and lead to prosperity.

The procession stands as a testimony of the master mechanics' ideas on politics, society, and economy in 1788, but it speaks less clearly about the concerns of the journeymen and apprentices, many of whom participated in the parade. Can we assert with authority that they understood or supported the Constitution? Might they have simply seized the opportunity to join in a display of their craft, have a holiday from work, and enjoy a dinner at someone else's expense? We may never have satisfactory answers to these questions.[7]

BAKERS

Headed by two masters, Messrs. John Quackinbos and Frederick Stymes.

Ten boys dressed in white, with blue sashes, each of them carrying a large rose, decorated with various colored ribbons.

Ten journeymen dressed in white, with blue sashes, carrying implements of the craft.

A stage, drawn by two bay horses decorated.

Four masters, with the federal loaf, 10 feet long, 27 inches in breadth, and 8 inches in height, with the names in full length of the ten states which have ratified the constitution, and the initial letters of the other three.

A flag, representing the declension of trade under the old confederation. Motto:

> "When in confusion, I was made,
> Without foundation was I laid;
> But hope the Federal ovens may
> My sinking frame full well repay."

7. Gilje, "The Common People and the Constitution"; Howard B. Rock, "'All Her Sons Join in One Social Band': Visual Images of New York's Artisan Societies in the Early Republic," *Labor's Heritage*, 3 (1991), 4–21; Alfred F. Young, "English Plebeian Culture and Eighteenth-Century American Radicalism," in Margaret Jacob and James Jacob, eds., *The Origins of Anglo-American Radicalism* (London, 1984), pp. 185–212; Sean Wilentz, "Artisan Republican Festivals and the Rise of Class Conflict in New York City, 1788–1837," in Michael H. Frisch and Daniel J. Walkowitz, eds., *Working-Class America: Essays on Labor, Community, and American Society* (Urbana, Ill., 1983), pp. 37–77; Whitfield J. Bell, Jr., "The Federal Procession of 1788," *New-York Historical Society Quarterly*, 46 (1962), 5–39; Sarah H. J. Simpson, "The Federal Procession in the City of New York," *New-York Historical Society Quarterly Bulletin*, 9 (1925), 39–57.

Figure 21. Taken from the iconography of the medieval English Blacksmiths' Society, the hammer in hand and the motto became the symbol of artisans in republican America. The sense of strength in the muscular arm and the idea of the centrality of the crafts were crucial to artisans' sense of their place in the early republic. Alexander Anderson, *With Hammer in Hand, All Arts Flourish and Stand*, Anderson Scrapbooks, vol. 3, p. 28, NYPL

On the reverse, the representation of their trade in a flourishing situation, with two ovens. Motto:

> "We are well built both sound and tight;
> We hope to serve the ships in sight
> With the best bread, bak'd with good flour
> When Congress have the Federal power."

In the centre, the spread eagle and crown, holding on the left the old confederation; on the right, the new constitution—Fame with her trumpet, over it—Followed by 80 masters, journeymen and apprentices, with white aprons.

BLACKSMITHS AND NAILERS

A flag with two smiths shops represented, in one, a number of men forging an anchor, in the other, men shoeing a horse and making nails. Their coat of arms, three hammers crowned; over which was seen an eagle; under the words, "The New Constitution." Between the two shops, a large anchor. Motto:

> "Forge me strong, finish me neat,
> I soon shall moor a *Federal* fleet."

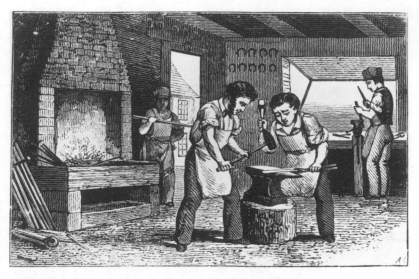

Figure 22. Anderson's depiction emphasizes the strength, simplicity, and virtue of the artisan. Alexander Anderson, *Blacksmiths at Work,* Anderson Scrapbooks, vol. 1, p. 71, NYPL

A man with his arm extended, with a hammer in it, with this motto:

> "By hammer in hand
> All arts do stand."

The number, 120 in order, headed by Mr. John M'Bain.

During the march the blacksmiths exerted themselves in the *Federal* cause. They began and almost completed, an anchor upon the stage—besides making a number of other articles, as hooks and thimbles, horseshoes, nails, etc.

PEWTERERS

Bearing an orange colored silk flag, on which was elegantly painted the United States colors; underneath which, the Pewterers' arms supported by two miners, holding burning lamps in their hands. Motto: '*Solid and pure,*' in gold letters; on the front part of the flag, the words, "Society of Pewterers," with the representation of a pewterer's

Figure 23. Pewterers' Banner (restored), Constitutional Parade, 1788, NYHS

workshop, in which the different branches were at work, and some of their work finished. Above this were the following lines; viz.:

> "The *Federal* plan most solid and secure,
> Americans their freedom will ensure;
> All arts shall flourish in Columbia's land,
> And all her Sons join as one social band."

"As Virtuous as the Generality of Mankind"
A DEFENSE OF THE BAKERS AND ARTISAN ENTERPRISE

The master bakers of early national New York were a proud, literate body of aspiring mechanic entrepreneurs whose middling economic standing was similar to that of coopers, carpenters, and other craftsmen in the middle strata of both mechanics and the city's populace. Their bakeries, though employing only a few hands, nonetheless required considerable capital. Major expenses included the purchase

Figure 24. Master craftsmen were ambitious entrepreneurs, trusting that the American Revolution would lead them to financial success equal to the political triumph of the new republic. They were inventive in their advertisements, utilizing newspaper ads, broadsides, and trade cards. The broadside of the Thomas Ash Chair Manufactory, with the cartman and ship displayed prominently, emphasizes the importance of expanding national and international trade to the mechanic. Broadside, Thomas Ash Chair Manufactory, MCNY

of flour, yeast, candles, and firewood; the salary, room, and board of a journeyman or two and an apprentice; the upkeep of a horse and cart; and yearly rent. In addition, bad flour and yeast could cost them as much as 3 percent of their yearly production.[8] Total expenditures, even for a small bakery, could easily run to over $10,000 a year, while costs at a larger enterprise could equal twice that much. Since bakers were men of moderate means, they often needed credit for

8. A detailed list of expenditures for a baker is published in the *Mercantile Advertiser*, November 19, 1801, and reprinted in Howard B. Rock, *The New York City Artisan, 1789–1825: A Documentary History* (Albany, 1989), p. 114.

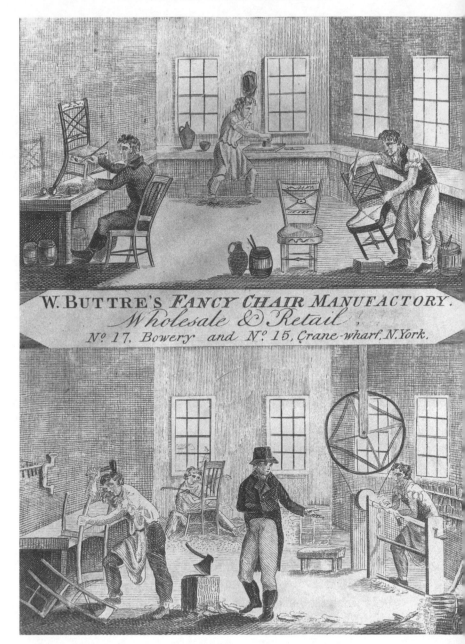

Figure 25. Buttre's Fancy Chair manufactory's trade label portrays consummate artisan skill and the careful supervision of the omnipresent master. Trade label, W. Buttre's Chair Manufactory, Courtesy of The Winterthur Library

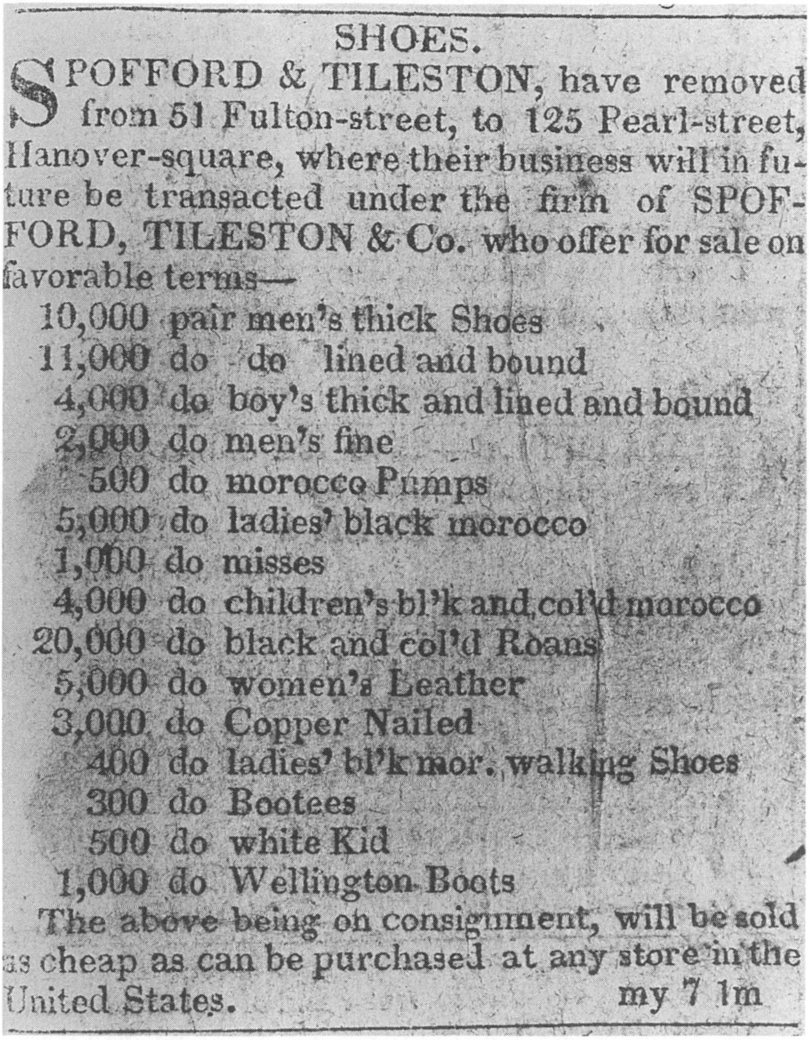

SHOES.

SPOFFORD & TILESTON, have removed from 51 Fulton-street, to 125 Pearl-street, Hanover-square, where their business will in future be transacted under the firm of SPOFFORD, TILESTON & Co. who offer for sale on favorable terms—

10,000 pair men's thick Shoes
11,000 do do lined and bound
 4,000 do boy's thick and lined and bound
 2,000 do men's fine
  500 do morocco Pumps
 5,000 do ladies' black morocco
 1,000 do misses
 4,000 do children's bl'k and col'd morocco
20,000 do black and col'd Roans
 5,000 do women's Leather
 3,000 do Copper Nailed
  400 do ladies' bl'k mor. walking Shoes
  300 do Bootees
  500 do white Kid
 1,000 do Wellington Boots

The above being on consignment, will be sold as cheap as can be purchased at any store in the United States.   my 7 1m

Figure 26. The Spofford and Tileston ad describes the immense capacity of preindustrial manufacturing in early national New York. Advertisement, Spofford & Tileston, Shoes, *New York Evening Post*, May 31, 1819

these expenditures. One man, James Stuart, continually negotiated thirty- to sixty-day notes from $150 to $1,000 for the purchase of flour.[9]

As experienced proprietors of shops that required their extensive production and marketing expertise, bakers were keenly concerned with making what they considered to be a fair profit. Since the seventeenth-century, however, American breadmakers had their profits controlled by the assize, a municipally regulated price that could be charged for a loaf of bread. When the price of flour rose or fell, the weight of a loaf costing one shilling was adjusted accordingly so that the baker's "advance" or profit was always the same. Flour inspectors were authorized to seize underweight bread, fine offending bakers, and give the confiscated loaves to the almshouse. This corporate practice, dating from medieval England, was based on the theory that the community's need for this vital foodstuff—the mainstay of the diet of the less well off—at a "just price" was of greater import than the artisan's right to operate unfettered in the marketplace.[10]

The economic restrictions imposed by the assize were in direct contradiction to the entrepreneurial aspirations among artisans and the increasingly popular liberal belief in free trade and free markets. Accordingly, bakers began in the 1790s to petition the common council for the cessation of the assize. In 1800 the common council allowed a free market in bread subject only to quality regulation. One year later popular opposition to this effort brought the controversy to a head and compelled city officials to reinstate the assize. In response, irate bakers organized a one-day work stoppage. Their action, in turn, moved the city's mercantile elite to establish a factory to secure a source of bread for the metropolis.[11] The founding of the New York Bread Company caused an outrage among bakers, and, indeed, much

9. Account book of James Stuart, June 24, 1790–October 29, 1808, Henry DuPont Winterthur Museum Library, Winterthur, Delaware.

10. For a discussion of the assize see Howard B. Rock, "The Perils of Laissez-faire: The Aftermath of the New York Bakers' Strike of 1801," *Labor History*, 17 (1976), 374. For traditional English practice of price regulation, see E. P. Thompson, "The Moral Economy of the English Crowd in the Eighteenth Century," *Past and Present*, 51 (1971), 76–136.

11. The board of directors included merchants Henry Rutgers, Jonathan Lawrence, David Lewis, William Bayard, Walter Borne, John B. Church (brother-in-law of Alexander Hamilton), auctioneer David Dickson, and former congressional candidate Gordon Mumford. This list encompassed both Federalists and Democratic-Republicans.

of the artisan community, as they cried out against monopoly and the challenge to virtuous and independent mechanics.[12] Aware of the danger that factory production, already introduced in England, posed to the small artisan entrepreneur, they launched a political attack against the Bread Company, arguing that it threatened both artisan enterprise and republican freedom in the United States. They formed committees in each ward to lobby against any kind of corporate charter for this company. The bakers' desire for a free market as a revolutionary right, they argued, was limited to artisan enterprises. If other threatening forms of enterprise were to appear, then, republican-minded artisans demanded that the public good be protected by their banishment.[13] An "Investigator" proposed a kind of compromise for the issue in the selection below from the *American Citizen*, January 19, 1802.

For the American Citizen
An Address to the Citizens of New York

It is probable, that the advantage contemplated to be derived from purchasing bread of the New-York Bread Company, at a lower price than that at which bread is now sold by the bakers, will induce many persons to purchase bread of that Company who have not seriously considered the consequences which must follow their patronising such an Association.

Admitting it to be true that the conduct of mankind is governed by a principle of self-love, and that but few of their actions are the effects of disinterested benevolence, yet there are certainly but few men so sordid as to persevere in a course of conduct that will add but little to their own happiness, and greatly diminish that of their neighbours, while they are conscious that their pursuits will have such a tendency.

The Bread Company, if it succeeds according to the expectations and wishes of its members, will probably be a lucrative concern, and supply the citizens with bread at a cheaper rate than that at which bread is usually sold; but these are advantages which can only be obtained at the expense of a class of men who perhaps are as virtuous

12. Two other arguments in this debate may be found in Rock, *The New York City Artisan*, pp. 151–154.

13. On the fear of monopoly by artisans, see Rock, *Artisans of the New Republic*, chap. 7; and Rock, *The New York City Artisan*, pp. 155–158.

as the generality of mankind; for supposing the Bread Company to be able to supply the whole of the inhabitants of this city with bread, and that the citizens were to transfer their custom from the bakers to the Bread Company, the necessary consequences would be that the bakers must abandon their business, or take refuge in other cities or towns, an evil which it is impossible to believe mankind would inflict, unless upon those who have been proved to be guilty of unparalleled crimes.

It is supposed, and perhaps believed by some persons, that the bakers have been guilty of monopoly and extortion. Admitting that they have committed those crimes, and that they have been adjudged guilty by an impartial jury, it does not appear that they have carried their rapacity to a very great extent, for were that the case, it is probable we should find them living in a similar style with those who have amassed much wealth by monopoly or other means; but it is, I believe, a fact, that they generally live in the humble style of mechanics and useful artisans, rather than in the sumptuous manner of the idle wealthy, and that they are daily employed, in preparing an article of food necessary to the subsistence of man.

But that the bakers are guilty of the crimes alleged against them has not, I presume, been proved to the satisfaction of impartial minds; for though there have been statements published representing the probable profits which they derive from their business, yet the accuracy of those statements is doubtful, having been written by persons who are unacquainted with the expenses necessary to conduct their business. The bakers, or some of them, have also published a statement, from which it appears that their profits are not greater than those of other professions. The competency of the bakers to make a just statement will not be disputed, and their veracity I suppose is equal to that of their co-temporaries. The supposition that the founders of the Bread Company were influenced by base motives to propose that institution, or that they design by it the destruction of all distinctions among men, excepting those of rich and poor, is most probably without foundation. The neglect of the bakers to furnish the citizens with bread for one day, suggested the utility of a Bread Company to prevent such an inconvenience in the future, and to countervail their supposed monopoly and extortion. But since it will operate materially against a class of citizens equally virtuous with every other class of men, and who, if their case were candidly considered, would be acquitted from the charge of guilt, it were much to be wished that the Company would employ their capital in a way that would not interfere with the useful pursuits of individuals; and as no bad effects can result from the Bread Company, if the citizens generally forbear to encourage it, it may reasonably be expected that they will continue to patronize the bakers who to present serve them with good bread, rather than seek a trifling advantage at the cost of a class of their fellow citizens. . . .

INVESTIGATOR.

"Arbitrary in the Highest Degree"
JONAS HUMBERT ARGUES FOR A RETURN TO FREE ENTERPRISE

The New York Bread Company went into operation in 1802, only to have its bakery destroyed in March 1803 in a spectacular fire. After the Bread Company's demise, the bakers resumed their attack on the assize. In 1814 prominent republican baker and politico, Jonas Humbert, a former bread inspector and Democratic-Republican political candidate, issued the following manifesto (printed in the *Columbian*, April 7, 1814), declaring that he would no longer go along with the assize. His appeal appeared during the War of 1812, a period in which there was some additional economic pressure to raise prices. With the threat of a factory gone, the argument for free enterprise as a republican right returned to prominence among the bakers. In addition, the Federalist *Evening Post* in 1819 came out against price regulation. The Council finally endorsed this policy and ended price controls in 1821.[14]

To the hon. Corporation of the City of New-York
Gentlemen — Duty that I owe to a large family, as well as other important considerations, compels me to present this address to your honorable body through the medium of public print.

Owing to the great advance of fuel, as well as every article to support life, I submitted to your consideration the propriety and justice of augmenting the profits on a barrel of flour. Several facts, un-

14. See Rock, *Artisans of the New Republic*, pp. 197 and 203, n. 33.

deniable in their nature, were substantiated, shewing the difficulties under which the bakers labored. Some short time after I signed a petition to your honorable body with a number of bakers, praying an additional allowance, and stating at the same time, the propriety and reasonableness of our requests. About four months now has elapsed and no redress is granted, although a committee reported an augmentation of six shillings per barrel.

Gentlemen — It is far from my creed to act in hostility to constituted authority. I however have always considered it strictly proper that every mechanic, as well as other persons in society, should judge for himself what profits would be a sufficient compensation for his time and labor and the articles furnished to those who employed him; if his profits were exorbitant his customers would soon quit him; if reasonable, and his bread was good, they would not complain: in this case is it not arbitrary in the highest degree, that any law shall interfere and compel a tradesman to labor for a less remuneration than what his patrons are willing he should have from them. In any case of combination, whatever, either of baker, or butcher, or grocer, or dry good merchant, to impose on the public, by monopoly intending to *create* a scarcity, for the purpose of extorting an extravagant profit, the honorable corporation would show their wisdom, prudence and just authority to interfere.

I have, gentlemen, for these years past, complied with the law regulating the weight of bread; during all this time no inspector or bread weigher, has ever weighed a loaf of my bread, at least in my bakery, because there was no need of it: this compliance has proved of great disadvantage, because it has deprived me the means of support.

After this statement the honorable corporation will not consider my determination as indecorous or offering an insult. By my business I must support a pretty large family; and I shall in future offer my bread for sale of the best quality that I possibly can manufacture, and as sweet and free from a disagreeable and unwholesome acidity as experience and experiment will warrant, at such price and such weight, as can be afforded; those who are disposed to take it, will be satisfied that I do not mean to be extravagant; on the contrary, those who think my bread good, but too small, will be under no necessity to buy it.

Considering all these circumstances, gentlemen, I hope you will not permit your inspectors to seize my property; the honorable corporation of New-York will not be the means of reducing a laborious mechanic, and his wife and children to beggary.

I am, gentlemen, your obedient and humble servant,

JONAS HUMBERT

"A Wife and a Numerous Family to Support by His Industry"
PRICE GOUGING BY A CARTMAN

Cartmen, the largest single group of tradesmen in the city, (numbering 1,200 in 1806) hauled merchants' and artisans' wares to and from the docks or to points in the city. They also removed garbage, collected manure, and assisted in street construction and paving. Entrance to this trade required no apprenticeship; in fact most of these tradesmen learned the requisite handling skills from their fathers, relatives, or friends. They were generally among the poorer of the city's workingmen, with limited economic horizons. Because they were required by law to own their horse and cart, they often had to save or borrow the few hundred dollars' purchase price. If he could find enough work, a driver could earn a better than subsistence living and perhaps save a thousand dollars in a lifetime. Illness to a horse or driver, however, could cause serious financial difficulties.[15]

The city's cartmen were under the strict supervision of the city, as both the mayor and the common council regulated their activities. The mayor issued licenses to drivers and disciplined violators of the city's various ordinances. The council set the prices cartmen could charge for hauling their loads. To avoid any possibility of monopoly or price gouging, the municipality strictly forbade cartmen from working for other men or from selling shares in their operations. They were also prohibited from selling wood to the public, and could cart it only after a buyer had paid for his cord at the dock. Before using his wagon on the city's streets, a driver had to secure a permit from the mayor and affix to the wagon a tag with the license number.[16]

15. Cartmen are discussed in Graham Russell Hodges, *New York City Cartmen, 1607–1850* (New York, 1986); and Rock, *Artisans of the New Republic*, chap. 8.

16. Regulations are found in *Laws and Ordinances Ordained and Established by the*

Figure 27. All cartmen were licensed by the mayor and worked under regulations passed by the common council. In return for obeying the city's rules, cartmen expected the municipality to protect their economic position. Nearly all cartmen owned horses, but a few worked with wheelbarrows and, consequently, received a "Hand-Cartman" license. George Hurst was the son of a ship captain born in London. After his father's death the family moved to New York in June 1825, when he received this license and purchased a used handcart for $12.00. Hand-cartman's License, 1825, MCNY

Municipal paternalism worked for the protection of both the public and the cartmen. The population expected the city to guard it against any violators seeking unjustified private gain. The prices that cartmen could charge were strictly regulated and openly published. Consequently, complaints that cartmen regularly collected more than the established fees brought cries of indignation and demands for punishment. Drivers however, often lived on the edge of subsistence. The number of haulers and the small amount of work in slow times presented constant financial crises for the families of these cartmen. The following letter to the editor of the *American Citizen* (April 7,

---

Mayor, Aldermen and Commonality of the City of New York (New York, 1799), pp. 29–39. Sidney I. Pomerantz, *New York: An American City, 1783–1803* (New York, 1938), pp. 172–178, 211–212, discusses the cartmen's legal status.

Figure 28. Cartmen were the most visible and most numerous of the city's independent proprietors. Though not skilled craftsmen, each man owned his own horse and cart and operated independently. *Cartman at Work, Picture of New York* (New York, n.d.)

1810),[17] in which a distraught cartman is caught exacting an extra shilling for his wood, is an example of the dilemmas faced by these men.

MR. CHEETHAM- - - -I had occasion some few days since to purchase a load of wood for my family, and employed a cartman to bring me one. When he called for his pay, he charged me eighteen shillings for the wood, and two shillings and two pence for the riding and inspection, which I paid him. — Within an hour or two afterwards another cartman called at my house and asked me if I would take some more of the wood, stating that I could now have it for sixteen

17. James Cheetham, an emigre English jacobin hatter, was editor of the *American Citizen*, a staunchly partisan Jeffersonian, Democratic-Republican newspaper.

shillings a load, as the Boatman was in a hurry to get away, adding that he and the other cartman who had brought me a load just before, had been riding from the same boat, that I might therefore be assured that the wood was the same in quality as the load I had then received. I told him that two shillings a load was a great reduction and I would take a cord of it. He then replied that the reduction was only *one shilling*, as he had been riding it all the morning at seventeen shillings. I told him the other cartman had charged me eighteen shillings—he replied that I was charged one shilling too much. In the afternoon I saw the cartman who had charged me the eighteen shillings, and reproached him for it. At first he denied that I had paid him more than he had to pay the boatman for it himself. I then told him that such a cartman, naming him, was now riding a cord for me from the same boat at sixteen shillings, and that he had told me the price of that which he had bro't me was only seventeen shillings— He now admitted that he had overcharged me one shilling. I reproached him for his breach of confidence and threatened to complain of him to the Mayor—he then burst out into tears and told me that he had a wife and a numerous family to support by his industry; that the Embargo and Nonintercourse Act had reduced the business of his employers[18] and that he could hardly earn enough to find bread for his children; that there were so many cartmen who had licenses. I think he said from twelve to thirteen hundred, so it was impossible for them from the reduced amount of work to keep their horses and to support their families upon their present earnings, unless they were a little before handed as he called it—that he was conscious that he had done wrong, and plead his necessities as an excuse for him. I told him this was no excuse for a fraud, for if he had told me his situation, 'altho but a poor man myself, I would have helped him and his family as far as I could do it without injuring mine. His repentance appearing to be sincere, and knowing the hardships which but too many of our cartmen labour under, I promised to let the affair drop, provided I should never hear of a similar occurrence. Permit me therefore to suggest to his Honor the Mayor, whether humanity and the good of

18. The embargo on shipping, passed by Congress to halt attacks on American vessels, virtually closed the Port of New York from late 1807 through March 1809, and the Nonintercourse Act (1809–1810) prohibited trade with England and France. Both acts created considerable unemployment. Cartmen, whose livelihoods depended on merchant trade, were severely affected.

our citizens do not dictate the propriety of reducing the number of cartmen, at least one third, and of limiting the number, say at most to eight hundred?

There are about twelve thousand families in this city, eight hundred cartmen would give one for every fifteen families, which I think would be amply sufficient—as I am informed their licenses will expire in May or June next, and it is hoped that his Honor will reflect upon the propriety of reducing their number, so as to give a better and more comfortable living to those who may be again licensed and in this way prevent any temptations to commit frauds upon the community when entrusted to buy their wood, as this article is at all times a very heavy part of the expenses of a family, without paying more than it actually costs.

A HOUSE KEEPER

"Rights, Liberties & Privalages"
THE CARTMEN AND THE IRISH ALIEN DRIVERS

Unlike the bakers, the cartmen did not attempt to free themselves from public regulation. For them, the economic heritage of the Revolution was the assurance that in return for their obedience to the municipality's code, and through that the public's welfare, the city would provide job security and protection. In this vein, they reasoned, it was the duty of the city fathers to prevent interlopers—such as the Irish, blacks, and farmers—from entering their trade.

The following document (City Clerk Filed Papers, Petition of Cartmen, June 1, 1818, NYCMA) focuses on these issues. Because of a labor shortage during the War of 1812, licenses had been issued to Irish immigrants, who as foreigners were technically ineligible for a permit. Many of these immigrants continued to haul after hostilities ceased. The cartmen considered these men to be inferior in ability and social standing, and lacking patriotism because of their failure to become American citizens. In addition, the aliens angered the cartmen by charging merchants less than the established rate and thus stealing away some of their customers. The mayor responded to the drivers' complaint by declaring that while he would no longer license aliens, it would be unfair to revoke the permits of those currently at work.[19] He promised to enforce regulations, but warned the drivers against taking matters into their own hands. In their reply printed below, the cartmen bitterly complain that their "Rights[,] Liberties & privalages" were being violated by an unfair municipal policy that broke the tacit compact between the city and its cartmen. The drivers believed that their republican rights as citizens, as well as the paternal protection provided by the licensor, were at stake.

New York June 1st 1818

To the honourable the Corporation of the City of New York in Common Council Convened,

We the Committee that represents the great body of Licenced Cartmen of this City having sometime since present to your honourable body a petition praying for an Amendment in the present Law which was passed for the better regulation of the licenced Cartmen of the City of new york

The Justness as well as the expediency of such a measure we Conceive to be fully Acknowledged by the honourable board in refering the petition to his honour the Mayor and thereby intended to answer the prayer of the petition, your petitioner conceives that it will not answer the purpose nor carry into effect the purposes for which our petition was presented. From the Just as well as the patriotick spirit that attends and marks your Deliberations in the Decisions made by your honourable Body we kneed but state that the Rights Liberties & privalages which we as a body of Citizens have prayed for are strictly and justly established upon the fact that our fathers having relinquished individual Interest & Substance with spilling theire Blood & Laying down theire Lives to obtain the Rights and privalages of free men and bequeathe the Inheritance to us theire offspring[. T]his they did having Respect unto the Reward more than the Gold of Brittain. With this petition we present the decision of his honour the mayor in our Case and at the same time beg Leave to state wherein it will not answer the purpose desired and for which it is Intended. In reflecting upon this your honourable body Cannot we trust but perceive that our Rights and Claims are founded upon the Broad Ground of Reason

19. See Rock, *The New York City Artisan*, pp. 164–165.

& Justice as may more clearly [be] understood by refering to the first Sentance expressed in the polite and Liberal answer of his Honour the mayor to our Communication to him on this subject. The words are as follows, I have attentively Considered your Communication of the 26th Inst. your reasoning with respect to the propriety of refusing Licences to unnaturalized foreigners appears to me to be perfectly Just.

Therefore after having fully established the principal that those rights and liberties [and] privalages are ours as free Citizens who have to bare the Burden and expences upon the Grounds of reason and Justice it remains with your honourable Body alone to say whether we shall enjoy them or whether those Disinterested shall divide them with us. Already have we been under the necessity of rallying around the standard of Liberty to maintain and support those verry Laws and Constitution that guarrenties them to us while at the same time we have beheld those verry men Instead of Casting in theire Lot with us shrink back and Claim the privalages of Aliens and enter into bonds and security which was much more trouble than Swaring Alegance to a Contry which they profess to have adopted by Coming to it to reside. your honourable body is not aware what material Injury we have sustained in these times of troubles by theire enjoying the priv-alages which as Citizens Could not and duty to our Contry should not in such a time that Claimed our Services in another way, we who was in employ by having to attend to the duties of a soldiers Life had to relinquish our Imployment they having the opportunity offered thereby and from the number of them have secured the principal part of the Merchants employ throughout this City your honourable body may rest assured that this fact is so well established that it needs no Comment. His honour having stated that the Course he had adopted to persue if after this should be strictly attended to (which we have no security for not knowing who may preside in time to come as Mayor) would Cease of Itself to this we would most humbly reply that owing to the number and the privalages they enjoy being exempt from all duties both as Citizens and Soldiers is Clearly mannifest to us will take some forty or fifty years before it would accomplish the De-sired end. His honour having further stated that it would be unjust to deprive them of Licence who have them they having expanded [ex-pended] all in establishing themselves in the Business. We would in answer to this Decision pray that it might be considered how much more unjust it is that we should Bare the Burden and pay of our hard earnt pittance to support them in such privalages and would venture to say that many of them Drives for men who follow other Business & Divide the proffit arising therefrom. To evade the Law under a fictitious sale of Both horse & Cart.[20]

We must acknowledge with no Small degree of gratitude and esteem it a great favour Confered upon us by his honour the mayor in his Candid Assurance of using every means to Check the evasions of the Law in which we pledge ourselves to render our cordial support. But the manner in which it is to be done will we feare exaust our patience for to Leave our daily employers whereby we obtain our Bread for our family and attend upon this part of our duty day after day while the Case is argued by councill before a Jury is more than our Circumstances will allow of we had Better all be Aliens— — — in this Case as well as many others if this is to be the end of our Informing against violation of the Sovereign Authority. . . .

John Butler Chairman
Wm. Coquillett Sec.

By order of the Committee.

"Employment in Their Own Country"
NEW YORK'S SHIPWRIGHTS APPEAL TO CONGRESS

One reason Stephen Allen and other master craftsmen supported their new federal Constitution was their expectation that a strong central government would do more to protect American trade and manufactures. This protection was considered part of the revolutionary promise to artisans of the nourishment and cultivation of their professions. For those in the maritime trades their lobbying led to a 10 percent reduction in duties for goods shipped in American vessels and a reduction in a special tonnage duty.[21] The possibility of losing

20. This was the practice of a merchant fictitiously selling a horse and cart to a driver to avoid the requirement that each cartman own his own horse and cart.

21. The original 10 percent reduction was part of the first tariff passed in 1789. The tonnage act imposed a special duty of fifty cents per ton on all foreign-built and foreign-owned ships; for American-built but foreign-owned ships, the levy was thirty cents per ton; and for those built and owned by American citizens, it was only six cents per ton. F. W. Taussig, The Tariff History of the United States (New York, 1888), p. 15.

this advantage caused anxious pleas to Congress (such as the one below, *The Memorial of the Mechanics* . . . [New York, 1803]) in which the artisans claimed that their trade would be quickly devastated and the promise of the revolution lost.

Communicated to the House of Representatives
January 27, 1803
To the Honourable the Senate and House of Representatives of the United States, the Memorial of the mechanics of the city of New York, and others concerned in the building of equipment of vessels, respectfully shews:

THAT your memorialists cannot observe, without much anxiety, that it is now proposed to Congress to repeal all discriminating duties between this country and Great Britain, so as to admit the vessels of that nation, and in the end, vessels of all foreign nations, to enter our ports on equal terms with our own. As it is certain, in the judgment of your memorialists, that foreigners can build their vessels cheaper, equip them cheaper, and navigate them cheaper than we can do; the consequence must be, that they can afford to enter, and will enter, all our ports, and take the carrying trade from our merchants, by underbidding them for freight; our carrying trade being thus shifted from our own to foreign countries, the necessary effect will be to produce a very material, if not a total stagnation in our ship-building; add that numerous classes of mechanics, who are concerned in either building or equipping of vessels, must cease to find employment in their own country, which they have hitherto done. They therefore pray that the proposed repeal may not take place.

THOMAS WRIGHT

New York, January 18, 1803   [followed by 173 signatures]

"Nursed by Guardian Care"
MASTER CRAFTSMEN ON THE NECESSITY OF PROTECTING AMERICAN MANUFACTURES

Masters expected that the American government, formed with their strong support, would do its share in protecting and encouraging domestic industries. In the appeal to Congress below (from Walter Lowne and Mathew Clark, eds., *American State Papers* [Washington,

D.C., 1832], vol. 1, *Finance* [1801], p. 694), they expressed their idea of the place of the mechanic arts in the future of America and in the responsibility of government to nurture those crafts through their early and most difficult stages. Greater domestic production, they argued, would not hurt commercial interests. Rather, merchants would either export nationally manufactured wares or invest their capital in other equally profitable ways. The welfare of the new republic depended on such support.

Protection of manufactures was a controversial issue in Jeffersonian America. Republican thought preferred an agrarian nation supplemented by free trade. The factories of Great Britain were to be avoided at all cost, as they turned cities into teeming metropolises marked by extremes of rich and poor. Yet Jeffersonians were zealous in their desire to be free of dependence on England and its goods. Thus there was an ambivalence in republican thought. New York artisans, many of them partisan Jeffersonians, sought ways to nourish their budding enterprises. Their emphasis on American independence from foreign manufactures challenged southern republicans who were far more sympathetic to agriculture and commerce and harbored a deep-seated fear of factories.[22]

To the Senate and House of Representatives of the United States, in Congress assembled, the memorial of the subscribers, mechanics and manufacturers, in the city of New York, respectfully sheweth:

Your memorialist, with deference to the superior discernment of Congress, entreat permission to call their attention to the subject of manufactures within the United States.

While the prosperity of agriculture and commerce are deservedly objects of national solicitude, the interest of the manufacturer is entitled to a share of attention.

It appears to your memorialist to be a principle of the most obvious policy, that the capital and labor of a state should be directed towards objects most conducive to the public prosperity.

A country so extensive as the United States, and comprehending

---

22. On tariff protection see Rock, *Artisans of the New Republic*, pp. 171–177, and *The New York City Artisan*, pp. 143–147. For a full discussion of the controversy between agrarian interests versus manufacturing, see Drew McCoy, *The Elusive Republic: Political Economy in Jeffersonian America* (Chapel Hill, N.C., 1980).

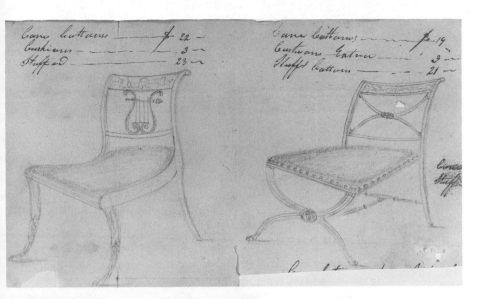

Figures 29, 30. Cabinetmaker Duncan Phyfe was probably the most renowned of early national New York's master craftsmen. A poor Scottish immigrant, he ultimately owned a warehouse, showroom, and workshop and employed one hundred journeymen. The figure above is a bill that includes sketches by Phyfe. Masters argued that early protection of their trades would allow more of them to develop to the prominence of such as Phyfe and to compete evenly in world markets. Duncan Phyfe Bill to Charles Bancker with Sketch, Courtesy of The Winterthur Library, Joseph Downs Collection of Manuscripts and Printed Ephemera

On the left is a likeness of the Scotsman with one of the tools of his trade, a frame saw. *Portrait of Duncan Phyfe,* detail, *American Collector,* May 1942

such varieties of soil and climate, must, necessarily, afford a proportionable variety and quantity of materials for the purposes of manufacture. Wool, cotton, flax, iron, indigo and numberless other articles, can, with care, be furnished in the greatest abundance; the addition of labor, only, is wanted, to convert them into valuable fabrics. Labor can be considerably facilitated by machinery, and the American genius is particularly adapted to mechanics.

Your memorialists do further respectfully represent, that the prosperity of a State is not only evidenced by its population, but that it likewise consists in the industry of its inhabitants; their usefulness to each other, and their independence of foreign Powers.

While destitute of manufactures, and dependent upon Europeans for a supply of those articles which nature or habit have classed among the necessaries of life, we hold some of our principal blessings upon a precarious tenure, of which war or shipwreck may deprive us.

So long as we remain a nation of farmers and merchants merely, we shall be tributary to the Europeans; we shall lavish upon them the wealth that may be retained at home, and pay to them a tax, which is multiplied in every hand through which it passes.

The value of the raw material frequently bears an inconsiderable proportion to that of the manufactured article. The iron, which costs a single cent, is worth an eagle[23] when moulded by the ingenuity of the artisan of Birmingham or Sheffield. To reward the labor of foreign artificers would be generous; but it would be just to remunerate the industry and ingenuity of our own countrymen and citizens.

With submission, your memorialists, represent, that the introduction of manufactures would not militate against the interest of the American merchant. The manufactures of Britain constitute the foundation of their commerce. Should any branch of manufacture, when fostered by the protecting hand of Government, rise superior to our internal necessities, we should trust to its excellence to furnish it with a market. Should any branch of commerce be affected by the origin of domestic manufactures, the activity and enterprise of the merchant will not fail to discover a new employment for his capital. The increasing population and wants of our country will prevent a diminution of foreign commerce, for a long time; while the introduction of manufactures will support a domestic commerce equally ad-

23. The eagle was an American gold coin worth five dollars.

vantageous to the merchant, because it will employ his capital at much less hazard; more beneficial to the community, because its profits will be distributed among our own citizens; more conducive to the prosperity of the Government, because the internal intercourse it will occasion, will tend to assimilate and strengthen the empire.

It is not on a sudden that manufactures can be established; they must be pursued with persevering diligence, and nursed by guardian care. They will have many obstacles to encounter, and will be opposed by those Europeans, whose interest it is to render us their perpetual tributaries. But this is a stage through which manufactures must inevitably pass. The weakness of infancy must precede the maturity and vigor of manhood; and unless a commencement is made, we shall have nearly the same obstacles to combat in the next century, that are opposed to us in the present. It appears, therefore, to your memorialists, to be the true interest of the United States to lay the foundation of infant manufactures, and to commence with such articles as can best be supported. When countenanced by the protection of the Government, they will gradually increase, and a new source of opulence and prosperity be opened to our country.

Nations the most polite and enlightened have ever bestowed the utmost attention upon manufactures; they have even cherished valuable fabrics by premiums and bounties, though your memorialists require not these inducements to call forth their enterprise and industry.

Your memorialists beg leave further to represent, that, by some fatal inattention, the breed and numbers of our sheep are now on the decline and with deference submit to the consideration of Congress, whether suitable measures should not be taken to encourage the raising and importation of these valuable animals.

And your memorialists do pray that Congress by imposing protecting duties, and by such other measures as they in their wisdom, may suffer, will afford encouragement to such manufactures and fabrics as may be most useful and most likely to succeed in the United States. Your memorialists take the liberty of suggesting, in a schedule, hereto annexed, such particular manufactures as they consider may be most successfully established, and your memorialists pray that such encouragement may be extended toward them, as, in the opinion of Congress, may be deemed proper and necessary.

And your petitioners, as in duty bound, will ever pray.

"Culpable Forgeries, Wicked Fabrications, and Malicious Calumnies"
THE CARTMEN AND THOMAS JEFFERSON

The political heritage of 1776—republican rights and responsibilities—was uppermost in the minds of master craftsmen. For no group was this legacy more meaningful than the cartmen. Many were war veterans and all were proud citizens who valued the rights of citizenship, particularly that of the ballot box. Cartmen had been eligible to vote from the colonial era (their status as "freemen" allowed suffrage privileges), and when united they composed one of the most formidable political blocs in the city.[24] No candidate or party could safely ignore them. They were, however, subject to considerable political coercion that came either from the mayor's office, with its power of issuing and revoking licenses to discipline offending drivers, or from the city's merchant class who hired the cartmen to move their goods throughout the metropolis. During the early national period the cartmen, inspired by revolutionary republicanism and the emergent Jeffersonian Democratic-Republican party, had an outlet to which they could direct their political clout against coercion. Elections became periods of intense contention for cartmen's allegiance as well as moments of exaltation and importance for this lowly echelon of city labor.[25]

Partisan politics unquestionably did much to enhance the standing and self-esteem of the artisan and cartman community. By and large the political candidates were not members of these classes, and they were willing to manipulate the mechanics' aspirations. Many appeals emphasized the intimidation of cartmen and tradesmen by merchants, including stories of blackmail or the repetition of common terms of opprobrium toward workingmen. One such appeal listed them as "Silver Heels, Leather Heads, Solemn Asses, Dough Heads."[26] These solicitations no doubt aroused craftsmen and cartmen to defend their political independence, but they also reinforced their insecurity as to the permanence of their revolutionary legacy.

The two documents in this section are republican appeals that decry the vicious belittling by the Federalists who used the licensing

24. Hodges, New York City Cartmen, chaps. 2–3, 7–9.
25. Ibid., chap. 8.
26. Public Advertiser, March 25, 1809.

power of Mayor Richard Varick to intimidate cartmen electors.[27] The Democratic-Republicans urged cartmen to vote their consciences for the Jeffersonian ticket.

The documents originally appeared in the militantly Republican *American Citizen* (April 28 and 29, 1800). The authors carefully touched issues of importance to cartmen, including the denial of their rights as citizens, the Alien and Sedition acts, and the establishment of an army to conduct a war against France. With the help of the cartmen, the Republicans carried New York City, electing an all-Jeffersonian slate to the State Assembly, which, in turn, proved critical to the election of Jefferson as President.

To the Cartmen of the City of New York,

Friends and fellow Citizens,

The die is at length cast. Your insolent oppressors no longer confine themselves to wheedling you out of your liberties, but you are now told that unless you vote for the men of their choice you are to be discarded from employ and abandoned to all the horrors of starvation. This has become the common language of your tyrants—but be not deceived. Your labour is as necessary to them as their money to you. They can no more dispense with your assistance than you can with theirs. The commerce of this city requires a certain number of cartmen, and as long as the business is not overdone you are certain of a subsistence. Therefore spurn the base and empty threats of these blusterers. Their wind may serve to make a sound in a hollow cask, but ought never to interrupt the tranquility of our honest cartmen. Applications are making daily to the mayor for licenses which shews that we have not cartmen enough. Four cart-wheels will continue to move over the pavements under burthens as heavy as your beasts can draw, without being indebted to those greater beasts who should dare to intimidate you out of your suffrages. Assert therefore my honest fellow citizens your independence. Attend the polls to a man, vote as your consciences dictate, but be assured that [it] is a bad cause which finds it necessary to call to its aid threats, bribery, corruption and lies at least so thinks a whig of seventy six who remains unchanged in
EIGHTEEN HUNDRED

27. Hodges, *New York City Cartmen*, pp. 96–97, 100–101; and Rock, *Artisans of the New Republic*, pp. 58–59.

FOR THE AMERICAN CITIZEN
To the Cartmen of New-York

Friends & Fellow Citizens,

It was with emotion of the strongest indignation, that I beheld the numerous base arts practised by the aristocratic faction in this city, at the last election, in order to promote the success of their riches.[28]

However ominous the friends of liberty might have considered an *alien, a sedition bill* and *an army establishment*, yet they were never so much alarmed by these measures, as to suppose them capable of undermining our national freedom; they depended on the good sense and virtue of the people as the best securities against the designs of ambitions or power.

But their fears were completely routed at the combination formed in this city last spring, not only to deprive you of the right of electing your representatives, but what was worse, to render you the instruments for *bolstering* up an heterogeneous faction, whose conduct has justly excited the suspicion and execration of all honest men. . . .

No stronger arguments can be produced of the badness of their cause, than the profligate means, which the federalists use to acquire popular support. Culpable forgeries, wicked fabrications, and malicious calumnies, are generally resorted to, to create dangerous prejudices and an improper *bias* in the public mind.

We have seen the peace of families disturbed, & sentiment of hatred excited in the credulous, by passionate declamations upon acts of atrocity which were never committed.[29]

We feel the pressure of accumulating taxes and now anticipate an increase in our national debt, while the present system of administration is pursued. Economy is recommended, but recollect what is practised. If you have a predilection for being saddled with burdens; if you are fond of public profusion; if you are inclined to serve those who pretend to despise you & are ever active to lop off your rights, in the

28. In the election of 1799, the Federalists recaptured the city's assembly seats through the use of intimidation by the Federalist merchants. Arthur I. Bernstein, "The Rise of the Democratic-Republicans in New York City" (Ph.D. diss., Columbia University, 1964), pp. 353–362.

29. In 1799 the Federalists filled their newspapers and broadsides with charges of French atrocities upon American ships. Bernstein, "Rise of the Democratic-Republicans," p. 353.

name of God, support the federal or aristocratic ticket, but if you wish for a plain and simple government zealous to avoid all unnecessary expences, and mindful of your interest, you will vote for a ticket, composed of veteran republicans, respectable for the purity of their private characters and meritorious for their adherence to the principles of our glorious revolution.

HEROES who fought and bled for your cause are the candidates for your suffrages. They are pledged to protect, what they succeeded in obtaining for you. Had our assembly consisted of such characters, we should not have been treated with contumely, nor would they have withheld from their constituents, the privilege of nominating the electors for President. You were charged by your federal representatives with being *too ignorant and vicious* to be entrusted with the exercise of that power.[30] If you have the spirit of men, you will resent the insult, if one spark of the patriotism of '76 exists among you, shew *your deriders, your would-be tyrants* that you are yet FREEMEN and will not be controuled.

PHILANDER

"Patriotism, Humanity, and the Love of Fat Beef"
TOASTS OF THE BUTCHERS' BENEVOLENT SOCIETY

The New York Butchers' Benevolent Society was a society of masters established to provide benefits to distressed or elderly members and to offer a fraternal and recreational outlet. Members celebrated national holidays as well as the anniversary of its founding. The toasts, published in the *New York Evening Post*, March 5, 1817, interweave allusions to the trade with patriotism and celebration of the profession and extol exemplary artisan republican ideals. They exhibit a proud strain of patriotism and loyalty to their republic—with a special remembrance for George Washington—as well as faith in the armed forces shortly after the conflict with Great Britain. There are affirmations of faith in the progress of American manufacturing, agriculture, literature, and, with the seeming demise of the two-party

---

30. The Jeffersonian attack on the deferential expectations and contemptuous sentiments of Federalists toward artisans and cartmen was the most significant cause of their downfall in New York City. See Rock, *Artisans of the New Republic*, chap. 2.

system, a sense of the coming age of harmony, friendship, and benevolence.[31]

FOR THE NEW-YORK EVENING POST

Anniversary of the Butchers' Benevolent Society. — The members assembled at an early hour on Monday, the 3d inst. when the officers
were elected for the ensuing year. The society then partook of a
handsome dinner, provided by Mr. J. Manold. After the cloth was
removed the following TOASTS were drank, accompanied with appropriate SONGS:

1. The day, and all who celebrate it.

2. The Butchers' Benevolent Society—Strengthened by the *joints*
of union, may it never be destitute of the *oil* of humanity.

3. The present anniversary— May it have the pleasing effect to
encourage social feeling, and *split* the rock of division on every *side*.

4. The memory of Gen. George Washington— A patriot the most
exemplary; who lived in the affections, died in the tears, and survives
in the hearts of his countrymen.

5. America— Let the fields, which fatten her numerous herds,
become the *shambles* and *graves* of her daring invaders.

6. The edge of party feeling— Blunted by the relations of civil life,
may it never be sharpened by the *bone* of contention.

7. Commerce— Let the *marrow* of industry, and the *sinews* of integrity, *nerve* the arm and hearts of every American tar.

8. The Corporation of the City of New-York— The guardians of
our rights, may we continue to receive from them that indulgence,
which we have ever had the happiness to experience.

9. The American navy— Strong *ribs* of oak, defended by hearts
still stronger.

10. The citizens of New-York— Celebrated for commercial enterprise, patriotism, humanity, and the love of *fat beef*.

11. Peace— The *rope* and the *axe*, to him who would wantonly
interrupt it.

12. The resources of our country— Ascertaining by industry, never
failing to reward it.

31. For a further discussion of artisan rituals and celebrations, see Wilentz, "Artisan
Republican Festivals," 37–39; Rock, *Artisans of the New Republic*, chap. 5; and Rock,
The New York City Artisan, pp. 4–14.

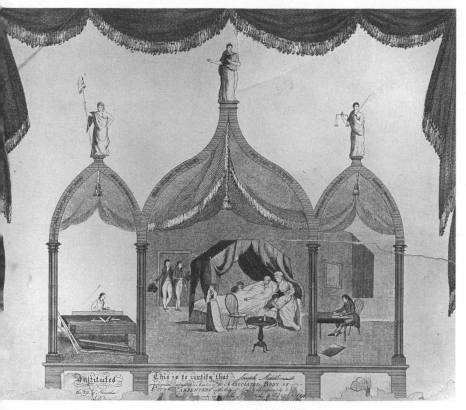

igure 31. Master craftsmen commonly associated for the promotion of their trade and for enevolent purposes such as death and disability benefits. This certificate of the House Carenters depicts both their craft and benevolence. Prominent as well are the classical women tuated atop the pinnacles, representing the republican symbols of liberty, wisdom, and jusce. The partially obscured motto reads: "Liberty may we ever feel and never abuse thy benign fluence. Firm United we stand our hope is in God. Justice and Benevolence Adorn Socity." Certificate of Membership to the New York Body of Associated House Carpenters, 1796, 1CNY

13. Internal improvement— The sure means of uniting all sections of the country, in harmonious intercourse.

14. Literature— The clouds of ignorance fly before it, peace and contentment follow its train.

15. The heroes of the revolution— Can those who reap the harvest, forget the hands that prepared the soil?

Hon. Peter H. Wendover,

Figure 32. One of the city's leading Democratic-Republicans, sailmaker Peter H. Wendover served as both alderman and assemblyman. *Portrait of Peter Wendover,* NYHS

16. Friendship— Like the blood which flows through congenial veins, may it be exhausted only in death.

17. Agriculture— The parent of our profession, and of every subsequent blessing which mankind have been permitted to enjoy.

18. The American Fair— In the offices of domestic life, tender as the lamb; in the defence of virtue, invincible as the lion.

"National Deliverance"
THE FOURTH OF JULY ORATION OF PETER WENDOVER, SAILMAKER

In this address given before master and journeymen organizations, as well as other citizens, Democratic-Republican sailmaker Peter Wendover, a prosperous Jeffersonian master craftsman who served both as an alderman and assemblyman,[32] invoked the classical republican spirit of public service and sacrifice, patriotism and community. Wendover outlined a vision of history that viewed the story of America as a progressive march toward liberty. From this perspective, the

32. Willis, "Social Origins and Political Leadership," 356.

Figure 33. The certificate of membership of the Master Sailmakers Society reveals the pride and centrality of the trade displayed in the motto, "Commerce Moves All," and in pictures of ships and sailmakers. The upper left corner represents a symbol of Liberty handing a certificate of emancipation to a slave. Although one-quarter of the artisan community owned slaves in 1796, clearly the sailmakers understood the paradox of a republican society peopled with slave owners. Certificate of Membership in the Society of Master Sail Makers of the City of New York, 1795, NYHS

colonists lived in a bucolic, egalitarian, and pristine new world, "uninterrupted by the broils of Europe." When a corrupted England attempted to introduce vice and to curtail "native privileges," Americans, aided by providential grace and the genius of Washington, revolted. Wendover portrayed the Constitution as a work of true republican spirit ("Free representation and equal rights") and both defended and lamented the French Revolution as a people's revolt following in American footsteps but crushed by both European potentates and a lack of virtue. Yet even with this disappointment, America, founded on "rational liberty" and administered "by the intelligence of Jefferson," remained a beacon for the world. Wendover concluded with a plea for continuing virtue and a reminder of the fate of Greece. Wendover's vision of the American republic allowed for no internal divisions. (Aspersions cast on Jefferson are denounced as "cruel slander.") Moreover, he recognized that the artisan community played a crucial role in the creation of the republic and retained responsibility for keeping the ship of state on course.[33]

BRETHREN, FRIENDS, FELLOW CITIZENS!

When you reflect on the occasion for which we are assembled, and consider for a moment why we have set apart this great anniversary; when you take a view of the scenes that are past, and retrospect to the circumstances which gave rise to our joys; while your hearts beat high with exultation, with me you will exclaim, the subject is highly momentous; the task too important for the Speaker of the Day.

Were I so vain as to flatter you that your hopes would be realized in hearing something to the purpose, or should I pretend to the exercise of talents equal to the duty assigned by me, you would *smile* at my *folly*, and *pity* my *weakness*. Untaught in the rudiments of language; not versed in the embellishments of diction, or strains of eloquence, I claim your indulgence for a short season, while I presume to remind you that the purpose for which we are collected, is not to *criticise* on the abilities of the *Orator*, but for mutual congratulations

33. This rendition of the document is based on the copy in the American Antiquarian Society's microcard collection, number S 11846. On the copy are several penned-in corrections of typesetting errors and a few changes of expression. None of these alterations changed the meaning of the sentences or oration. Because some of the corrections so obliterated the original, in the interests of consistency the corrected version has been followed here. Peter Wendover, *National Deliverance. An Oration . . . Delivered in the New Dutch Church, The Fourth of July,* 1806 (New York, 1806).

that COLUMBIA IS FREE![34]

The custom of celebrating important events, and holding national festivals, is so ancient, and become so common, that some have adopted it on the slightest occasions. The defeat of an army, the deposing of an usurper, and the coronation of a monarch, have all been made use of to encourage the practice; even when the people that pursued it were groaning under the *vilest oppression*.

Among the various occurrences in which civil society can feel an interest, the EMANCIPATION of a Nation appears to be the greatest; and the annual celebration of such an event is doubtless a duty of public importance. This duty is not only founded on rational principles, but is sanctioned by the oracles of truth.

If we compare our former situation and happy deliverance with that of the Israelites of old, who were commanded not only to keep a day as a memorial, but to inculcate on their children the propriety of the injunction; we shall readily discover, that while we prize our enjoyments, we are bound to *improve* them.

With these ends in view, looking to the historian to record, with scrupulous exactness, the rise and progress of the revolution, and the improvements of our country, we shall, in a cursory manner, attempt to revive them in the following respects.

First; the wonderful deliverances wrought in our favour, and the invaluable previleges we have attained.

Secondly; the obligations we are under to hand them down to *posterity unimpaired*.

It would not comport with our present engagements to enter into a detail of the situation of our progenitors who fled from the tyranny of Britain to seek an asylum in this *Western World*; let it be remembered that their love of liberty was rational, and founded on the boasted professions of a nation where it did *not exist*.

Uncontaminated with the vices of the old world, and separated from the scene of pageantry and adulation by the waters of the Atlantic, they fondly imagined that *they* and *their children* would be permitted to cultivate the arts of peace, uninterrupted by the broils of Eu-

---

34. A common theme in mechanic orations and literature is to admit the lack of literary abilities at the same time that one affirms that such intellectual accomplishment was but a secondary achievement. Patriotism, leadership, and contribution to the nation did not require such skills or training. Artisans were at the least equal to the better educated in their support of the new republic.

rope, and undisturbed by the *satellites of power*. Not over solicitous for the exercise of external self-government, and firmly attached to the country from which they had emanated, they were obedient to its sovereign, and respected its laws. Justly appreciating the blessings conferred on them by a bountiful Providence, their hearts glowed in high expectation of *future prosperity and long repose*. But, alas! tyranny, ever insatiable, unhallowed ambition, for ever on the rack, not content to wave the sceptre in peaceful sway, the court of Britain seemed to suspect that the benignity of Heaven would lavish its bounties on these favored climes. Well aware that the happiness of the subject would not comport with the views of the monarch, a pretext was sought to curtail our native privileges, and make us submit to terms of the *greatest degradation*.

To you, O America! is directed the threatened vengeance, and Britain resounds with the clarions of war. Unhappy Britain! Not called to repel from your Island a *proud invader*; not arrayed in defence of your country, and the rights of conscience; but tyranny is alarmed, and you are commissioned to enforce the dreadful mandates of the *Hydra of Despotism*. Behold

> *The monster raves, determined to prevail,*
> *And in oppression, takes a sweet regale:*
> *Envy enrag'd, like dread Vesuvius burns,*
> *The nations wonder, lo! Columbia mourns!*

Beholding in anguish a formidable armament preparing for the destruction, Americans pondered. Unwilling to enter on this impious work of slaughter, not disposed to imbrue their hands in a brother's blood, or to fall by the hands of their British brethren, they renewed their supplications, and again presented their entreaties to a cruel Sovereign, but presented them in vain! It suited not the designs of an unprincipled ministry to spare the lives of the subjects, who dared to believe that a *Monarch could do wrong*. The dictates of reason were treated with derision. The voice of philanthropy was hushed to silence.

The Fleets and Armies of England, composed of the slaves of tyrants from home, and purchased vassals from abroad, arrived in splendor, and debarked on our shores, with the instruments of death. Not inured to the tactics of war, untaught in the practice of barbarity, not accustomed to the clang of arms, America trembles; all awake to foreboding fears. All alarmed at the clouds that thicken, *Americans collect*. The crisis is truly distressing—*Death is a terror*, but *slavery is death*.

Driven by dire necessity to act on the defensive, and conscious of the justice of their cause, the persecuted citizens of Columbia, appealing for protection to the SOVEREIGN of the UNIVERSE, they prepared for the conflict, and met the merciless foe, already entered on the work of cruel devastation, attended with circumstances of *unparalleled horror*.

Flushed with a few successful attacks on an unarmed yeomanry, and elated with the pride of military prowess; with their hearts steeled to the voice of humanity, Britons exult in the hope of conquest. But, trembling Americans, mark the event! Those well disciplined armies, destined by Britain to subjugate your country, are stopped in their march— The valour of Englishmen is put to the test—Infatuated Britain must humble. Her armies must yield. —For WASHINGTON COMMANDS!

Frustrated in their hopes of conquest by open warfare— Failing in their application of the coffers of corruption; and finding the soil of America fertile to liberty, the *minions of royalty*, in remorse and confusion, *departed* our shores, and *peace* and *independence* crowned our struggles.

Here we might point to the *instruments* of our deliverance, and with mingled emotions of gratitude and pain, remember their woes. Here we might rehearse the deeds of dauntless heroes, early fired in their country's cause: Who nobly ventured, and so nobly fell! The faithful *historian* shall record their valour, while Americans inherit the price of their blood. Here we might descant on the services of our worthy sires, who for us contended, and for us prevailed. Spared for a season to reap the fruit of their labours, at the end of *thirty revolving years* we behold them mostly numbered with this kindred dead. How dear their *memory*! How deserving our praise! Ye venerable sages, who yet survive the ravages of time—called *this day* to celebrate the achievements of your veteran compatriots, you shall share our *highest plaudits*! Your wasting frames and hoary locks indicate your short continuance, and speak to us a solemn lesson! Long fatigued in the arduous warfare, and often burthened with the cares of your country— now looking forward to the hour of dissolution, you seem to say, "*Beloved countrymen, continue virtuous—You'll long be free!*" —Ye soldiers of liberty, who braved the dangers of the raging battle, on this day of happy triumph we remember your sufferings, we feel for your wrongs! Your *seven years* toil and valiant feats were known to your country—she sought to requite you, but, betrayed by the avarice of man, she became *ungrateful!*

Having struggled through a long and arduous contest, and obtained a rank among the nations of the earth; it was left for Americans to convince the potentates of Europe, that the end of all *just governments* was the *happiness* of the *governed.* And finding by experience that a temporary compact could not be productive of permanent advantages, the Genius of America, ever watchful for the interests of posterity, suggested an improvement, exhibiting competent energy, combined with FREE REPRESENTATION and EQUAL RIGHTS.

Too long made the sport of ambition to invite the artifices of political adventurers; and having too long waded the fields of blood to risk the evils of anarchy; the sages of our country approached, with cautious steps, to the convocation of *statesmen*—while the hardy sons of liberty denounced *extermination* and *death* to the *daring* mortal who, with polluted hands, should touch the *repository* of their *rights.*

Thus enveloped in the shades of political twilight, and fearful the gathering clouds would burst in convulsions, the war-worn patriot wept for his country; while the enemies of man, filled with envy, counted on a triumph. But the event is known— The *assembled wisdom* of *Freemen*, and the *combined virtue* of *Americans*, overruled by the goodness of PROVIDENCE, warded off impending evils; and the invaluable rights of the Citizen were placed on a solid basis.

Advancing on in pursuit of peace and national felicity, we were again arrested with surrounding dangers. —The same year in which the government of the Union became consolidated, we beheld the commencement of a revolution, *sublime* in its *origin*, but dreadful in its *effects*. The subjects of the French King, having long groaned under the burden of oppression, taking example from the *courage* and *magnanimity of Americans*, burst their chains and nobly contended for the RIGHTS OF MAN.

Alarmed at the enthusiasm of a powerful people, the monarchs of Europe trembled for the consequences; and the peaceful citizens of Columbia, sympathising with the advocates for freedom, feared an entanglement in the general *commotion*. But here we were again permitted to see a happy deliverance—*Peace* was preserved to our favored country, while, with indescribable profusion, *all Europe* was drenched in human gore. Shall we digress for a moment to lament the *fury* of the nations, and the *wretchedness* of man? Shall we grieve for the departed glory of Frenchmen, once struggling to be free? O France, thy efforts for liberty were truly astonishing—but learn, that LIBERTY and VIRTUE are forever inseparable!

But, my countrymen, assembled to celebrate the *heroism* of our citizens, and to recount the blessings of our inheritance, let us remember the high obligations we are under to acknowledge that GOD, who interposed for our country, relieved us from *thraldom*, and saved us with an omnipotent arm. On every return of this happy day we are bound to recollect his MERCIES, and teach the rising youth to proclaim his *praise*.

Under his propitious care we have been permitted to raise up the fair fabric of EQUAL LAWS, and to cement our dear-bought rights under a CONSTITUTION, founded on the broad basis of *rational liberty*; unalloyed by hereditary absurdity, or regal power; and well calculated to promote the *happiness* of the nation when *sceptres* and *despots* shall lose all their charms!

Let us congratulate our country that, at *this* day, when the nations of Europe are *deluged* with *war*, and held in *bondage*, *we* enjoy *peace*. Governed by laws emanating from the people, and faithfully administered by the wisdom of a JEFFERSON—Excellent citizen—enlightened statesman! In vain shall cruel slander attach the epithet *Infidel!*[35] Thy FAME shall live in the breasts of *Freemen*— Thy VIRTUES and REPUBLICANISM, shall be celebrated by the *world*, and with the glories of WASHINGTON, descend to unborn millions; and the tongue of calumny shall confess, that *infidelity* in *thee*, consists solely in opposing the doctrine, that "A *government by Nobles is the most stupendous fabric of human invention!*"

Let us rejoice that, amidst the profuse blessings of an extensive and fertile country, we enjoy, unawed by tyrants, the sacred right of *elec-*

---

35. An allusion to the charges made against Jefferson for his views of Christianity. Wendover was following the deistic artisan tradition of Thomas Paine that would give way during the Second Great Awakening to fundamentalism. Despite the seeming neutrality of the speech, Wendover, as noted, was an ardent Jeffersonian. The artisan community had moved from strong Federalist allegiance in the 1790s to a large majority in favor of the Jeffersonians by 1806. See Wilentz, *Chants Democratic*, pp. 77–87; and Rock, *Artisans of the New Republic*, chaps. 1–2.

tive franchise. Let us ever recollect, that the *preservation* of our liberties depend, under *Providence*, on the *purity of legislation*, and the *morality* of the *people.* Can it ever be contended that *corrupt* measures will produce *pure* effects? Or that men, morally dishonest, may *safely* be trusted with our invaluable rights? Or will even absurdity insist, that citizens, vicious in their practices, are calculated to promote principles of *morality*, so very essential to public happiness? Let it be indelibly written in our political creed, that PUBLIC LIBERTY and PUBLIC VIRTUE are indissolubly connected—and that where the latter is extinct, the former must expire. Let our children be early and faithfully taught, that acts to be *rightful*, must ever be *just.* That republican principles and true patriotism, can only be promoted by the practice of the *moral virtues* and *conscious integrity.* Let Americans remember, with the Grecians of old,

> That "*Wanting* VIRTUE, *life is pain and woe,*
> That "*Wanting* LIBERTY, *even virtue mourns,*
> "*And looks around for happiness in vain!*"

But, fellow-citizens, shall we for a moment allay the ardor of our ecstatic joys, and on *this* day of national festivity, chide our countrymen for the encouragement of a growing evil,* *impious* in its nature and dreadful in its consequences? Shall we weep over our beloved country to behold a people, who when oppressed by an open enemy, gloried in sparing the lives of their *vanquished* foes—becoming signalized in barbarity, and in single combat, spill a brothers blood? Shall an American, contending for the right of government by the *voice of the people*, assume the prerogative to slay a fellow man? Shall our citizens be permitted with impunity to *stain* the heroism of Columbia, with the name of murder? Forbid it patriotism! Forbid it morality! No more let savage gratification, and pretended honor, be suffered to sacrifice the principles of *humanity* and a sense of *moral*

———*The Author intended, under a suitable head, to have mentioned some other vices of our day, which he has ever considered the bane of Republican principles—but having exceeded the limits originally contemplated, he ventured to make this digression to expose the practice alluded to as one of the most inconsistent.

obligation at the shrine of *revenge!*

Let us ever recollect, that we are accountable for the improvement of our privileges to that GOD who governs the nations, and awards the destinies of men. And remember, that for our advantage he affords us the inestimable blessings of the GOSPEL OF PEACE—the precepts of which, above all others, are eminently calculated to inculcate that excellent maxim, of "doing to others as we wish them to do unto us." These will not fail to promote the best *interests* of our COUNTRY and the *happiness* of MAN, "How admirable," (says an excellent author) "is that religion, which, while it seems only to have in view the felicity of the *other* World, constitutes the happiness of *this!*"

Friends and Fellow Citizens!

Called to review the happiness of our lot; and descrying the nations from afar in shackles of bondage—let us sympathize with their sorrows, and solemnly reflect on the *astonishing contrast.* Saved from the chains of *infuriated Monarchs,* we *this* day hail our country *the land of the free!*

Constrained, by every endearing motive, to protect the sacred deposit of *civil and religious* liberty, may we and our children be a potent example of *virtue and magnanimity.* May we soon realize the glorious era, in which the *banners of freedom,* unfurled in the *West,* shall travel onward and encircle the globe. And may succeeding ages enhance the *intrinsic excellence* of the *Heavenly boon,* TILL THE LATEST POSTERITY INHABIT THE EARTH.

4

WATERFRONT WORKERS:
Afloat and Ashore

The American Revolution had a mixed impact on waterfront workers. There is no doubt that sailors played a crucial role in politics "out-of-doors" (riots and street demonstrations), which marked American seaports in the years of resistance to British imperial measures during the 1760s and 1770s.[1] Sailors contributed to the war effort by serving aboard privateers and other vessels during the struggle for independence, and became an important national symbol during the years of the early republic.[2] Moreover, their labor remained crucial to the great commercial expansion of the United States as American shipping assumed a major position in international trade.[3] Yet, although sailors and others on the waterfront at times adopted the rhet-

1. In the eighteenth century both the generic "Jack" and the term "Tar" (tar coated most everything aboard ships, including the sailors' clothes) became standard names for the stereotypical sailor. Often they were combined. Jesse Lemisch, "Jack Tar in the Streets: Merchant Seamen in the Politics of Revolutionary America," *William and Mary Quarterly*, 3d ser., 25 (1968), 371–407.

2. Jesse Lemisch, "Listening to the 'Inarticulate': William Widger's Dream and the Loyalties of American Revolutionary Seamen in British Prisons," *Journal of Social History*, 3 (1969), 1–29; Samuel Eliot Morison, *The Maritime History of Massachusetts, 1783–1860* (Boston, 1979; orig. pub. 1921); James Fulton Zimmerman, *Impressment of American Seamen* (Port Washington, N.Y., 1925).

3. Robert Greenhalgh Albion, with the collaboration of Jennie Barnes Pope, *The Rise of New York Port, 1815–1860* (New York, 1939); Albion, "New York Port in the New Republic, 1783–1793," *New York History*, 21 (1940), 388–403.

oric of the new republican ideology, they remained trapped in near poverty, and their lives often reflected a reality that belied republican ideals and created a negative stereotype.

This traditional view of sailors' lives can be misleading and must be overcome if we are to get a clear picture of work and life along the waterfront in New York City. The typical sailor, so the stereotype dictates, belonged to a special fraternity: he wore different clothes, spoke a peculiar argot, was committed to profanity, drank too much, spent his money freely, patronized prostitutes, got into brawls, and then signed aboard his next voyage. According to the stereotype, the sailor's presence on the waterfront was ephemeral: quite likely, he was here today and gone tomorrow. Like many stereotypes, there is some truth to this thumbnail sketch of the "jolly tar." There is also much that is wrong with it. Sailors and waterfront workers were a diverse lot. Some fit the stereotype. Many did not.[4]

People who lived along the waterfront drifted in and out of different occupations. They might go off on a voyage for a few months, and, upon their return, work as riggers or stevedores for a few months. Some men served aboard ships for only a couple of years and then turned to other ways of earning a living. (Indeed, in a port city like New York many men no doubt had some deep-water sailing experience.) Others, however, became entrapped in a lifestyle of hard work aboard ship, relieved only by excess on shore.

The following documents depict this variety and the impact of the new republican and commercial revolutions on work experience along the waterfront. The first document addresses the experience of a typical sailor during the Revolutionary War in an effort to show how mariners contributed to the creation of the American Republic. The sacrifice that participation in the War of Independence entailed became emblazoned into the consciousness of those who labored on and by the sea. That consciousness may not be fully evident in the second document, where we get a glimpse of waterfront life from the reminiscence of Horace Lane, but several of the documents reveal the connections between the sailor's world and the political and economic revolutions of the age. George Little's description of the conditions of labor at sea included a recognition of the centrality of the

4. Marcus Rediker, *Between the Devil and the Deep Blue Sea: Merchant Seamen, Pirates, and the Anglo-American Maritime World, 1700–1750* (Cambridge, 1987).

sailor to the American economy. The efforts at reform that Little mentions and that inspired Richard Henry Dana, Henry Chase, and the American Seamen's Friend Society were in part generated by the awareness that sailors contributed to the birth and the growth of the American nation. Equally important, however, were the actions taken by the waterfront workers themselves. Building upon their awareness that they, too, were "citizens," these workers demanded economic relief during the embargo and struck for wages when conditions were better.

"Scenes of Wretchedness, Disease, and Woe"
ABOARD THE PRISON SHIP JERSEY

The waterfront districts in all American ports were busy during the Revolutionary War. Prices were high in both British- and whig-occupied cities, so wages were good for sailors and dockside workers. Those who signed aboard privateers on either side could make a fortune, but these workers also ran risks. Although American privateers captured hundreds of thousands of tons of shipping during the war, many sooner or later encountered a British warship and were taken prisoner. Eleven thousand men died aboard prisoner-of-war hulks like the *Jersey* in Wallabout Bay, across the East River from New York City. Some escaped, others were exchanged, and countless others were pressed into British service even before they reached the prison ships. For all American sailors the rotting hull of the *Jersey* hung over their war experience like a dark cloud. It marked their sacrifice in lives, and it represented their helplessness before forces beyond the tars' control. Because generals and politicians on both sides could not come to an agreement on an equitable system of exchange, many sailors remained in the *Jersey* until their shriveled corpses were joined with the bones of other sailors buried in mass graves on the Brooklyn shore.[5]

5. Eugene L. Armbruster, *The Wallabout Prison Ships, 1776–1783* (New York, 1920); Charles H. Metzger, *The Prisoner in the American Revolution* (Chicago, 1971); Catherine M. Prelinger, "Benjamin Franklin and the American Prisoners of War in England during the American Revolution," *William and Mary Quarterly*, 3d ser., 32 (1975), 261–294; Louis H. Roddis, "The New York Prison Ships in the American Revolution," *United States Naval Institute Proceedings*, 61 (1935), 331–336.

Figure 34. A depiction of the scene inside the Jersey. Engraving of the Jersey Prison Ship in Albert Greene, Recollections of the Jersey Prison Ship from the Manuscript of Capt. Thomas Dring New York, 1961)

Thomas Dring was lucky: he survived the ordeal of the Jersey. His release in 1782 resulted from a private deal struck between the State of Rhode Island and the British for an all-too-infrequent exchange of forty prisoners. Dring recounts the horror of arriving aboard the Jersey and his first dreadful night in that place. (Albert Greene, Recollections of the Jersey Prison Ship from the Manuscript of Capt. Thomas Dring [New York, 1961; orig. pub. Providence, 1829], 11–16.)

We had now reached the accommodation ladder, which led to the gangway on the larboard [port] side of the Jersey; and my station in the boat, as she hauled alongside, was exactly opposite to one of the air-ports in the side of the ship. From this aperture proceeded a strong current of foul vapor, of a kind to which I had been before accustomed, while confined on board the Good Hope;[6] the peculiarly dis-

6. Dring had been captured in 1779 and placed aboard the Good Hope in the North (Hudson) River. After four months he escaped by swimming to the Jersey shore. Albert Greene, Recollections of the Jersey Prison Ship, pp. 5–6.

THE IMPRESSMENT OF AN

American Sailor Boy,

SUNG ON BOARD THE BRITISH PRISON SHIP CROWN PRINCE, THE FOURTH OF JULY, 1814
BY A NUMBER OF THE AMERICAN PRISONERS.

THE youthful sailor mounts the bark,
    And bids each weeping friend adieu :
Fair blows the gale, the canvass swells :
    Slow sinks the uplands from his view.

Three mornings, from his ocean bed,
    Resplendent beams the God of day :
The fourth, high looming in the mist,
    A war-ship's floating banners play.

Her yawl is launch'd ; light o'er the deep,
    Too kind, she wafts a ruffian band :
Her blue track lengthens to the bark,
    And soon on deck the miscreants stand.

Around they throw the baleful glance :
    Suspense holds mute the anxious crew—
Who is their prey ? poor sailor boy !
    The baleful glance is fix'd on you.

Nay, why that useless scrip unfold ?
    They damn'd the " lying yankee scrawl,"
Torn from thine hand, it strews the wave—
    They force thee trembling to the yawl.

Sick was thine heart as from the deck,
    The hand of friendship wav'd farewell ;
Mad was thy brain, as far behind,
    In the grey mist thy vessel fell.

One hope, yet, to thy bosom clung,
    The captain mercy might impart ;

Vain was that hope, which bade thee look,
    For mercy in a Pirate's heart.

What woes can man on man inflict,
    When malice joins with uncheck'd power ;
Such woes, unpitied and unknown,
    For many a month the sailor bore !

Oft gem'd his eye the bursting tear,
    As mem'ry linger'd on past joy ;
As oft they flung the cruel jeer,
    And damn'd the " chicken liver'd boy."

When sick at heart, with " hope defer'd,"
    Kind sleep his wasting form embrac'd,
Some ready minion ply'd the lash,
    And the lov'd dream of freedom chas'd.

Fast to an end his miseries drew :
    The deadly hectic flush'd his cheek :
On his pale brow the cold dew hung,
    He sigh'd, and sunk upon the deck !

The sailor's woes drew forth no sigh ;
No hand would close the sailor's eye :
Remorseless, his pale corse they gave,
    Unshrouded to the friendly wave.

And as he sunk beneath the tide,
    A hellish shout arose ;
Exultingly the demons cried,
    " So fare all Albion's Rebel Foes !"

Figure 35. This broadside, published during the War of 1812, focuses on the American sailor as victim of the British. Impressment was one of the most dramatic and compelling of the causes of the War of 1812, and the sailor became an important American symbol of the war. Broadside, "Impressment of Tars," 1813, NYHS

gusting smell of which I then recollected, after a lapse of three years. This was, however, far more foul and loathsome than any thing which I had ever met with on board that ship, and produced a sensation of nausea far beyond my powers of description.

Here, while waiting for orders to ascend on board, we were addressed by some of the prisoners, from the air-ports. We could not, however, discern their features, as it had now become so dark that we could not distinctly see any object in the interior of the ship. After some questions, whence we came, and respecting the manner of our capture, one of the prisoners said to me, that it was "a lamentable thing to see so many young men in full strength, with the flush of health upon their countenances, about to enter that infernal place of abode." He then added, in a tone and manner but little fitted to afford us much consolation, — "Death has no relish for such skeleton carcasses as we are, but he will now have a feast upon you fresh comers."

After lanterns has been lighted on board, for our examination, we ascended the accommodation ladder, to the upper deck, and passed through the barricado door; where we were examined, and our bags of clothes inspected. These we were permitted to retain, provided they contained no money or weapons of any kind.

After each man had given his name and the capacity in which he had served on board the vessel in which he was captured, and the same had been duly registered, we were directed to pass through the other barricado door, on the starboard side, down the ladder leading to the main hatchway. I was detained but a short time with the examination, and was permitted to take my bag of clothes with me below; and passing down the hatchway, which was still open, through a guard of soldiers, I found myself among the wretched and disgusting multitude, a prisoner on board the *Jersey*.

The gratings were soon after placed over the hatchways, and fastened down for the night; and I seated myself on the deck, holding my bag with a firm grasp, fearful of losing it among the crowd. I had now ample time to reflect on the horrors of the scene, and to consider the prospect before me. It was impossible to find one of my former shipmates in the darkness; and I had, of course, no one with whom to speak during the long hours of that dreadful night. Surrounded by I knew not whom, except that they were beings as wretched as myself; with dismal sounds meeting my ears from every direction; a nauseous and putrid atmosphere filling my lungs at every breath; and a stifled and suffocating heat, which almost deprived me of sense, and even of life.

Previous to leaving the boat, I had put on several additional articles of apparel for the purpose of security; but I was soon compelled to disencumber myself of these; and was willing to hazard their loss, for a relief from the intolerable heat.

The thought of sleep did not enter my mind: and at length, discovering a glimmering of light through the iron gratings of one of the airports, I felt that it would be indeed a luxury, if I could but obtain a situation near that place, in order to gain one breath of the exterior air. Clenching my hand firmly around my bag, which I dared not leave, I began to advance towards the side of the ship; but was soon greeted with the curses and imprecations of those who were lying on the deck, and whom I had disturbed in attempting to pass over them. I however persevered, and at length arrived near the desired spot; but found it already occupied, and no persuasion could induce a single individual to relinquish his place for a moment.

Thus I passed the first dreadful night, waiting with sorrowful forebodings for the coming day. The dawn at length appeared, but came only to present new scenes of wretchedness, disease, and woe. I found myself surrounded by a crowd of strange and unknown forms, with the lines of death and famine upon their faces. My former shipmates were all lost and mingled among the multitude, and it was not until we were permitted to ascend the deck, at eight o'clock, that I could discern a single individual whom I had ever seen before. Pale and meagre, the throng came upon deck; to view, for a few moments, the morning sun, and then, to descend again, to pass another day of misery and wretchedness.

"Some Drinking, Some Swearing, Some Fighting, Some Singing"
GOTHAM'S WATERFRONT DANCE HALLS

When Horace Lane wrote The Wandering Boy, Careless Sailor, and Result of Inconsideration in 1839 he had spent much of his fifty years as a sailor. Too worn-out to go to sea, and with no marketable skill ashore, he did the one thing that sailors do best: he told the marvelous tale of his life. His intention was reform, and he spun his yarn as a republican morality lesson, depicting the evils of a wandering disposition, drink, and carousing.

The outlines of Lane's tale are incredible. He served in several different navies—American, British, and Dutch—as well as sailing aboard privateers and regular merchant vessels. Ashore he was a misfit, failing at an apprenticeship and being imprisoned four different times for a variety of crimes. At sea he roamed the world. From New York City, which served as the closest thing to a home port, he traveled to Europe, Africa, the West Indies, and the East Indies.

The excerpts from his book (Horace Lane, *The Wandering Boy, Careless Sailor, and Result of Inconsideration. A True Narrative* [Skaneateles, N.Y., 1839], pp. 68–70, 103–104) which follow depict a youthful Lane ashore in New York City between voyages. The first passage describes his experiences in 1804 when he was sixteen years old and, despite several years at sea, relatively fresh-faced and innocent. The second covers Lane's fall to iniquity and inebriation at age twenty. Both selections describe an important part of New York's waterfront life—the dance halls and drinking establishments that rang with merriment and excitement, attracting sailors and those living near the docks and wharves.

We shaped our course for New-York, having nothing to fear but boisterous weather, and French privateers; the former we had plenty of, but luckily avoided the latter.[7] Our sturdy crew soon raised a breeze among the grog-shops and dens of infamy, when we arrived. It was knock down, and drag out, every thing in human shape that opposed or thwarted their notions. As yet, I had not allowed myself to partake with them in their most vicious career; I kept from debauchery and inebriation. One evening, a shipmate, a young fellow that boarded in the house where I did, asked me to take a walk with him. I went along, having an idea that he was intending to take me to some house where some of our shipmates boarded. After turning a few corners, I found myself within the sound of cheerful music. As we drew near to a door, where all was bustle and confusion within, I lagged back. My consort perceived my timidity, and began to shame

7. They had to avoid French privateers because the ship was illegally engaged in trading munitions to Haiti, which had been a colony of France and was then struggling to maintain its independence.

me. "What!" said he. "You going to be a sailor, and afraid to go into a dance-house! Oh, you cowardly puke! Come along! What are you standing there for, grinning like a sick monkey on a lee backstay?"[8] I was a coward, but did not like to be called one; so, to wipe off the stain, I mustered spunk enough to enter. The first opposition I met was a thick fog of putrified gas, that had been thoroughly through the process of respiration and seemed glad to make its escape. It was a small room, well filled with human beings of both sexes. There was a big darkie in one corner sweating, and sawing away on a violin; his head, feet, and whole body, were in all sorts of motions at the same

Figure 36. After months, even years at sea, sailors were prone to excess, and scenes like this were not uncommon. *Drinking Scene,* in Samuel Wood, *Proof Book* (New York, 1821), NYHS

8. Backstay is "part of the standing rigging of a sailing vessel to support the strain on all upper masts." The lee backstay is the rope that runs from the upper part of the mast to the rear and lee (away from the wind) of the vessel. Peter Kemp, ed., *The Oxford Companion to Ships and the Sea* (London, 1976), pp. 52, 473, 707–711.

time. To increase vigour, and elate the spirit of fun, there stood by his side a tall swarthy female who was rattling and flourishing a tambourine with uncommon skill and dexterity; and to complete the scene of action, there were six or eight more on the middle of the floor, jumping about, twisting and screwing their joints and ankles as if to scour the floor with their feet. It was "Hurrah for the Sampson!" (the ship I had performed the last voyage in.) There were some drinking, some swearing, some fighting, some singing; some of the soft-hearted females were crying, and others reeling and staggering about the room, with their shoulders naked, and their hair flying in all directions. "Ah!" thinks I; "Is this the recreation of sailors? Let me rather tie a stone to my neck, and jump from the end of the wharf, than associate with such company as this!" and I made a glad retreat. Had I been allured into some of the more decent recesses of debauchery, it would have had a different effect on my mind, and most likely I should have been induced to keep such company, and practice their vices sooner than I did; but I had seen enough to last me several years.

As I was rambling along the wharves one day, I fell in with captain John May. This gentleman had been first lieutenant of the Connecticut, the first ship I sailed in from New-London. He commanded a vessel then nearly ready to sail, and solicited me to go with him, offering me good wages. I agreed, purchased a chest, and a good stock of clothes. We set sail, and proceeded to Guadaloupe.

[Lane tells of another trip to New York four years later.]

I had a letter from the second mate of the Flora, to deliver to a dame that resided with the celebrated French Johnny, who kept a dance-house in a street then called George's, now Market. I rejoiced in having this opportunity and excuse to visit this place of recreation, as I had often heard its merits spoken of by sailors. I found the house; it was beset without by a multitude of the baser sort of young people. "These," thought I, "are the fag-end of creation," as I forced my way among them to the door, feeling as if my object was noble. The door was closed, and kept so by a man with a chain. For a shilling I was permitted to pass in. Never was there a greater invention contrived to captivate the mind of a young novice, than presented itself on my entrance. A spacious room, illuminated with glittering chandeliers hanging in the centre, and lamps all around; three musicians on high seats well skilled in using their instruments; about fourteen (apparently) damsels, tipped off in fine style, whose sycophantic glances and winning smiles were calculated only to attract attention from such as had little wit, and draw money from their pockets; and I was just the man. This was felicity indeed.

> So I spent my money while it lasted,
>   Among this idle, gaudy train;
> When fair elysian hopes were blasted,
>   I shipped to sail the swelling main.

The inducements of the above described den of infamy were so captivating to my silly mind, that I gave loose to the reins of self-government, and fell in with their practices, not without some reluctance, especially to their base language. A glass of hot punch was only 25 cents; it was sweet, and not very strong; and by sipping a little pretty often, I soon got so that it tasted good. But alas! my race was short; for

> When madam finds Jack's money's gone,
>   To him she tells her mind;
> Saying, "My dear, you must away,
>   More money for to find.

> "You know it well, my dear," she says.
> "There's charges on the shore;
> It grieves my heart that we must part,
>   Perhaps to meet no more."

"A Matrass Made of Cattails"
ON THE CHARACTER AND CONDITION OF SEAMEN

George Little was a New England boy who went to sea at age sixteen in 1807. During the next twenty years he sailed in and out of a variety of United States cities and visited foreign ports from Canton to the West Indies. Although surprised at first at the work constantly demanded by the officers (he had thought that sailors had "nothing to do but eat, drink, sleep, and look out"), Little eventually became one of those few seamen who worked their way to the command of a ship.[9] Little also paid a heavy price for the hardships he experienced at sea: he went blind before his fortieth birthday.

Clearly inspired by Richard Henry Dana's *Two Years before the Mast* and the efforts to reform the sailor's life that began after 1810, Little strove to give a sympathetic and knowledgeable portrait of the world of the sailor. In an age when the ideals of equality spawned by the American Revolution were being applied to more and more elements in society, Little's book joined the effort to include sailors in this new egalitarianism. To help make this case, Little was not shy about singing paeans to the contributions of seamen to commerce and to the American nation. But the main thrust of the section included below (Little, *Life on the Ocean*, pp. 369–374), and the main thrust of Little's book, was to make known to the reader what the sailor's life at sea was really like.

Not many years have elapsed since sailors were considered a class of isolated beings, scarcely worthy to be ranked among the lowest and most degraded of human kind; —when it might truly have been said, that "no man cared" either for their souls or their bodies; and even up to this hour, there are many in our community that look upon poor Jack as a kind of wild animal, dangerous to society, and who ought not to be suffered to roam at large.

Although the moral sense of the Christian public has been aroused to engage in the benevolent enterprise of meliorating the temporal and spiritual condition of seamen, yet, when this philanthropic object is presented for the consideration of our countrymen, a vast majority treat it as a scheme perfectly chimerical, and they will neither lend their influence, nor means, to accelerate this praiseworthy object. Such do not consider the relative importance of seamen, either for the advancement of commercial pursuits, or for the protection of our country's rights, or for the maintenance of our national honor. They do not consider that seamen are the great links of the chain which unites nation to nation, ocean to ocean, continent to continent, and island to island; and it is a matter of astonishment, when such people are reminded that seamen are the instrumentalities who

9. George Little, *Life on the Ocean; or Twenty Years at Sea: Being the Personal Adventures of the Author*, 14th ed. (New York, 1843), pp. 31–39.

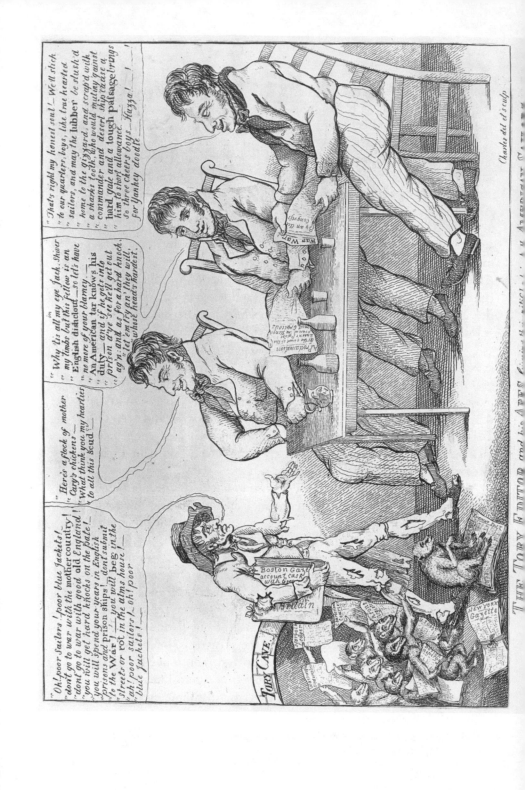

fill our nation's treasury, enrich the coffers of the merchant, build the stately warehouses which overflow with the fabrics of every clime, erect the magnificent and splendid mansions which beautify and adorn our seaports, and construct the most beautiful specimens of naval architecture that float over the ocean. It is seamen that give employment to the shipwright, the ship-joiner, sailmaker, blacksmith, blockmaker, &c. In a word, it is seamen who must fulfil Scripture prophecy, by carrying the glad tidings of salvation, and planting the standard of the cross in the dark regions of idolatry and superstition. Yes; it is by their indefatigable exertions, that the light of the glorious gospel is to shine upon the benighted hearts of the heathen, until this moral darkness shall have been every where dissipated by the rising beams of the Sun of Righteousness.

It must not be understood that it is meant that sailors are, naturally, better than landsmen; yet an experience of twenty years with their traits has given me an intimate knowledge of their character; and, although I am compelled to say that there are some among them who disgrace human nature, yet, in general, they are brave, generous, manly, and unsuspecting. The sailor's insight of human nature is limited, and drawn altogether from the objects constantly before him; he is apt to think all mankind candid, open, honest, and void of trickery, because he himself is so. Jack is unpracticed in the arts of acquiring, or preserving, property, or improving his condition in life. He attaches no other value to money than as a means of procuring him present enjoyment. No class of men obtain their little money with more hardship and difficulty. This, one would think, would lead them to estimate it at its proper value. But such is not the case. They scatter it with profuseness, as if they were ardently desirous of getting rid of an encumbrance; and, consequently, it does not trouble them long.

The generosity of a sailor is proverbial. Although he acquires his dollars amid toils and dangers from which a landsman would shrink

Figure 37. During the Napoleonic Wars, American sailors were subject to impressment by the British Navy, a major issue between the pro-French Democratic-Republicans and the pro-British Federalists. The poor American sailor or "tar," subject to sudden capture, was the symbol of British cruelty and was used against the Federalists, as in this political cartoon. William Charles, "The Tory Editor and His Apes Giving Their Pitiful Advice to the American Sailors," engraving, 1812, NYPL

with affright, he can feel deeply for the wants of others, and has a hand ever ready to assist the distressed. He will share the last copper with the wretch who is in need of pecuniary assistance, and will combat manfully in behalf of the victim of oppression. It is certainly true, that the general conduct of sailors, when on shore, compels us oftentimes to turn away from them in disgust; and one would naturally suppose that, after a long absence, the weather-worn voyager would take care of the small pittance which he had so dearly earned, or, at least, expend it in providing himself with some appendages to assist him in gaining useful information, or in the enjoyment of some rational amusement, which might, at the same time, relax his mind and furnish him with instruction that would prove to be useful to him in after life. But such, however, is not the case; for they often seek to indulge their sensual appetites, at the expense of all that is moral and intellectual. The thoughtlessness of these sons of the ocean is not, however, to be wondered at, when we look at their privations, and peculiar habits of a sea life which, in port, they are compelled to lead. For example, see that gallant ship just about to cast off her moorings, bound for the East Indies; go on board, and you may, perhaps, see a dozen seamen; then range your eye for-and-aft the decks, which may be one hundred and thirty feet long, and thirty feet broad; this, then, is the whole length and breadth of Jack's world—his only associations for one year at least. Did I say one hundred and thirty feet? —No, you must take off thirty or forty feet for the quarter deck; for, in all well-regulated vessels, a hand before the mast is not allowed to set foot on the quarter deck, except to take his turn at the helm, repair the sails, or to perform some act of duty about the mizzen-mast, &c. Thus, then, about ninety feet is the extent of his outdoor rambles. Now, let us take a look into the forecastle, a spacious apartment of about twelve feet in length, and about the same in width, when deducting the breadth of two berths, —the whole tapering off to nothing, forward. Here, then, is his dining and dressing room, bedchamber and parlor. And now let us examine the furniture. The chests, which are closely stowed, present a surface nearly as level as the deck, and perform the office of a table; then, there are kids [small wooden tubs], tin pots, iron spoons, and, perhaps, two horn tumblers, which answer the double purpose of first measuring out to each his allowance of grog, and then taking the place of the vinegar cruet. Now, cast your eye towards the bowsprit-bits, and you will see,

—not a magnificent chandelier, —but an old tin lamp with a long spout, filled with slush, serving the purpose of oil, and an old rag, slack-twisted, for wick. This splendid piece of decoration serves to illuminate the obscure forecastle. Let us now examine the bunks where Jack sleeps. The bed, gentle reader, is not composed of down; but lo! a matrass made of cattails, the bulk of which, rolled up, might be stowed in a large bandbox, first strikes the eye; and then, instead of the snow-white sheets, there is a blanket, which has been Jack's companion for many a long voyage, and for which he has so great an affection, that, in order to preserve the precious relic, it has been heavily quilted throughout with yarn; and it now answers the twofold purpose, with the help of his pea-jacket, of blanket and quilt; and his canvass bag, well stowed with dunnage within, and well coated with tar without, is the pillow, to complete the whole trappings of a forecastle bedding. . . .

[For meals sailors] are generally allowed beans, peas, rice, potatoes, as a change. Salt pork is also given instead of beef. With this kind of living, it not unfrequently happens, that they are obliged to work all day, and then are called up perhaps two or three times in their watch below at night. They are not only frequently exposed to storms and tempests, wet and dry, sudden transitions of heat and cold, but it sometimes happens that, from stress of weather, calms, or otherwise, they suffer incredibly for want of provisions and water. Add to all this, it is often the case that a sailor does not receive a kind or pleasant word from his officers during a voyage; and, although there are many honorable exceptions in commanders of vessels, yet I am compelled to acknowledge that there are many who look upon a common hand as nearly allied to a brute, and, consequently, treat him as such. At best, a sailor's life is full of hardship and peril; and if to these are added hard living, hard usage, and hard words, it may be imagined that his life at sea is not very desirable.

"To Put a Marlinspike in a Man's Hand"
RICHARD HENRY DANA DESCRIBES AN ABLE SEAMAN

Work aboard a sailing ship was difficult. It also required a certain level of skill. As the following selection by Richard Henry Dana shows (*The Seaman's Friend* [Boston, 1851], 158–163), there was a

Figure 38. Alexander Anderson, *Sailor near Docks*, Anderson Scrapbooks, vol. 1, p. 73, NYPL

strict sense of hierarchy in skill that was sustained not only by the masters and owners of ships, but by the seamen themselves. Dana, a rich Boston brahmin who immortalized his own experience as a sailor in a classic of American literature, *Two Years before the Mast*, also championed the cause of the common sailor. As part of that effort he wrote *The Seaman's Friend* as a guidebook to seamanship. Although it appeared in 1851, the book reflects the essential work responsibilities as they existed for at least the previous half century and thus offers a good guide to the responsibilities of sailors at sea.

Sea-faring persons before the mast are divided into three classes, —able seamen, ordinary seamen, and boys or green hands. And it may be remarked here that all green hands in the merchant service are termed *boys*, and rated as such, whatever may be their age or size. . . .

The crews are not rated by the officers after they get to sea, but

. . . each man rates himself when he ships. The shipping articles, in the merchant service, are prepared for so many of each class, and a man puts his name down and contracts for the wages and duty of a seaman, ordinary seaman, or boy, at his pleasure. Notwithstanding this license, there are very few instances of its being abused; for every man knows that if he is found incompetent to perform the duty he contracted for, his wages can not only be reduced to the grade for which he is fitted, but that something additional will be deducted for the deception practiced upon all concerned, and for the loss of service and numerous difficulties incurred, in case the fraud is not discovered until the vessel has gone to sea. But, still more than this, the rest of the crew consider it a fraud upon themselves; as they are thus deprived of a man of the class the vessel required, which makes her short-handed for the voyage, and increases the duty put upon themselves. If, for instance, the articles provide for six able seamen, the men expect as many, and if one of the six turns out not to be a seaman, and is put upon inferior work, the duties which would commonly be done by seamen fall upon the five. The difficulty is felt still more in watches; as, in the case I have supposed, there would be in one watch only two able seamen instead of three, and if the delinquent was not a capable helmsman, the increased duty at the wheel alone would be, of itself, a serious evil. The officers also feel at liberty to punish a man who has so imposed upon all hands, and accordingly every kind of inferior and disagreeable duty is put upon him; and, as he finds no sympathy from the crew, his situation on board is made very unpleasant. Indeed, there is nothing a man can be guilty of, short of a felony, to which so little mercy is shown on board ship; for it is a deliberate act of deception, and one to which there is no temptation, except the gain of a few dollars.

The common saying that to hand, reef, and steer makes a sailor, is a mistake. It is true that no man is a sailor until he can do these things; yet to ship for an able seaman he must, in addition to these, be a good workman upon rigging. The rigging of a ship requires constant mending, covering and working upon in a multitude of ways; and whenever any of the ropes or yards are chafing or wearing upon it, it must be protected by 'chafing gear.' This chafing gear consists of worming, parcelling, serving, rounding, &c.; which requires a constant supply of small stuffs, such as foxes, sennit, spunyarn, marline, and the like, all of which is made on board from condemned rigging and old junk. There is also a great deal of new rigging to be cut and fitted, on board, which requires neat knots, splices, seizings, coverings, and turnings in. It is also frequently necessary to set up the rigging in one part of the vessel or another; in which case it must be seized or turned in afresh. It is upon labor of this kind that the crew is employed in the 'day's work' and jobs which are constantly carried forward on board. A man's skill in this work is the chief test of his seamanship; a competent knowledge of steering, reefing, furling, and the like, being taken for granted, and being no more than is expected of an ordinary seaman. To put a marlinspike in a man's hand and set him to work upon a piece of rigging, is considered a fair trial of his qualities as an able seaman.

There is, of course, a great deal of difference in the skill and neatness of the work of different men; but I believe I am safe in saying

Mariner.

Figure 39. Sailor in Civilian Dress, 1821, courtesy of Mystic Seaport Museum

that no man will pass for an able seaman in a square-rigged vessel, who cannot make a long and short splice in a large rope, fit a block-strap, pass seizings to lower rigging, and make the ordinary knots, in a fair, workmanlike manner. The working upon rigging is the last thing to which a lad training up to the sea is put, and always supposes a competent acquaintance with all those kinds of work that are required of an ordinary seaman or boy. A seaman is generally expected to be able to sew upon a sail, and few men ship for seamen who cannot do it; yet, if he is competent in other respects, no fault can be found with an able seaman for want of skill in sailmaking.

In allotting the jobs among the crew, reference is always had to a man's capacity; and it is considered a decided imputation upon a man to put him upon inferior work. The most difficult jobs, and those requiring the neatest work, will be given to the older and more experienced among the seamen; and of this none will complain; but to single out an able seaman and keep him at turning the spunyarn winch, knotting yarns or picking oakum, while there are boys on board, and other properly seaman's work going forward at the same time, would be looked upon as a punishment, unless it were temporarily, or from necessity, or while other seamen were employed in the same manner. Also in consideration of the superior grade of an able seaman, he is not required to sweep down the decks at night, slush the masts, &c., if there are boys on board and at hand. Not that a seaman is not obliged to do these things. There is no question but that he is, just as much as to do any other ship's work; and if there are no boys on board or at hand at the time, or from any other cause it is reasonably required of him, no good seaman would object, and it would be a refusal of duty to do so, yet if an officer were deliberately, and without necessity for it, when there were boys about the decks at the time, who could do the work as well, to order an able seaman to leave his work and sweep down the decks, or slush a mast, it would be considered a punishment.

In working the ship, the able seamen are stationed variously; though, for the most part, upon the forecastle, at the main tack or fore and main lower and topsail braces; the light hands being placed at the cross-jack and fore and main topgallant and royal braces. In taking in and making sail, and in all things connected with the working of a ship, there is no duty which may not be required of an able seaman; yet there are certain things requiring more skill or strength, to which he is always put, and others which are as invariably assigned to ordinary seamen and boys. In reefing, the men go out to the yard-arms, and the light hands stand in toward the slings; while in furling the bunt and quarters belong to the able seamen, and the yard-arms to the boys. The light hands are expected to loose and furl the light sails, as royals, flying jib and mizzen topgallant sail, and the men seldom go above the cross-trees, except to work upon the rigging, or to send a mast or yard arm up or down. The fore and main topgallant sails, and sometimes the flying jib of large vessels, require one or more able seamen for furling, but are loosed by light hands. In short, as to everything connected with working ship, making and taking in sail, &c., one general rule may be laid down. A seaman is obliged to obey the order of the master or officer, asking no questions and making no objection, whether the duty to which he is ordered be that which properly belongs to an able seaman or not; yet an able seaman alone can do the more nice and difficult work, the light hands, in their turn, are expected to do that which requires less skill and strength. In the watch on deck at night, for instance, the able and ordinary seamen steer the ship, and are depended upon in case of any accident, or if heavy sails are to be taken in or set, or ropes to be knotted or spliced; and in consideration of this, if there is light work to be done, as coiling up rigging about the decks, holding the log-reel, loosing or furling a light sail, or the like, the boys are expected to do it, and should properly be called upon by the officer, unless from some circumstance it should be necessary to call upon a man. . . .

No man is entitled to the rate or wages of an able seaman, who is not a good helmsman. . . .

An able seaman is also expected to do all the work necessary for reefing, furling, and setting sail, to be able to take a bunt or earing, to send yards and masts up and down, to rig in and out booms, to know how to reeve all the running rigging of a ship, and to steer, or pull an oar in a boat.

"A Wretched and Undone Sinner"
THE REVEREND HENRY CHASE AND THE MARINERS' CHURCH

The Reverend Henry Chase came to the Mariners' Church on February 14, 1821, in an effort to bring religion to the waterfront. Located at 75 Roosevelt Street, the Mariners' Church was part of a large-scale reform movement to extend Christianity to what the middle class perceived as one of the lowest elements of society. In the early nineteenth century, middle-class professionals and businessmen became increasingly preoccupied with instilling within those men who worked for them their interpretation of the Revolution's republican values, an ideology emphasizing the virtues of self-discipline and the willingness to perform hard work.[10] Chase's efforts are a part of this movement; he saw himself as a missionary among pagan hordes in the rough dockside neighborhoods. The reverend labored hard at his mission, visiting homes, attending prayer meetings, and officiating at religious services. His diary (Reverend Henry Chase, "Diary, 1821–1828," NYHS) records the variety of his experience: Chase had to comfort families with sick members or with husbands lost at sea. He also listened to the religious yearnings of those on the waterfront. The stereotype of the drunken sailor seldom appears in his diary; instead there are hard-working men and women, many of whom were very serious about religion. Chase thus provides a different view of the waterfront. Here there are long-term relationships, families holding together, women supporting one another in their time of need, and religious sailors who recall their conversion experience.[11]

Visits to the Families of Mariners . . . Dec. 18 [1821], to Jan. 18 following.[12]

18 Mr. Smith 96 Henry—gone to sea—been expected home some-

---

10. Eugene T. Jackman, "Efforts Made before 1825 to Ameliorate the Lot of the American Seaman: With Emphasis on His Moral Regeneration," American Neptune, 24 (1964), 109–118. For a general discussion of middle-class values, see John S. Gilkeson, Jr., Middle-Class Providence, 1820–1940 (Princeton, 1986); Paul E. Johnson, A Shopkeeper's Millennium: Society and Revivals in Rochester, New York, 1815–1837 (New York, 1978); Mary P. Ryan, Cradle of the Middle Class: The Family in Oneida County, New York, 1790–1865 (Cambridge, 1981); Anthony F. C. Wallace, Rockdale: The Growth of an American Village in the Early Industrial Revolution (New York, 1972).

11. An outline of some of this evangelical effort can be found in The Sailor's Magazine and Naval Journal, 1, Sept. 1828 and April 1829.

· 12. Chase did not write down the exact date of every visit in this period; he listed them instead by number. The numbers at the beginnings of these entries, therefore, indicate to which visit in this period he is referring. The number 18 therefore refers to his eighteenth visit in the month between Nov. 18 and Dec. 18.

time—heard unfavorable news from the ship—fears he is lost—I endeavored to comfort his family—left one Herald[13] and two tracts[.]
19 Mrs. Conner 6 Harmon—saw her at Mr. Smiths—husband per-
ished off Cape Cod a year ago last Christmas—she attended M. C.
[Mariners' Church] gave her two tracts—appear something serious—
husband used to attend M. C.
20 Mrs. Wood & Mrs. Head 97 Henry—both husbands lost at sea—
very cordial—had quite a religious conversation—left one Herald
and three tracts—attend M. C. when can—son of Mrs. Head just
going to sea.

Thursday 2 [January 1823 . . . Visited Mr. Peter Smith, Seaman, near
the corner of Grand and Allen. Not in, but his wife, who is anxious,
stated to me something of his exercises of mind, and what an interesting meeting they had last Thursday night, in which her husband
told his experiences. They both think very much of sailors meetings,
and attend them as often as possible. He is soon to go on a voyage to
sea, and had prepared his books to take with him, bible, tracts, and
other religious books. I could not but notice one thing as deserving
observation, which showed his anxiety for religious books and pam-
phlets. The family purchased some article at a store, which was
wrapped up in paper. He found the paper to contain some hymns,
and with great care, he had preserved the paper, and prepared it to
take with him on his voyage.

I attended prayer meeting in the evening at Mrs. Mansfields 21
Pike Street. Mr. Clark, a sailor, opened the meeting by reading a
Psalm from the Bible, which he followed by a prayer and some remarks. Among other things he exhorted parents to take their children one by one alone, and there talk to them and pray with them.
He was followed by Mr. ————, a Norwegian and a sailor, who commenced by speaking of the sincerity and solemnity with which we
should perform our religious exercises, for God is a consuming fire.
He adverted with much feeling, to his former wickedness when he

13. Probably refers to *The Christian Herald and Seaman's Magazine*, 1816–1824,
published in New York City by John E. Caldwell, one of the founders of the American Bible Society. The paper is listed in Jean Hoornstra and Trudy Heath, eds.,
American Periodicals, 1741–1900: An Index to the Microfilm Collections (Ann Arbor,
Mich., 1979), p. 55.

followed the sea, and frequently prayed to God to send the ship, cargo, captain, and crew all to the Devil. He said he was saved from the consequences of his own prayers, by the contrary prayers of his friends upon the shore. After him, Mr. Peter Smith, sailor, spoke a few words and offered up a prayer with much apparent humility and sincerity. I made some remarks and closed by prayer. There were not many present, but the meeting was very solemn and interesting. After meeting was closed, a sailor said, "If you have patience, I will sing a few verses," and then began in a clear shrill musical voice.

"From whence doth this union arise, that hatred is conquered by love,
It fastens our souls in such ties, that nature and time can't remove."

We then separated, and some left the place with much reluctance. On my way home I had some conversation with Mr. Smith, who professes lately to have experienced religion. Some time last winter on a voyage his mind was solemnly arrested by the fall of two men overboard, one particularly almost with an oath in his mouth, both met a watery grave. When he arrived home, his mind was yet more powerfully arrested by finding his wife anxious, who, by attending the Mariners' Church (under religious exercises) had become anxious about her soul. A few weeks ago he professes to have found peace, having previously seen himself to be a wretched and undone sinner, justly exposed to hell and deserving to be cast off forever. He now views Jesus Christ as the only savior, to whom he has been able to flee for refuge. I plainly told him the temptations to which he would be exposed, and exhorted him to perseverance and to set a good example before his shipmates, and do all the good he can in the world.

"How and Where Mr. Landlord Chooses to Send Him"
THE MARINERS' BOARDINGHOUSE

The American Seamen's Friend Society, organized in 1828, was modeled after similar reform groups in England and attempted to consolidate the efforts of local mariners' churches. Its message was clear:

sailors were an exploited labor force because they drank and mis-behaved on shore. Like the sponsors of the Mariners' Church, these reformers wanted to reorient the sailor's world more in line with the values of sobriety, industry, and hard work. Although it appeared to be an effort to liberate sailors from a type of bondage, the unspoken agenda of the reformers was to create a more tractable and disciplined labor force. As ministers like Henry Chase gained a more intimate knowledge of the waterfront, they began to identify the boarding-house keeper as an evil and corrupting influence upon American tars.[14] These landlords, as "Advance Wages" (*Sailor's Magazine*, 2 [December 1829], 111–113) makes evident, acted as recruiting agents for merchant vessels. The boardinghouse keeper lent money to his boarders and then arranged for the sailor's next voyage, pocketing most of the sailor's advance as repayment. Many a mariner trying to regain his sea legs and struggling with a hangover on the first day back at sea cursed his landlord as a crimp or landshark.

Oddly enough, however, the same sailor, upon returning to port, sought out the familiar outlines of his friend, the boardinghouse keeper. With pockets bulging from his wages, Jack was welcomed with a warm greeting, and the cycle would begin again. In the pe-ripheral world of the waterfront the boardinghouse keeper provided key services: plenty of drink, a warm bed, new clothes, and perhaps a liaison with a prostitute. The boardinghouse keeper may have ex-tracted his pound of flesh as the reformers claimed, but he was a permanent and crucial part of the waterfront world.

ADVANCE WAGES

I am surprised that among all the topics of improvement in the concerns of sailors, nothing has ever been said about their advance wages. The custom of paying sailors, in all cases, a month's advance, and when engaged for long voyages, two, and even three months, has grown out of the habitual improvidence of this class of people. There is nothing in the nature of the case, so far as I can see, which makes it more proper to pay sailors in advance, than to pay mechanics and laborers in advance.

14. Hugh H. Davis, "The American Seamen's Friend Society and the American Sailor, 1828–1838," *American Neptune*, 39 (1979), 45–57.

Figure 40. A view of New York's docks. Sailors lived in boardinghouses nearby, and shops supplying ships fronted Water Street, which is in the background in the figure. Boatmen and various waterfront laborers walked here every morning to work. William P. Chappel, *The Old Ferry Stairs to Brooklyn,* oil on cardboard, MMNY

The workman is worthy of his hire,
and
*He is a good paymaster who pays when
the work is done.*

The thing grows out of the sailor's debts to the landlords. The landlord first encourages, or at least permits him to run a little in debt. Then he lets him go deeper and deeper, until it will do to strike. And then poor Jack must ship, just how and where Mr. landlord chooses to send him. Consequently shippers resort to the landlords for hands, because they know that these men have this power over them, to make them ship just when they think proper. And when the articles are signed, the landlord stands by as bondsman, the landlord certifies his character, and the landlord receives the month's advance.

DETRIMENT TO OWNERS

One ill effect is exemplified in a recent case. The brig ————, shipped a crew for Lima, with two month's advance. Just off the Hook it was discovered that she leaked, and the captain returned to the quarantine ground to overhaul and examine.[15] But no sooner had they come to anchor, than the men utterly refused to obey his orders; saying they were not going to sea again in such a ship. And the owner, who went down, was actually obliged to call in authority, and confine them in the *lock-up*. The reason of it undoubtedly was, that they wanted to get away, and cheat the owner out of his two month's advance.

In the case of vessels going coastwise, this custom is the source of continual vexation. A crew is shipped to a southern port, New Orleans for instance, at fourteen dollars a month, and receive a month's wages in advance. By the time the month is half expired, they reach that port, where there is frequently, in the business season, a scarcity of hands, and find that they can get fifteen dollars. I am told it is no unusual case for vessels to be left by their whole crews. And at other

15. "The Hook" refers to Sandy Hook, outside New York Harbor, and the quarantine ground was an area off Staten Island where quarantined ships moored.

times the hands come to the master and tell him they will quit unless he will advance their wages.

The necessity of hauling vessels out into the stream, the day before sailing, in order to keep the men on board, arises in a great degree from the advance money. If they are not too much in debt to the landlords, the use they make of their advance is commonly, to get so drunk that they are crazy. A ship lying in the North [Hudson] River the other night, had two men jump overboard, and were taken up with difficulty. No doubt many are drowned in this way, and go drunk to a watery grave, and to the bar of God; and no notice is taken of it. For such is the general recklessness about sailors, that a poor fellow might very well jump overboard in the stream the first night, and his place be supplied in the morning, with not a word said about it.

DETRIMENT TO SAILORS

It [advanced wages] serves as a facility for their running in debt. Landlords know that they have this security in the case of sailors, which they have not in the case of other laborers who have no property. And therefore they are more willing to trust them. But it is a great damage to a poor man to be in debt. He thereby parts with his liberty, and becomes a slave to his creditor. In fact the whole business of shipping a crew is often a good deal like a bargain and sale, where the landlord brings his slaves to market, and sells them to the highest bidder.

This advance money very seldom does a sailor any good. It commonly goes to pay an old debt; and a debt too, which he would not have contracted if it had not been for this usage. Or if not to pay an old debt, he has no use at all for it. Sailors very seldom care to take money to sea with them. Indeed they have a prejudice or superstition against it, and have been known to throw money into the dock rather than keep it in their pockets, when going on board. Of course, when a sailor gets his advance, if he has not already mortgaged it, he must contrive some way to spend it. And as he has commonly but a day or two between signing and going on board, it follows that he must spend fast to get rid of his cash. And so he dashes into some scene of frolic, dissipation, and sin, whence he comes out, as any one can see for himself who will be present when a crew go on board for a foreign voyage.

At any rate, he gets no good of all his advance money. I do not suppose there is one case in ten where this goes for any useful purpose, but only to support a set of unprincipled crimps and harlots, who delight in the plunder and ruin of sailors.

THE REMEDY

I should not think it worth while to bring forward such a catalogue of evils, if I supposed there was no remedy. To complain of things, which we can do nothing towards mending, is very much like complaining against divine Providence.

But to my mind it seems wrong, in this age of the world, to talk of any *moral* evils, as too bad to be cured. In the present case, we may be sure the evil *will not cure itself*. If shipping merchants and masters of vessels, tamely fold their arms, and say, "There is no help for it, we must do as others do, we cannot break in upon ancient usages," and the like, then nothing can be done.

The evil is not to be remedied by mere force and power. It must be, to a good degree, voluntary on the part of sailors themselves. It must begin among those sailors who take care of their money, and who pay as they go, who are ready to ship themselves before they get in debt to the landlords, and who are so steady and sober, that they do not want a beastly drunken frolic before they sail.

Let masters of vessels, when making up a crew, look out for such characters, and offer good wages: and then offer, say a dollar a month in addition, to those who will go to sea without claiming their advance money. Steady sailors, that is, the best and most trusty sailors, will soon be found, who will jump at the chance of getting a dollar a month higher wages than others. And certainly, with additional comfort and security of the voyage, the diminished risks, and the lower rates of insurance which would soon be adopted for such vessels, would more than compensate the owners for this small addition to seamen's wages. And above all, those who adopt this course will have the sublime satisfaction of striking a blow very near the root of the monstrous evils that pervade the maritime system in this country.

"Not Objects of Pity Yet"
THE SAILORS AND THE EMBARGO OF 1808

In January 1808 President Thomas Jefferson, irate over the British attack on an American warship and disgusted over the countervailing trade restrictions issued by the warring French and British governments, decided to punish both those nations by closing down American exports. The President was confident that virtuous Americans would sacrifice this trade and that the embargo would convince the French and the British to cease harassing American ships. But the cost of this experiment in diplomacy was high. Grass soon grew on wharves that had bustled with activity.[16] Merchants were in dire jeopardy of losing the great profits they had earned in the neutral carrying trade, but they at least had an economic cushion to fall back on. The men who worked along the docks and aboard ships confronted a harsher reality. Winter was always a slow time for them with work scarce and wages low. The stoppage of trade threatened to propel them and their families below subsistence levels. Without a modest income there would be no wood for the stove to keep them warm, no food for their stomachs, perhaps no roof over their heads.

These workers, however, were citizens of the American republic and as such they had the right to petition and to congregate in a mass meeting. Jeffersonian politicians in New York City were not thrilled about the prospect of the boisterous and rough types of the waterfront gathering in a crowd, and, as the minutes of the common council make clear (*Minutes of the Common Council of the City of New York, 1784–1831* [New York], 4:699–704), they struggled to prevent the gathering.[17]

Fortunately for all concerned the meeting occurred without serious mishap. The waterfront workers presented a "memorial" letter that contained a veiled threat, but was straightforward and humble about asking for assistance. The common council reacted quickly, passing measures that would help sailors and dock workers to find employ-

16. Henry Adams, *History of the United States of America during the Second Administration of Thomas Jefferson*, vol. 2 (New York, 1909), p. 278.

17. The common council was the ruling body of the city, consisting of aldermen, assistant aldermen, the city recorder, and mayor. This group is the "Board" and the "Corporation" referred to in the document.

Figure 41. Although their lives were subject to sudden death, and although they were away from port often, mariners managed to form a benevolent society. Symbols on the certificate include representation of the work of sailors in calm and in storm, benevolence and unity as well as a crest that includes classical symbols of republican liberty. John Edwards was a rigger living on Catherine Street in 1794. (Riggers often went to sea, working as common sailors.) Certificate of Membership in the Mariners Friendly Society, 1795, MCNY

ment, provide jobs at public works, and set up relief for the poor and a "Soup House."[18]

In Common Council. *January 8th, 1808*
The Mayor informed the Board that he had called a special meeting of the Common Council in consequence of a Notice published in

18. George Daitsman, "Labor and the 'Welfare State' in Early New York," *Labor History*, 4 (1963), 248–256; Paul A. Gilje, *The Road to Mobocracy: Popular Disorder in New York City, 1763–1834* (Chapel Hill, N.C., 1987), p. 183; Frank Folsom, "Jobless Jack-Tars, 1808," *Labor's Heritage*, 2 (1990), 4–17.

the *Daily Advertiser* of this morning "inviting the Seamen in the vicinity of this city to assemble in the Park[19] tomorrow at 11 o'clock, for the purpose of enquiring of him what they are to do for their subsistence during the Winter." That he wished to consult with the Board on the measures that might be proper to be adopted to prevent any unpleasant consequences.

Whereupon, the Mayor was requested to publish the following Notice in all the Daily papers and to circulate the same in Hand Bills, viz.

Notice.

The Mayor decidedly disapproves the mode of application recommended in a Morning paper, to be pursued by the Sailors of this port for relief.

He informs the public that the Corporation[20] will, on the present emergency, as they have done on former occasions, provide for the wants of every person, without distinction, who may be considered proper objects of relief.

The Mayor cannot conclude this Notice, without exhorting all classes of Citizens to refrain from assembling in the mode as proposed, and especially dissuades the Sailors from meeting in the Park.

In Common Council. *January 11, 1808*

. . . The Mayor laid before the Board the following Memorial, which had been presented to him by the Seamen assembled in the Park, on Saturday morning last, who quietly dispersed on being assured by his Honour that the Corporation would take their case into consideration.

To the Honorable the Mayor of the City of New York.
Honorable Sir.

Our situation is not only distressing, but truly alarming. The Embargo lately levied upon our shipping, has not only destroyed all employment by Sea, but rendered it impossible to gain a subsistence by our labor on shore. Our humble petition, to you Sir, is to know how we are to act in this case, and to beg of you to provide some means for our subsistence during the winter, should not the embargo be immediately taken off. What has America to boast of but her Agri-

19. The "Park" refers to the area directly south of the present City Hall. This common land had been a locus of political meetings since the 1760s.
20. The city government.

culture and Commerce? The destruction of one, will be the ruin of the other.

The greatest part of the wages due us from our last voyages is already expended, and more, we are already indebted for our boarding. By what means shall we discharge these debts? Should we plunder, thieve or rob, the State prison will be our certain doom.

In a handbill, this morning, You tried to dissuade us from our purpose, mentioning that provision was made for objects of pity. We are not objects of pity yet, but shall soon be, if there is not some method taken for our support. We are the most part hale, robust, hearty men, and would choose some kind of employment rather than the poor house for a livelyhood. We humbly beg therefore, you will provide some means for our subsistence, or the consequences may not only prove fatal to ourselves, but ruinous to the flourishing Commerce of America, as we shall be necessitated to go on board foreign vessels.

The Committee of ways and means
Report

That in order to provide for the subsistence of the Seamen of this port, thrown out of employment in consequence of the existing embargo, they have conferred with Captain Chauncey of the U^d States Navy who has consented to receive the Sailors in the Navy Yard, on condition of signing the Articles of the U^d States Navy, to continue in service, during their own pleasure, and perform duty agreeably to his orders, the Corporation agreeing to pay the amount of their maintenance, at the rate of twenty cents per ration for twenty four hours which includes victuals, drink, fuel, candles, and accommodation for lodging. Soap for washing to be an extra charge.

The Committee recommend this arrangement to the Common Council, as thereby every Sailor in distress will be comfortably supported, and being removed from town, and subject to the orders and discipline of the Navy, no ill consequences can result to the peace of the city, from their tumultuous associations. This meritorious class of citizens, it is confidently presumed, will be perfectly satisfied with this plan for their immediate support. Whenever they can do better they will be at perfect liberty to leave the navy yard and work for themselves.

Should the Common Council approve the measure, the Committee will arrange the details with Capt. Chauncey for the admission of the Seamen and charge of the rations.

To provide for that class of citizens, who are capable of labouring and who are destitute of occupation, the Committee have directed the Street Commissioner to examine how many Carmen and hands to load carts can be advantageously employed to fill the collect, and the means of providing earth for the purpose: and to report Ordinances to compel proprietors of low grounds in the vicinity to co-operate with the Corporation.[21]

The Committee likewise contemplate the expediency of reducing Inclenberg hill on the Boston road, provided the frost shall not oppose insuperable obstacles.[22]

They will likewise direct the Street Commissioner to examine the situation of Streets and lots that may require to be regulated and raised in the vicinity of Corlaers Hook,[23] and, if practicable and not too oppressive to the proprietors, to report ordinances for regulating and filling the same.

These various objects may employ a considerable number of industrious persons at moderate wages, which may enable them to support their families without becoming a public burthen.

For the maintenance of that class of citizens for whom labour cannot be provided and who are incapable of labouring, the Committee propose to issue rations of Soup and meat, four times a week, in proportion to the numbers of their respective families, agreeably to the accompanying plan.

To conduct this measure, with the greatest possibly economy, the Committee are providing a Soup House in the Alms House, which will be completed by Thursday next; in the mean time partial supplies are provided, adequate, it is presumed, to the present demand. . . .

Resolved that the Committee of ways and means be empowered to adopt such measures for the support of the Seamen and labouring

21. "The collect" was a large pond just north of the present city hall which by 1808 had become thoroughly polluted. The Committee recommends here a public works project for the unemployed seamen in which the collect was filled in and houses quickly built on top of it.

22. Inclenberg Hill was on Manhattan Island, north of the city. The public works project proposed here was to reduce the size of the hill to make travel easier.

23. Corlears Hook was on the East River; today, it is approximately where the Williamsburg bridge enters Manhattan.

class of the community, thrown out of employment in consequence of the existing embargo, and of the indigent poor, by furnishing labour or means of subsistence, as in their judgment may appear most expedient; And that the said Committee keep a regular account of all expences incurred by them, in fulfilling their engagements, and report, weekly progress of their proceedings to this Board.

John Bingham
Chairman

"Traversed the Docks with Drums and Colors"
THE SAILORS ON STRIKE IN 1802

Most strikes in the early national period were by skilled artisans, but sailors occasionally bonded together to demand an increase, or to prevent a cut, in wages. In October 1802 New York sailors joined together, marched along the docks, and threatened violence to get more money. For all their talk, though, their actions remained limited. Under the command of designated leaders, the sailors merely unrigged vessels that were preparing for departure and had signed up crews at less than the demanded fourteen-dollar wage.

If the strikers demonstrated restraint, city officials did not. Intervening on the side of the merchants, magistrates and peace officers ended the strike by arresting the leaders, who were "committed for trial."[24] The first article appeared in *The Spectator*, October 23, 1802, and the second in the *New York Evening Post*, October 22, 1802.

COMBINATION OF SEAMEN

Two white sailors, why [who] styled themselves *commodores*, addressed a letter to the landlords and landladies of the sailor boarding-houses, enjoining them to ship no seamen for less than fourteen dollars a month, under the penalty of ten dollars for each offense. The black seamen in the port united in the combination, under the direction of two *black commodores*, who acted in concert with the *white*, they in a subordinate capacity. The more effectually to support this

24. Gilje, *Road to Mobocracy*, pp. 180–183.

combination, they, for several days, have traversed the docks with drums and colors—on these expeditions, the hats of the *commodores* were decorated with ribbons and feathers. Their numbers being deemed sufficiently formidable, they yesterday took possession of a schooner just ready for sea, and with great coolness and order proceeded to dismantle her of her sails and rigging, which they carefully stowed away in the hold.

The Mayor being informed of this movement immediately summoned the peace officers, who attended him to quell the disturbance. On their arrival at the dock, they found that a considerable number had retired to a rendezvous house hard by, where they were regaling themselves after their exploits.

The greater part of them were apprehended, and conducted to the police office for examination. The *ringleaders*, we are informed, were committed to Bridewell, and the rest discharged.

Combination of Seamen

For some days past the Streets along the Wharves have been infested by a riotous gang of seamen, parading with drums beating and [colors] flying, for the purpose of extorting from [the] merchants and ship-owners an augmentation of wages from *ten* to *fourteen* dollars. — To carry this illegal imposition into effect, they boarded several vessels in the harbour preparing for sea, whose crews were disposed to sail at their current wages, and by threats and violence compelled many heedless sailors to abandon their employment and join their standard. The brig Sally, Capt. Lord, belonging to Mr. I. Wright, just ready to sail for Wilmington, N. Carolina, was boarded yesterday [in an] un[warran]table manner, and the crew forced to [leave] her. To such extremities did these licentious sailors proceed, as to demand the ship's papers from the captain. To suppress [this] evil which was daily increasing to an alarming degree, the Mayor, attended by the Magistrates of the Police, and Peace Officers, waited [on] these maritime insurgents yesterday morning who held their rendezvous at one Rose's in [   ] street, a number of whom were taken into custody with resistance, and the ringleaders, we understand, have been committed for trial.[25]

25. The condition of this document prevents precise rendering. Brackets indicate words that are illegible in the text. Where there are words inside the brackets, the

"Guilty of Some Irregularities"
THE DOCKWORKERS ON STRIKE IN 1828

By the late 1820s laborers became more aggressive in wage disputes. Although organizations such as the Workingman's Party
(formed in 1829) and the General Trades Union (1833) were led by
skilled journeymen, less skilled workers could also unite in labor confrontations. In 1828 hundreds of dockworkers—including riggers and
stevedores—stormed along the wharves, using force and violence to
persuade all to join them. Unlike the striking sailors described above,
these workers were willing to destroy property and to come to blows
over their labor demands. Their militancy met with strong opposition. Not only did some ship captains resist the human tide of
strikers, but city officials interceded by sending dozens of peace officers and a troop of cavalry to stop the rioting strikers. At least twenty
dockworkers were arrested.[26]

The following documents include a newspaper article describing
the strike in general terms (the *New York Evening Post*, July 14, 1828)
and court depositions that indicate the involvement of specific
workers (District Attorney Papers, Sessions Records, Municipal Archives, Department of Records and Information Services, City of
New York). The latter documents are of great importance to historians because, although they do not provide the entire story, they do
offer a rare glimpse of individuals and their actions.

Between two and three hundred riggers, stevedores and laborers,
depending upon employment connected with shipping, assembled
this forenoon in a body, and were guilty of some irregularities. They
went along the docks in a body, and on board of some vessels, and
forced the men employed in discharging or loading them, to quit
their work because their wages had been lowered. They attacked the
Havre packet Sully, Capt. Macy, with a shower of paving stones, one
of which struck Capt. Clark, of the ship Don Quixotte, who had
repaired on board to assist in preventing their boarding the ship and

---

word represents what was probably in the text. Where the bracket is empty, the word
cannot even be guessed at.

26. Ibid., pp. 183–186.

withdrawing the men from her. The ship Florida and a number of others were visited in turn, but no serious injury was done. A posse of constables from the Police Office soon appeared in their train, & the mob very prudently dispersed.

Deposition for the New York Court of General Sessions City of New York . . . John J. Dawson of No. 53 Broad Street being duly sworn says that this day at the foot of Old Slip, 1st Ward, a mob entered on board of a ship that lay there and the persons on board appeared to try to keep them off and in the affray deponent [i.e., Dawson] endeavoured to make peace, and in so doing was beaten and knocked down by Wm. Buller one of the rioters now in Bridewell. . . .

July 14, 1828

City of New York . . . Owen Callers, now of No. 119 Lombardy St., being duly sworn says that Jas. Williams and James Crawford and Nicholas Crohn now here were among the rioters abetting and encouraging them. Sworn the 14 of July.

City of New York . . . John Peters of No. 101 Washington Street being duly sworn says that John Norgaux of Robinson St., rigger was engaged yesterday as one of the rioters and was with them on the East river side and till they were stopped at the ship *Sully* near foot of Carlisle Street. Sworn 15th of July 1828.

City of New York . . . Zachariah Atwell the 3rd mate of the ship *Pallas* lying foot of Carlisle St. being duly sworn says that yesterday during the riot he was knocked down and thrown in a cellar by one of the rioters said to be named Jno. Jackson. Sworn 15th of July 1828.

City of New York . . . Joseph Woodward No. 139 Front St. being duly sworn says that Peter Henry Feil the man now here was at the head of the gang of rioters yesterday who were on Murrays Wharf next to Coffee House Slip, 1st Ward when men were taken out of a vessel and he went from there with the gang and as they went they gave three cheers. Sworn 15th of July.

City of New York . . . John J. Schoonmaker No. 32 Lumber Street, Inspector of the 1st ward, being duly sworn deposith and saith that Lewis Jackson (a Black) (now here) was yesterday engaged as one of a large crowd of rioters at South Street near Whitehall Slip at the first ward and deponent further saith that the said Lewis Jackson was also yesterday among the rioters at the foot of Carlisle Street in the 1st ward. Sworn the 15th July 1828.

5

AFRICAN AMERICANS:
Extending the Bounds of Republicanism

The fifty-one years between July 4, 1776, and July 4, 1827, mark one of the most crucial eras in the history of New York City. During that time, New York moved from a slave to a free society, and although not sudden, the transformation was dramatic. British occupation during the war brought freedom to many slaves as they escaped from their masters to fight for their liberty under the banner of King George. Others joined the side of the rebels. After the Revolutionary War, many Americans, inspired by the logic of the Declaration of Independence, called for the end of all bondage. While several other northern states moved to emancipate slaves, New York, with a 10 percent black population, hesitated. Even so, the number of free blacks swelled because of individual manumissions, runaways, and the arrival of many refugees escaping the racial turmoil in the West Indies during the 1790s. In 1799 the state legislature passed a gradual emancipation law that, with later amendments, ended slavery in New York State by July 4, 1827. Most of the city's thirteen thousand African Americans, however, had achieved freedom before that date.[1]

---

1. Arthur Zilversmit, *The First Emancipation: The Abolition of Slavery in the North* (Chicago, 1967); Edgar J. McManus, *A History of Negro Slavery in New York* (Syracuse, N.Y., 1966); Gary B. Nash, "Forging Freedom: The Emancipation Experience

How did this change in status affect laboring blacks? The end of slavery had not altered the work patterns of New York African Americans. Before emancipation most of the city's slaves were domestic servants, and afterward large numbers of blacks remained as servants within white households. Artisans also owned slaves and probably taught their trade to the blacks in their workshops. In the 1790s and early 1800s, many free blacks continued to work as artisans, and some even became small proprietors. Just over one-fourth of all free black heads of households identified in one sample (a total of 75 out of 262) were artisans in 1810, and their crafts ranged from hairdressing to shoemaking, tanning to cabinetmaking. Blacks also operated countless small cook and oyster shops throughout the city.[2]

Figure 42. Many African Americans could find no employment other than by wandering the streets as a peddler. Alexander Anderson, *Buttermilk Seller*, Anderson Scrapbooks, vol. 1, p. 66, NYPL

of Northern Seaport Cities, 1775–1820," in *Slavery and Freedom in the Age of the American Revolution*, Ira Berlin and Ronald Hoffman, eds. (Charlottesville, Va., 1983), pp. 3–48; Leo H. Hirsch, Jr., "The Negro and New York, 1783–1865," *Journal of Negro History*, 16 (1931), 382–473.

2. Shane White, *Somewhat More Independent: The End of Slavery in New York City, 1770–1810* (Athens, Ga., 1991), chap. 6; White, "'We Dwell in Safety and Pursue Our Honest Callings': Free Blacks in New York City, 1783–1810," *Journal of American History*, 75 (1988), 445–470; New York City Jury List, Fourth Ward, 1819, Historical Documents Center, Queens College, City University of New York; Paul A. Gilje, *The Road to Mobocracy: Popular Disorder in New York City, 1763–1834* (Chapel Hill, N.C., 1987), pp. 143–170; Gary B. Nash, *Forging Freedom: The Formation of Philadelphia's Black Community, 1720–1840* (Cambridge, Mass., 1988).

Figure 43. Blacks often worked either as servants or slaves for artisans, as did this man wh assists a cartman. *Customs House,* engraving, 1796, detail, NYPL

Liberated from the legal chains that bound them, and offered new opportunities of employment, many free blacks seized the chance for greater geographical mobility. Approximately four in ten adult male free blacks worked as either mariners or day laborers in the first decade of the nineteenth century. These men quickly and easily interchanged occupations. They might ship out to sea for several months, return to port to find some job as a day laborer for awhile, and then change positions again. This floating population lacked permanence, yet also exhibited a freedom of movement that was impossible under slavery.[3]

By the 1820s conditions for African Americans began to change. The same rising tide of democracy that opened the franchise to all adult white males led to increased political restrictions on free blacks. The state's Democratic forces sought to exclude free blacks since they

3. White, *Somewhat More Independent*; White, "'We Dwell in Safety.'"

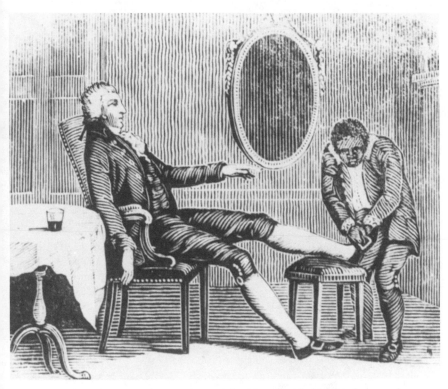

Figure 44. The most common occupation for New York's blacks, slave or free, was domestic service. They worked in elite homes such as this and in the homes of middling artisans. Alexander Anderson, *Domestic Servant or Slave,* Anderson Scrapbooks, vol. 2, p. 5, NYPL

tended to vote Federalist. Simultaneously, black laborers encountered more barriers that limited job opportunities. They had difficulty maintaining their small property holdings, and the proportion of black artisans decreased. Many of the following documents attest to these developments.[4]

Yet the African-American community was resilient. Despite intensifying racial hostility in the early nineteenth century, black New Yorkers continued to create and maintain a sense of community. African-American identity flourished in benevolent associations and in

4. Gilje, *Road to Mobocracy,* pp. 143–170; Nash, "Forging Freedom," in Berlin and Hoffman, eds., *Slavery and Freedom,* pp. 3–48; Hirsch, "The Negro and New York"; Dixon Ryan Fox, "The Negro Vote in Old New York," *Political Science Quarterly,* 32 (1917), 252–275.

Figure 45. Women in the poverty-stricken African-American community had no choice but to work. Aside from domestic service, peddling was the most common profession. Niccolino Calyo, *Hot Corn Seller*, gouache, MCNY

separate, self-created African churches. It also appeared in free schools for blacks, in institutions like the African Grove Theater, and in other black-run businesses. The growing African-American identity is evident in the following documents, which were chosen to delineate the story of black workers in a variety of settings and to demonstrate their versatility in both slavery and freedom.[5]

"A Decided Advocate for American Independence"
REVEREND PETER WILLIAMS, JR., RECALLS HIS FATHER

The memory of the American Revolution was very important to black New Yorkers. Confronted by a ferocious race riot in July 1834

5. Gilje, *Road to Mobocracy*, pp. 143–170; Nash, "Forging Freedom," in Berlin and Hoffman, eds. *Slavery and Freedom*, pp. 3–48; Hirsch, "The Negro and New York."

that demolished his church, the Reverend Peter Williams, Jr., conjured up a patriotic image of his father's participation in the war and thereby asserted his own American identity. During the riot, mobs controlled whole sections of the city, beat blacks, and ransacked their homes and institutions. This disturbance was triggered in part by increased abolitionist activity—abolitionists were believed by many to be associated with the British—and, in part, by deeply imbedded racial hatred and fear of labor competition that was intensifying. In the wake of this tumult, with his own church in ruins, Peter Williams, Jr., felt compelled to offer testimony to his Americanism as he defended the cause of abolition.[6]

What role did blacks play in the American Revolution? According to the following document, an open letter from Rev. Williams that was published in the *New York Evening Post*, July 15, 1834, blacks supported the "cause of liberty." Actually the situation was much more complex and the overall record of African Americans was mixed. Some blacks did side with the movement for independence; many others fought with the British. Their loyalties were often decided on the basis of which side offered the best chance for personal freedom. Thousands of blacks ran away from their American masters to British lines. New York City, occupied by the British from September 1776 to November 1783, became a haven for these black runaways.

Peter Williams's case was different. His master was a loyalist living in New York City. Freedom for Williams meant breaking away from his tory owner; but he did not run away, and at the end of the war he was working in his master's tobacco shop. When his master prepared to evacuate the city with the British, Williams's Methodist friends agreed to buy Williams and allow him to pay them back over the next few years. Contrary to his son's statement below, Williams never felt like a free man until that debt was paid. Subsequently, he became a successful tobacconist and an important African-American leader who was largely responsible for founding the first independent African church in New York City.[7]

We have no way of knowing whether the incident reported in this document was true or not. Peter Williams, Sr., may have spent some time during the war in New Jersey, probably away from his master.

6. Gilje, *Road to Mobocracy*, pp. 143–170.
7. Roi Ottley, *Black Odyssey: The Story of the Negro in America* (New York, 1948), pp. 87–88; Ottley and William J. Weatherby, eds., *The Negro in New York: An Informal Social History* (New York, 1967), pp. 53–56.

He may, too, have had his ride, much like Paul Revere, to warn that British were coming. The central issue, however, was that he probably told his son, Peter Williams, Jr., this story. In turn, Peter Williams, Jr., confronted with a severe challenge to his national identity, decided to present the story to the public.[8]

Rev. Mr. Williams
To The Citizens of New York

My father was born in Beekman street in this city, and was never, in all his life, further from it than Albany. . . . In the revolutionary war, my father was a decided advocate of American Independence, and his life was repeatedly jeopardized in its cause. Permit me to relate one instance, which shows that neither the British sword, nor British gold, could make him a traitor to his country. He was living in the State of Jersey, and parson Chapman, a champion of American liberty, of great influence throughout that part of the country, was sought after by the British troops. My father immediately mounted a horse and rode round among his parishioners, to notify them of his danger, and to call them to help in removing him and his goods to a place of safety. He then carried him to a private place, and as he was returning a British officer rode up to him, and demanded in the most peremptory manner, "Where is parson Champon [Chapman]?" "I cannot tell," was the reply. On that he drew his sword, and raising it over his head, said, "tell me where he is, or I will instantly cut you down." Again he replied, "I cannot tell." Finding threats useless, the officer put up his sword and drew out a purse of gold, saying, "if you tell me where he is, I will give you this." The reply still was, "I cannot tell." The officer cursed him and rode off.

This attachment to the country of his birth was strengthened and confirmed by the circumstances that the very day on which the British evacuated this city, was the day on which he obtained his freedom by purchase through the help of some republican friends of the Methodist Church, loaning him money for that purpose, and to the

8. The document is reprinted in *Journal of Negro History*, 11 (1926), 181–185. It originally appeared in several New York newspapers as a letter addressed to the citizens of New York. See *New York Evening Post*, July 15, 1834; and *Commercial Advertiser*, July 15, 1834.

last year of his life he always spoke of that day as one which gave double joy to his heart, by freeing him from domestic bondage and his native city from foreign enemies. . . .

Hearing him talk of these and similar matters, when I was a child, filled my soul with an ardent love for the American government, and made me feel, as I said in my first public discourse, that it was my greatest glory to be an American.

A lively and growing interest for the prosperity of my country pervaded my whole soul, and led to the belief, notwithstanding the peculiarly unhappy condition of my bretheren in the United States, that by arriving to become intelligent, useful and virtuous members of the community, the time would come when they would all have abundant reason to rejoice in the glorious Declaration of Independence. . . .

Peter Williams
Rector of St. Philip's Church, Centre St.

New York, July 14, 1834

"An Ignominious Death"
THE LIFE OF JAMES JOHNSON

James Johnson briefly became famous in New York when he was convicted of murder in October 1811 and executed in January 1812. The murder itself was unspectacular. Johnson and his wife ran a dance hall and oyster cellar for blacks. One evening a dispute with a customer led to a brawl during which Johnson grabbed an oyster knife and stabbed Lewis Robinson in the leg. When Robinson died from the wound, Johnson went to trial. The jury found him guilty of first degree murder, although he probably should have been charged only with manslaughter. The judge sentenced him to death. Johnson's execution, along with the execution of another murderer in a separate case, were the first such punishments in a decade in the city. That in itself was news. In the last days before the two convicted killers' executions, dozens of ministers visited them, urging them to repent. When Johnson experienced a last-minute religious conversion, he became even more of a celebrity. Publishers quickly turned out chapbooks describing both trials and offering brief sketches of the killers' lives.[9]

The following document, taken from one of those chapbooks (*A Correct Journal of the Conduct of Two Unfortunate Prisoners, Sinclair and Johnson* [New York, 1811], p. 15), is short, but it contains the outlines of a black worker's life, showing the variety of employment and the twisted career path followed by many African Americans as they moved from slavery to freedom.

Biography of Johnson

Johnson, the unfortunate criminal who is to be executed this morning, was born at Greatneck on Long-Island, on the first of February, 1780. His mother, at that time, lived in the service of Mr. Jules Setrea, who at his death, which took place in 1796, ordered all his slaves to [have] their freedom granted them.

The unhappy subject of this biography, acquired his liberty when about 16 years of age, and after that period went to live with Mr. Pascule, a weaver, near Rockaway, where he remained with credit and reputation for 7 years—after which he went to Hempsted, where he worked on different farms about two years—leaving it he commenced boating with Mr. D. Darling, for two and an half years more; then quitting him, housed with Hogeboom, on the North River, which he continued to do within a short time of his committing the fatal act, for which he is to atone, by the sacrifice of his life by an ignominious death. . . .

"Stripped like So Many Squirrels"
A MOB ATTACKS THE AFRICAN GROVE, A BLACK THEATER

As racism intensified in the early nineteenth century, African Americans turned inward and developed their own institutions. Although in some ways this development circumscribed black opportunities, in other ways it opened up avenues of employment that might otherwise have been denied to blacks. One such area was the

---

9. A chapbook was any small pamphlet sold inexpensively for popular consumption. See William Sampson, *Murders, Report of the Trial of James Johnson, a Black Man, for the Murder of Lewis Robinson, a Black Man* . . . (New York, 1811).

theater. New York City's expanding population sustained several different playhouses during the 1820s which catered to different audiences. The affluent patronized the Park Theater with its national and international casts, and the working class attended circus shows at the Lafayette Amphitheater to watch dancing girls and to cavort through short skits. Black entrepreneur Allen Royce opened the African Grove on Mercer Street, which catered to a black clientele and employed black performers and stage crew. Like other black-owned businesses, such as oyster stands and drinking establishments, the African Grove came under frequent attack from white rowdies. The following document (from the *New York Spectator*, August 20, 1822) describes such an episode. It reveals African Americans, fueled by the entreprenueral spirit of the age, approaching creatively the racist world that surrounded them by asserting themselves and establishing institutions like the African Grove, but it also reveals the price that they sometimes paid in the process. Ultimately, this harassment occurred with such frequency that city officials closed the African Grove in 1829.[10]

Unmanly Outrage. Saturday night a gang of fifteen or twenty ruffians, among whom was arrested and recognized one or more of the circus riders, made an attack upon the *African Theatre*, in Mercer Street, with the full intent, as is understood, to break it up root and branch; and the vigour of their operations is reported to have corresponded fully with their purpose. First entering the house by regular tickets, they proceeded, at *quick time*, to extinguish all the lights in the house, and then to demolish and destroy every thing in the shape of furniture, scenery, &c. &c., it contained. The *actors* and *actresses*, it is said, were fairly stripped like so many squirrels and their glittering apparel torn in pieces over their heads: the intruders thus completely putting an end to the play for the night. Eight or nine of the band were secured on the spot, and sent to the watch house, and held to answer, in proper sureties, by the Police next morning.

But the matter should not be spoken of in the spirit of *badinage*. Among the persecutions that wretched race is necessarily subjected

10. Gilje, *Road to Mobocracy*, pp. 156–157, 246–253; George C. D. Odell, *Annals of the New York Stage* (New York, 1927–28), 3:34–37; David Grimsted, *Melodrama Unveiled: American Theater and American Culture, 1800–1850* (Chicago, 1968), pp. 52–56.

to, by the delicacies and proprieties of refined life, exclusion, or virtual exclusion, from our theatres and other places of amusement, is one. In this condition, they devise amusements of their own, and are satisfied with them; and though they have been hunted with a malice as mean as it seems to be unmitigable, in every attempt they have made to form a permanent establishment; those who view the subject rightly, will array themselves on their part. And had it been displayed against the assertion of their rights in almost any other possible modification than that of carrying on theatrical entertainments, it would have excited more whole societies than one, to uphold them. Theatrical performances, are, indeed of questioned utility; but then theatricians themselves boast so loudly of the ennobling influences of the drama to refine, ennoble, and exalt the soul, will they deny those benign influences in awakening the mind of the poor African from the dormitude of ages—in shedding a little intellectual life on the forlorn, down trodden race "on whose heads" in the elegant and pathetic language of our Manumission Society "falls no light but that which issues from beyond the grave"? But if the *pride* of their persecutors is to be touched, what was the state of our own legitimate drama, let it be asked, even in the era of the immortal Shakespeare?

BROWN, the manager, we understand, was considerably beaten; and that attempts have been made at a compromise, which the public prosecutor, so far as the public are concerned, with a very laudable spirit, declines.

"B"

"A Torrent of Clamarous Abuse"
TUBMEN DISTURB THE NEIGHBORHOOD

Because of the shifting political and economic scene of the early republic, job opportunities for blacks decreased. Certain occupations, however, were left exclusively for blacks, and these jobs were often dirty and offensive, especially the work of the "necessary tubmen." These individuals drove their carts through town at night and in the early morning, emptying out the city's privies at a minimal fee for each customer. They would then drive their carts into the countryside and sell to farmers their collectings as either fill or manure. Clearly, their jobs were important to the urban community before the advent of effective sewer systems.

Figure 46. Blacks were responsible for the collection of garbage and wastes. By 1810 the common council employed twenty-five cartmen "to go daily through the sections that are not sweeping for the purpose of Collecting the Garbage and Offals from Yards and Kitchens for which purpose they shall Ring the Bell at Suitable Distances to Notify the Inhabitants to bring out the same and put it into the Carts" (1799 ordinance). This illustration depicts Potpye Palmer ringing his bell at the corner of Elizabeth and Pump streets as he carries out that task. The building at the right was the William and Groddy paint factory. William P. Chappel, *Potpye Palmer with His Garbage Cart & Bell,* 1805, oil on cardboard, MMNY

During the quiet of the night or early morning, the tubmen would shout and make noise in an effort to attract customers, but many, including the artisans who signed the following petition (City Clerk Filed Papers, August 12, 1817, NYCMA), found their racket disturbing. Moreover, a number of tubmen would apparently brace themselves for their labor with alcohol. When liquor flowed through their system, the tubmen sometimes became even louder and more obnoxious.

To the Honorable Corporation of the City of New York
The Subscribers inhabitants of the first ward of the said city
—Respectfully represent—

That a practice has modernly prevailed in the part of the city where your memorialists have their dwellings which would be disgraceful to any community having the least pretensions to be civilized, or even to decency.

A number of vagabond negroes who have taken upon themselves the business of nightmen exercise their functions in such a manner as is excessively offensive and outrages all propriety. These persons scream through the streets all hours of the night with such vociferation as to disturb everyone within reach of their detestable cries— The sick are tormented by their noise, and if any appeal is made to them on this account the evil is only increased by a torrent of clamarous abuse— They transact their business often at a very early hour in the evening while the streets are full of passengers— The first shilling they earn is commonly spent on rum and before their work is over they are generally in a state of intoxication owing to this or from carelessness they sometimes drop their loads where it is left overnight and for many hours of the morning to poison all in its vicinity— It is not only their savage yells that are offensive but they are in the habit of bawling out such expressions as are most shockingly indecent— They commonly go in pairs and perform a duet of this description, but a person in the neighborhood of Franklin Square may often hear a dozen or twenty of them at once vieing with each other in such noise & indecency as no stranger would believe could be tolerated anywhere but in an Encampment of Savages.

These people do not frequent Broadway, Park Place, State Street or other Genteel parts of the town. If they did they would not be endured for a single week.

But your memorialists humbly presume to hope that the industrious part of the community are as much entitled as any other to the enjoyment of their rest, to preserve their health and to prevent their families from being exposed to such violation of decency as are the present subjects of complaint.

It is true that these people are employed in a work that cannot be dispensed with. But it is not necessary that it should be performed after their manner.— The evidence of this is that well within these three or four summers there has been no ground for complaints on this subject.—

Your memorialists therefore hope that not only in regard to them but for the sake and *character* of the *city* your honorable body will adopt such regulations as may correct the evils of which they complain.

and your memorialists as in duty bound will
always pray that your honors may be
Philetic Havens, John M. Malkes, and twenty others.

"These Disagreeable Screamings"
THE HOWLS OF THE CHIMNEY SWEEPS

The following two documents address the same issues as the previous document. First, they demonstrate the dominance of black workers in an undesirable trade—the sweeping and cleaning of chimneys. Second, they show the dislike many citizens expressed for their advertising methods. Like the tubmen, many chimney sweeps cruised the streets soliciting customers. They had their apprentices (also blacks) do the calling, which began at an early hour, and the resulting din, as different youths competed with one another, could be quite disturbing. What is exceptional about these documents is that both the original petition and the chimney sweeps' reply represent that part of the past that is most difficult to study—the ideas and concerns of men and women who could not sign their own name and who therefore probably could not read. The first document, a petition to city officials from Adam Marshall, a black man who had a chimney-sweeping business that did not depend on street calling (City Clerk Filed Papers, August 26, 1816, NYCMA), describes a problem that contributed to the general disorder of the streets. Marshall may have had ulterior motives, however: limiting the activities of the street-bawling chimney sweeps would mean more business for his sweep office at 177 Duane Street.

These two documents need to be approached carefully. In both cases the petitioners obviously asked a scribe to compose their messages. Thus, the language and syntax of both are more formal and legalistic than if their sentiments had been expressed directly by the individuals; yet the documents expose the concerns of those involved. Take note, too, of the three female names on the second document (City Clerk Filed Papers, December 2, 1816, NYCMA), indicating that women competed for these jobs.

Figure 47. In New York City blacks labored as chimney sweeps, cleaning out the city's various chimneys. The trade was divided between masters and apprentices who, like this boy, would ply the streets bawling for work. Although regulated, the business was crowded, unhealthy, and dangerous, and many of the lads barely eked out a living. Niccolino Calyo, *Chimney Sweep at Rest,* gouache, MCNY

To the Honourable the Mayor, Aldermen, and Commonality of the City of New York.

The petition of Adam Marshal Inspector of Chimney Sweeps for himself and his associates, most respectfully showeth,

That in his opinion, there can be no use in the practice, which is now common of boys, who are apprentices to chimney sweeps, making a noise, particularly in the morning, for the sake of getting employment. To those who are sick, the screams of those boys must be particularly distressing and they cannot, at so early an hour, be otherwise than very unpleasant to those who are in health and, who, at

Figures 48, 49. The first of these two woodcuts depicts a master and two apprentices with their tools; the second depicts a sweep falling off a roof. Alexander Anderson, *Apprentice Sweeps with Master,* Anderson Scrapbooks, vol. 2, p. 1, NYPL; Alexander Anderson, *Chimney Sweep Falling off Roof,* BA

that time may wish to enjoy repose. The boys are, likewise frequently subject to abuse in consequence of this bawling, which for reasons which your petitioner most respectfully begs leave to suggest, may be injurious; but cannot be of any possible benefit to the community.

There are now in this city twenty nine offices where persons may call or send to have their chimneys registered by the year or half year, or swept from time to time, agreeably to the terms which Your Honourable Board have been pleased to allow and for which your petitioner, for himself as well as all the others engaged in the same business, begs leave to return their most grateful acknowledgment. There cannot, therefore be any necessity for these disagreeable screamings by which our citizens are so greatly annoyed at the time when they wish to enjoy their rest.

Your petitioner recollects that some years ago, there was a resolution passed by your Honourable Body to prevent the bawling of chimney sweeps, in the morning; but which has been either rescinded or for some time past, not carried into effect.

Your petitioner, therefore prays, that for the sake of the public quiet, you will fix a penalty upon the masters of any sweep or upon any sweep himself, who shall disturb the citizens by making a noise in the manner now so common as in duty bound. . . .

Adam Marshall X his mark

To the Honourable the Mayor and Corporation of the City of New York

The undersigned persons holding licenses under your honourable body to sweep chimneys in the city of New York— Humbly pray that your honourable body will reconsider an Ordinance pass'd some time since prohibiting their crying out in passing through the streets of the City—as your honourable body have seen it good to enact such prohibition your petitioners from Delicacy and the defference due forbear using any argument going to lessen the apparent evils attending their so crying out—but trust that your honourable body will take the subject in consideration when they inform you that the means of gaining a living for themselves and their families is very much lessened thereby—fully trusting in the kindness and wisdom of the body we address—we hope for a favourable [reply] from your [honors].

Richd. Garveston X mark, Hercules Selurman X mark, Jacob Cortwright X mark, Edwd. Baily X mark, James Morris X mark, Hannah Moore X mark, Peter Mark X mark, Henry Smith X mark, John Hunt X mark, Betty Henry X mark, Nathan Bryant X mark, Henry Lawson X mark, Charles Dodge X mark, Timothy Smith X mark, Thos. Shepard X mark, Chs. Patterson X mark, James Simmonds X mark, Susan Johnson X mark, [and others].

"Contending for the Prize"
"SHAKE-DOWN" DANCING AT THE CATHERINE MARKET

The author of the following selection was one of New York City's leading butchers in the mid-nineteenth century. Looking nostalgically at the smaller city of his youth, Thomas De Voe wrote a classic and comprehensive account of the various markets that existed or had existed in New York. Although his approach may have been antiquarian, De Voe researched prodigiously. The resulting book offers glimpses of a world that might otherwise have been lost.

Unlike many of his fellow butchers, who often participated in rowdy behavior and formed some of the city's earliest gangs, De Voe represented the genteel values that came to define the middle class in his period. His view of blacks was paternalistic. He recognized the evil of slavery, and believed it fortunate that New York law ended it in the opening decades of the nineteenth century. Yet he also feared that manumission brought with it a degeneration in the living conditions of many blacks. His reminiscence about days gone by, when black slaves entrusted with the produce of their master's farm arrived in the city from the surrounding countryside and attended the city's markets, provides a brief view of life and labor for African Americans under slavery.

The selection here, however, reveals much more than that. In De Voe's account of the "shake-down" dances on boards at the market (*The Market Book Containing a Historical Account of the Public Markets* . . . [New York, 1862], pp. 344–345), we see the intersection of black and white culture. Public "negro dancing" represented an important component of African-American identity and self-expression, as well as serving as a form of amusement for the blacks, both slave and free, who participated. It also was a means of employment by which this otherwise economically marginal group drew attention to itself and earned some money.

In addition, this selection is one of the few documents indicating the celebration of the Pinkster holiday in New York City. Pinkster, a corrupted term for the Dutch word for Pentecost, *Pfingsten*, was a cultural holdover from the Dutch which New York blacks transformed into their own special holiday in the eighteenth century. Albany and other towns in the colony celebrated the holiday, and New York City blacks seized upon Pentecost in June to take a few days off from their normal routine and participate in a variety of rituals, including the one De Voe describes below.[11]

---

11. E. A. A., "Sassafras and Swinglingtow; or, Pinkster Was a Holiday," *American Notes and Queries: A Journal for the Curious*, 6 (1946), 35–40; A. J. Williams-Myers, "Pinkster Carnival: Africanisms in the Hudson River Valley," *Afro-Americans in New*

Figure 50. Blacks working at the city's markets often found recreational outlet and financi⟨al⟩ reward in dancing. *Shake-Down Dancing at the Market,* in Augustine E. Costello, *Our Firem⟨en⟩* (New York, 1887)

The first introduction in this city of public "negro dancing" no doubt took place at this market [Catherine Market]. The negroes who visited here were principally slaves from Long Island, who had leave of their masters for certain holidays, among which "Pinkster" was the principal one; when, for "pocket-money," they would gather up ev-

York Life and History, 9 (1985), 7–17; White, Somewhat More Independent, pp. 95–106. See also James Fenimore Cooper's fictionalized description in Satanstoe, or the Littlepage Manuscripts, A Tale of the Colony (New York: G. P. Putnam's Sons, n.d., orig. pub. 1845), pp. 65–74.

erything that would bring a few pence or shillings, such as roots, berries, herbs, yellow or other birds, fish, clams, oysters, &c., and bring them with them in their skiffs to this market; then, as they had usually three days holiday, they were ready, by their "negro sayings or doings," to make a few shillings more. So they would be hired by some joking butcher or individual to engage in a jig or break-down, as that was one of their pastimes at home on the barn-floor, or in a frolic, and those that could and would dance soon raised a collection; but some of them did more in "turning around and shying off" from the designated spot than keeping to the regular "shake-down," which caused them all to be confined to a "board," (or shingle, as they called it,) and not allowed off it; on this they must show their skill; and, being several together in parties, each had his particular "shingle" brought with him as part of his stock in trade. This board was usually about five to six feet long, of large width, with its particular spring in it, and to keep it in its place while dancing on it, it was held down by one on each end. Their music or time was usually given by one of their party, which was done by beating their hands on the sides of their legs and the noise of the heel. The favorite dancing-place was a cleared spot on the east side of the fish market in front of Burnel Brown's Ship Chandlery. The large amount collected in this way after a time produced some excellent "dancers;" in fact, it raised a sort of strife for the highest honors, i.e., the most cheering and the most collected in the "hat." Among the most famous in their day was "Ned" (Francis,) a little wiry negro slave, belonging to Martin Ryerson; another named Bob Rowley, who called himself "Bobolink Bob," belonging to William Bennett, and Jack, belonging to Frederick De Voo, all farmers on Long Island; (the latter owned a farm of 20 odd acres of ground in the centre of what is now Williamsburgh, fronting on the river, running easterly between 7th and 8th Streets.) Jack was a smart and faithful man, and when he was set free by the laws, he became, after a time, a loafer, and died at this market. He was brought to Mr. De Voo, who thought a good deal of him, and on the day when he was made free, he fitted him out in a new suit from "top to toe," and then said to him: "Jack, if you go home with me, you shall never want; but if you leave me now, my home shall never more know you." Jack could not be persuaded to return home by many of the butchers and others, but would stay in the city. It was not long before his former master was importuned by several persons to take him back, but his answer was: "The laws set him free and he left me—now let the laws take care of him." Many New Jersey negroes, mostly from Tappan, were after a time found among them, contending for the prize, and oftentimes successfully too; they were known by their suppleness and plaited forelocks tied up with tea-lead. The Long Islanders usually tied theirs up in a cue with dried eel-skin; but sometimes they combed it about their heads and shoulders, in the form of a wig, then all the fashion. After the Jersey negroes had disposed of their masters' produce at the "Bear Market," which sometimes was early done, and then the advantage of a late tide, they would "shin it" for the Catherine Market to enter the lists with the Long Islanders, and in the end, an equal division of the proceeds took place. The success which attended them brought our city negroes down there, who, after a time, even exceeded them both, and if money was not to be had, "they would dance for a bunch of eels and fish." I have been often told that much of this dancing took place on Sunday mornings; but this was not so, although there were always large collections on that day with their trifles to sell, and their friends to meet or visit.

"Admitting Very Disorderly Persons"
WILLIAM BROOKS KEEPS AN UNRULY OYSTER HOUSE

Despite growing racism in the early nineteenth century, blacks and whites continued to live in close proximity. The following complaint comes from white neighbors of a black keeper of an oyster cellar. The document (District Attorney Sessions Papers, June 24, 1819, NYCMA) reveals several important facets of black work and culture. First, William Brooks, the black man, ran a small independent business selling both oysters and liquor, an operation similar to other such small-scale businesses in the city. Frequently these oyster shops were owned by blacks and located in cellars of buildings.

Second, illicit activity occurred in Brooks's shop. Like many New York blacks who were pushed to the periphery of the economy and often denied legitimate opportunities to earn a living, Brooks became involved in an underworld counterculture. But it would be a mistake to label that underworld simply African-American. Number 26 Banker Street became objectionable to its neighbors not only for the type of activity occurring in Brooks's oyster cellar, but also for the drinking and rowdiness in a white man's retail shop in the same building. What we see here, then, is a complex world that reveals the intersection of race, work, and leisure. Both a black man and a white man occupied Number 26 Banker Street, and to earn a living they countenanced the intermingling of races, sold food and liquor, and seemed to accept, even encourage, the public disorder that ensued almost every night. Confronting these budding entrepreneurs were two mechanics and their families, who resented the disruption of their homes and insults coming from the building next door.

Finally, in the late 1810s Banker Street was not a very respectable neighborhood. It was full of "rum holes" and oyster shops like the two described below. In their struggle for respectability, the mechanics, Jacob McCrea and Archibald Megershell, were fighting a losing battle. Their only real hope for relief was to follow the path of other aspiring mechanics and seek out a more refined neighborhood.[12]

James B. McCrea of No. 24 Banker Street[,] Shoemaker[,] and Archibald Megershell of No. 24 Banker Street[,] Mason[,] being severally sworn and each for himself saith that William Brooks a black man of No. 26 Banker Street who keeps an Oyster Stand is in the habit of admiting very disorderly persons in his house[,] that men and women as white as black of evil name and fame frequent there at all hours of the night to the great Annoyance of Deponents families[,] that very indecent language is used to Deponents wives[,] that last night about ten o'clock a mob collected at the door in consequence of disputes and disturbances at said hour[.] They also swear that Patrick Maxwell who keeps a retail shop where liquor is sold in the upper part of the same house also is in the habit of admitting disorderly persons there to drink at late hours of the night[,] that last night there was a great crowd collected disputing and quarreling[,] that the stoop of Deponents house was filled with some of the crowd to the great annoyance of their families[.] Therefore surety of the Peace is required of said William and Patrick and that they may be bound to answer said complaint at the next court.

James McCrea   Archibald Megershell
Sworn before me this 24th Day June 1819
J. Hopson

12. Gilje, *The Road to Mobocracy*, pp. 236–241.

Figure 51. Alexander Anderson, *Black Family*, BA

"They Must Not Suffer the Man to Be Taken Away"
THE AFRICAN-AMERICAN COMMUNITY AND FUGITIVE SLAVES

Could a slave negotiate the conditions of his labor? Sometimes—especially if he decided to run away. New York City, like other northern urban centers, became a haven for escaped slaves. The increasing size of the free black population, as northern states manumitted slaves, allowed blacks to melt into a sea of anonymity. Moreover, the city offered employment opportunities despite racial barriers, as well as the chance to participate in an active African-American community.

But cities also became prime hunting grounds for the slave catchers, or "blackbirders." On several occasions New York City blacks forcefully resisted the removal of recaptured slaves. What is compelling about the following account (District Attorney Sessions Papers, July 2, 1819, NYCMA) is that the slave had escaped from an owner in New York State, where slavery had been doomed to extinction by the state legislature. In addition, the crowd that came to the assistance of Thomas Hartlett, the escaped slave, represented a cross section of New York's black community. Indeed, one of those arrested in the rescue attempt, John Dyos, was a propertied black artisan living in the Barclay Street neighborhood in which the disturbance took place.

City of New York, . . . John McManus[,] one of the marshalls of the said City[,] being duly sworn says that on the 19th June 1819 a black man named Thomas Hartlett was brot. [brought] up to the Police Office and charged with being a runaway slave from a Mr. Hall of Montgomery County in this State[,] and on Examination and enquiry the Black man confessed himself the Slave and that he had run away. Whereupon an order of Removal was made and given to the agent of said Hall which agent stated that he could not get the said slave to the north river or to where he might secure him in order to take him to Montgomery County as he would be beset by the Blacks &c. who would as he supposed rescue the said slave and asked aid and assistance of the magistrate. Whereupon deponent as an Officer attached to the Police was told to go with the agent and accordingly on their way down[,] viz. in Barclay Street thus, they were beset with a crowd of Blacks, boys, &c. several of which blacks declared that the man[,] viz the slave[,] should not go or words to that[,] and that some of the Manumission Society had told them or said that they had no right to take away said man[,] and that they must not suffer the man to be taken away. That deponent and the agent of the owner of the slave requested to come back to the Office with the slave which was objected to by some of the Crowd or Mob and an attempt was made to rescue said Slave and deponent was seized in a violent manner by a Black man named John Dyos and it was with the utmost difficulty that they got back to the Police Office with the said Slave.
John McMannus
Sworn the 2d of July 1819
Charles Christian

"Don't Carry Your Head Too High"
TRADESMEN AND THE SEARCH FOR RESPECTABILITY

This document, from *Freedom's Journal*, April 20, 1827, articulates an interesting set of values concerning work and the place of African Americans in society. It outlines ideas that Benjamin Franklin might embrace: hard work and frugality as the surest avenues to success, merits that were connected to revolutionary republicanism and notions of virtue. For the men who lived through the Revolutionary War, virtue often meant self-sacrifice for the common good. By the 1820s and 1830s, however, many defined virtue as working hard for your own personal good. In this scheme, any success that one achieved, in some unseen manner, contributed to the good of the whole. Middle-class whites, who worked as merchants, lawyers, master craftsmen and in other entrepreneurial activities, espoused these ideas and centered their new morality around them. For black and white workers further down the economic scale, however, the message of self-help and social climbing became muted by those who warned against aiming too high. This caution had special meaning for African Americans because of the limitations that racial prejudice placed upon them. Evident in the author's story of the failure of his three friends is the message that perhaps black workers ought to be content with what they had achieved rather than to strive for a goal that was beyond their station.

This document also reminds us that blacks often sought respectability as they struggled to achieve a modicum of success as cobblers, as barbers, and as cabinetmakers. Here we see three young black tradesmen who strove to better their lot in life. The author disapproves of their effort, but the fact that the editors published the story suggests that some blacks, successful in their respective trades, sought a life-style and a means of employment that carried their "head[s] too high."

The article appeared in *Freedom's Journal*, a newspaper that began publication in 1827 and that was edited and published by blacks. An African-American identity appeared in every issue of the paper, so the apparently compromising message of Ned's communication is not necessarily submission to white racism. Subscribers to *Freedom's Journal* read stories about the history of the black revolution in Haiti, the biography of successful black shipowner Paul Cuffee, as well as the various efforts to abolish slavery throughout the nation. Editors John Russwurm and Samuel E. Cornish proclaimed in the first issue that "Useful knowledge of every kind, and every thing that relates to Africa, shall find a ready admission into our columns," in an effort to strengthen African identity and assert the equality of blacks. The editors declared in their prospectus that "all men are equal in their nature" and stated that they had established the paper to "bring into operation all the means that our benevolent CREATOR has endowed us, for the moral, religious, civil and literary improvement of our race."[13]

Don't Carry Your Head Too High

"Ned my boy," said my poor old grandfather to me one day, (he is dead now, "rest and bless him,"). "Ned, my boy, mind and *don't carry your head too high*." I was quite young then, and did not at the time know what the old gentleman meant; but I never forgot his words, and a life of observation has fully convinced me of their truth. The years of my boyhood flew rapidly away, and the more busy ones of manhood succeeded. Yet amid all the fun and frolic of youth, that season of real enjoyment, when the whole heart is glad, and the head is full of nothing but sport and merriment, the words of my grandfather, every now and then, would come across my mind, *don't carry your head too high*. In the course of time, the associates of my youth became settled men, and took themselves help-mates. And then it was, I discovered the meaning of my grand-father's saying.

Dick Thompson, one of my school fellows, was as nice a cobler, as ever put awl into his hands. He had a good shop, plenty of work, and was well to do in the world. But then Dick took it into his head, 'twas a low business for a fine fellow like him, to be every day measuring the length and breadth of a man's foot. So he broke up his shop, sold his tools, attended the auction of a shoe-merchant, bought all his stock, and set up a large shoe-store. Dick was no more cobler now, he got him a sign and the following words painted on it, in large gilt letters.—

RICHARD THOMPSON, *Shoe-Merchant.*

Two or three months after I went into Dick's store, when a man with a long pole came in, tipped Dick on the shoulder, seized every thing in his store, and carried him off to jail.[14] So thought I, this is what my grandfather meant, when he said, *don't carry your head too high*.

Tom Parker was another schoolmate of mine. After he left school, his father bound him to a barber. His master took a liking to Tom, as

13. The first issue of the paper carried a detailed prospectus, and subsequent issues often ran an abbreviated prospectus. The paper began publishing on March 16, 1827.

14. The sheriff or constable might have a staff, or pole, to indicate his office. He would be the one to enforce the collection of loans with a court order issued at the demand of creditors.

he was a smart active lad, gave him his shop and custom. Tom now began to feel like other rich men, and every dollar in his pocket added an inch to his consequence. It was not at all proper for a man of Mr. Thomas Parker's wealth, to be doing nothing else all the days of his life, but holding men's noses. Puh! 'twas shameful. So away went Tom's razors, down fell the barber's pole, and in its stead was seen a large fancy store. He was now in his glory, and he could be seen daily, dealing out spices and perfumery to ladies and fine gentle-men, who of course gave him plenty of smiles and little cash. And who cannot live on ladies' smiles? —so thought poor Tom. It was food for his mind, meat for his body, and cash for his pocket. But quarter day [when bills were due] came and went, and still Tom got nothing but—ladies' smiles. He sent in bills; the ladies, sweet crea-tures, gave him smiles, the gentlemen, promises. —Tom owed money, the day of payment was near, but he had not the where-withal. He made over his goods to his creditors, and "shut up shop." I met him the other day, his face was lean and thin, his clothes shabby and ragged. He was employed as a journeyman by a barber in the neighborhood. I thought of my grandfather,—*don't carry your head too high.*

Charles Smith was my bosom companion. We had stuck together in many a boy's frolick, and our attachment grew with our years. He had served his time as a cabinet maker, and his father dying soon after he came of age, left him in the possession of handsome property. He opened a shop of his own, and such was his attention to his business, that he soon had a great run. In short, few young men ever began life with fairer prospects of making the descent into the vale of life, smooth and easy. He married a girl of great beauty and many accomplishments. She could sing, play music, and dance. In the height of his love he determined that she should want nothing which money could procure, and she like other young ladies wanted every thing that money could purchase—Mrs. Sally Jackson had a piano with a drum, and triangle, and forthwith Mrs. Charles Smith's was laid aside as unfashionable, and one with a drum and triangle was put in at the petty cost of $500. Then Miss Collins had a beautiful harp, and she should so like to play on one, besides it looked so pretty to lean on a harp and touch the strings with the end of one's fingers; O dear me, Mr. Smith, so get me a harp; won't you my love? Charles was not the man to withstand the entreaties of his pretty wife, so [he] got her a harp and a master to give lessons. Thus things went on, and what with the piano, harp, and dancing master, French teacher, &c. &c. Charles' purse was drained pretty low. People began to talk of the extravagance of Mrs. Smith,—they wondered at the imprudence of Mr. Smith. His customers dropped off one by one. Want of business produced shortness of cash, this again produced shortness of credit. In short, Charles Smith was a ruined man. He saw his folly when it was too late, and in a fit of delirium put an end to his life. Poor fellow, he suffered his wife to *carry her head too high*.

NED.

"If He Cut Coloured Men"
SEGREGATION IN A BARBER SHOP

From Alexis de Tocqueville to Harriet Martineau, European travel journals remain one of the most trenchant sources on American social and cultural history in the antebellum period. Even though most of these accounts date after the 1830s, the genre was well established before that date. In 1819 Henry B. Fearon published his *Sketches of America*, which he based on a ten-month tour on behalf of thirty-nine families that were contemplating migration to the United States (Henry B. Fearon, *Sketches of America* [London, 1819], 58–60). Like other Englishmen in the nineteenth century, Fearon had a high opinion of himself and his country and eagerly honed in on the weaknesses and inconsistencies of the American social scene. In the following selection, Fearon describes a visit to a barber shop and offers some poignant commentary on American race relations.

Operating a barber shop was one of the handful of enterprises that remained opened to blacks in the early nineteenth century. A black could thrive, become a "boss," and own a business. To do so and ensure gentleman customers, however, the black entrepreneur had to subscribe to the white man's racial barriers. A black man could hire other blacks to cut the hair of whites, but he could not then cut the hair of members of his own race. Struck by the incongruities of American race relations, Fearon offered his tale as an object lesson of how the "laws of the mind" were far more potent than those of "the statute book."

Soon after landing I called at a hair-dresser's in Broad-way, nearly opposite the city-hall: the man in the shop was a negro. He had nearly finished with me, when a black man, very respectably dressed, came into the shop and sat down. The barber enquired if he wanted the proprietor or his *boss*, as he termed him, who was also black: the answer was in the negative; but that he wished to have his hair cut. My attendant turned upon his heel, and with the greatest contempt, muttered in a tone of proud importance. "We do not cut coloured men here, Sir." The poor fellow walked out without replying, exhibiting in his countenance confusion, humiliation, and mortification. I immediately requested, that if the refusal was on account of my being present, he might be called back. The hair-dresser was astonished: "You cannot be in earnest, Sir," he said. I assured him that I was so, and that I was much concerned in witnessing the refusal from no other cause than that his skin was of a darker tinge than my own. He stopped the motion of his scissars; and after a pause of some seconds, in which his eyes were fixed upon my face, he said, "Why, I guess as how, Sir, what you say is mighty elegant, and you're an elegant man; but I guess you are not of these parts." —"I am from England," said I, "where we have neither so cheap nor so enlightened a government as yours, but we have no slaves." —"Ay, I guessed you were not raised here; you salt-water people are mighty grand to coloured people; you are not so proud, and I guess have more to be proud of; now I reckon you do not know that my boss would not have a single ugly or clever gentleman come to his store, if he cut coloured men; now my boss, I guess, ordered me to turn out every coloured man from the store right away, and if I did not, he would send me off slick; for the slimmest gentleman in York would not come to his store if coloured men were let in; but you know all that Sir, I guess, without my telling you; you are an elegant gentleman too, Sir." I assured him that I was ignorant of the fact which he stated; but which, from the earnestness of his manner, I concluded must be true. . . . At the dinner-table I commenced a relation of this occurrence to three American gentlemen, one of whom was a doctor, the others were in the law: they were men of education and of liberal opinions. When I arrived at the point of the black being turned out, they exclaimed, "Ay right, perfectly right, I would never go to a barber's where a coloured man was cut!" Observe, these gentlemen were not from the south; they are residents of New York, and I believe were born there. . . .

The most degraded white will not walk or eat with a negro; so that, although New York is a free state, it is such only on parchment: the black Americans are in it *practically* and politically slaves; the laws of the mind being, after all, infinitely more strong and more effective than those of the statute book; and it is these *mental* legislative enactments, operating in too many cases besides this of the poor negroes, which excite but little respect for the American character.

"All Men Are Born Free"
CELEBRATING THE ABOLITION OF THE SLAVE TRADE

Black New Yorkers did not avoid politics. During the early republic an articulate and influential leadership emerged to guide the New York African-American community. One of their central concerns

Figures 52, 53. Blacks were aware of republican values. The ad for the African Mutual Instruction Society reveals their interest in self-improvement, and James Gilbert's ad for his clothing and tailoring store, with its eagle insignia, reveals an ambitious black artisan who used identification with American values as his marketing strategy. *Freedom's Journal,* February 1, 1828

remained slavery—both within and beyond the state boundaries. This document reveals how important national and international issues of slavery were for blacks.

The Constitution of the United States prohibited any congressional action against the slave trade for twenty years after it was written. When that term ended, Congress quickly passed a law against the further importation of slaves. It was to celebrate that federal law that "the Africans and their descendants" held their meeting on December 2, 1807.

The following resolutions, published in the *New York Evening Post*, December 16, 1807, demonstrate not only how African Americans inculcated and utilized the rhetoric of the Revolution, declaring "the *undeniable principle*, that all men are born free," but also their willingness to assert themselves in politics. The form and language of the following resolutions mirror the form and language coming from other political meetings of the era. The message, however, represented a challenge to white prejudices.

MEETING OF AFRICANS

At a numerous and respectable meeting of the Africans, and their descendants, of the city of New-York, held the 2d December, 1807, at the African School Room, Cliff-Street, for the purpose of taking into consideration, the propriety of celebrating the day, on which the Acts, passed by the Congress of the United States, for the Abolition of the Slave Trade, took effect, when the following resolutions were adopted.

JOHN TEASEMAN, was called to the chair, Peter Williams, Jun., Sec'ry

Resolved Unanimously, That, having been the unhappy victims of a trade, which has deprived us of our best and most valuable enjoyments; and convinced as we are, of the *undeniable principle*, that all men are born free, we view the abolition of this Traffic, "so abhorrent in its nature to every just and tender sentiment," with inexpressible satisfaction.

Resolved Unanimously, That the day which terminates the Slave Trade in this country, ought to be celebrated by *us, in particular*, with demonstrations of gratitude and thanksgiving.

Resolved, Unanimously, That the tribute of our warmest gratitude is due to those friends of humanity, who have interested themselves in our favour, and whose exertions, through Divine assistance, have contributed, in no small degree, to bring about this happy event; And also to that government, which has so cordially and so honorably co-operated with them in this cause, and availed itself of the first practicable moment for arresting the progress of this great moral and political evil.

Resolved, Unanimously, That a Committee of Twelve persons be appointed for the purpose of making suitable arrangements for carrying the foregoing Resolutions into effect.

Resolved, Unanimously, That the Committee consist of the following persons, viz:

PETER WILLIAMS	WILLIAM GREEN	ISAAC FORTUNE
DANIEL BERRY	ROBERT SIDNEY	WILLIAM HAMILTON
THOMAS MILLER	WILLIAM BROWN	NICHOLAS SMITH
ABRAHAM GORDON	JOHN TEASEMAN	THOMAS SIPKINS

JOHN TEASEMAN, Chairman
PETER WILLIAMS, Jun., Sec'ry

"The Attempt to Disenfranchise People of Color"
DEFENDING SUFFRAGE

Free New York blacks voted throughout the antebellum period, but many whites frequently challenged their right to do so. Black voters persisted in maintaining their allegiance to the Federalist leadership that had been instrumental in the passage of the gradual emancipation law in 1799 and continued to act as guardians for the African-American community. Indeed, the roster of New York's Manumission Society reads like a *Who's Who* of the state's Federalist politicians, including Alexander Hamilton and John Jay. The problem for black voters in the nineteenth century was that the Federalists lost ground to their more democratic opponents, and, as the Federalist political power waned, so did their ability to protect blacks. Calculating Jeffersonian and Democratic politicians knew that curtailing the number of blacks at the polls would only enhance their own political clout. These men thus used white racist assumptions to argue against further black participation in elections. To smear their opponents Jeffersonians in 1808 prepared a campaign song that began "Federalists with blacks unite." They passed a law to limit the black franchise in 1811, and in the wake of the War of 1812, which was a political disaster for the Federalists, they renewed efforts to limit black voting even further. In 1821, when the state's new constitution provided universal manhood suffrage for whites, property qualifications were retained for blacks. By that time, however, the efforts at intimidation had been very successful and only a small percentage of the city's blacks bothered to go to the polls.

The following document represents a constitutional appeal in 1815 to retain the voting rights of the city's blacks. It appeared in a leading Federalist newspaper (*New York Evening Post*, April 25, 1815), and, as in many political articles of the period, the author hid his identity behind a pseudonym—"Wilberforce," the name of the great English abolitionist. Given its source, the author was probably a white Federalist.[15]

The attempt to disfranchise people of color, —Article 5th of the Constitution of the United States, provides, "that no person shall be deprived of *life, liberty* or *property* without due *process* of law." By the Bill of Rights of this state it is declared (chapter 1st, clause 5th) "That no persons of what state or condition soever, shall be put out of his or her *franchise* or freehold, unless he or she be duly brought to answer, and be *fore-judged* of the same by *due course* of law; and if anything be done contrary to the same, it shall be void in law and holden for none."

The meaning of the terms "process of law," "course of law," are well ascertained to signify the regular course of *judicial proceedings*, not the *arbitrary act* of any man or body of men whatsoever. The right to vote is emphatically called the *elective franchise*, and was vested in all citizens of color, at least in those who had obtained certificates before the passing of the unconstitutional law at the last session. —By what *course*, by what *process of law* have they been *brought to answer* and forejudged of this franchise? By what authority is it subjected to new and burdensome conditions? By none! Will the citizens of color then submit to this daring outrage on their rights? Can the respectable boards of inspectors do otherwise than consider that act as a violation of the Bill of Rights, as "done contrary to the same" and therefore decide that "it is void in law and holden for none?"

WILBERFORCE

15. Fox, "Negro Vote," 275.

"We Stand Redeemed from a Bitter Thraldom"
ABOLITION and the SPIRIT OF '76

Slavery was the most important labor issue for blacks in the early national period. Completion of emancipation in New York State on July 4, 1827, signaled a milestone in the realization of the American Revolution for New York blacks. In a Fourth of July oration, William Hamilton, a leader in the city's African-American community, linked the events of 1776 with the emergence of blacks as a free labor force in New York. Although he quoted the Declaration of Independence, extolling the virtues and the ideal of liberty, Hamilton's knowledge of the African-American experience in the state went well beyond Independence Day hoopla. He may have dwelt on the principles of "the glorious sons of '76," but he also emphasized how many slaves achieved their freedom during the upheaval of the Revolutionary War by siding with the British and leaving the country as refugees.

Hamilton reached even further into the past and reminded his black audience of the "Negro Plot" of 1741. At that time white New Yorkers, fearing a slave rebellion and using the legal mechanisms of the state, burned thirteen black men at the stake and hanged seventeen others.[16] Hamilton also recited some of the horrors of slavery, which many of his listeners had undoubtedly endured, and, as they knew, others were yet suffering. The oration, reprinted in *Freedom's Journal*, October 12, 1827, thus suggests the outlines of the intimate and complex relationship between slavery and freedom in the years after the American Revolution.

Extract From an ORATION,
Delivered in the African Church, in the City of New-York,
on the Fourth of July, 1827, in Commemoration of the
ABOLITION of DOMESTIC SLAVERY, in this State.
By William Hamilton

Liberty! kind goddess! brightest of heavenly deities that guide the affairs of men.

Oh Liberty! where thou art resisted and irritated, thou art terrible as the raging sea, and dreadful as a tornado. But where thou art listened

16. Thomas J. Davis, *A Rumor of Revolt: The "Great Negro Plot" in Colonial New York* (New York, 1985).

to, and obeyed, thou art gentle as the purling stream that meanders
through the mead; as soft and as cheerful as the zephyrs that dance upon
the summer's breeze, and as bounteous as autumn's harvest.

To thee, the sons of Afric in this once dark, gloomy, hopeless, but
now fairest, brightest, and most cheerful of thy domain, [we] do owe
a double oblation of gratitude. —Thou hast entwined and bound fast
the cruel hand of oppression—thou hast by the powerful charm of
reason, deprived the monster of his strength—he dies, he sinks to
rise no more.

Thou hast loosened the hard bound fetters by which we were held;
and by a voice sweet as the muse of heaven yet strong and powerful
reaching to the extreme boundaries of the state of New-York, hath
declared that we the people of colour, the sons of Afric, are FREE!

My bretheren and fellow-citizens, I hail you all. This day we stand
redeemed from a bitter thraldom. Of us it may be truly said, "the last
agony is o'er," THE AFRICANS ARE RESTORED! No more shall
the accursed name of slave be attached to us—no more shall the
negro and *slave* be synonymous.

Fellow citizens, I come to felicitate you on the victory obtained—
not by sanguinary conflict with the foe—there are no fields teeming
with blood; not a victory obtained by fierce-flaming, death-dealing
ordinance, vomiting forth fire and horrible destruction—no thousands made to lick the dust—no groan of the wounded and dying.
But I come to felicitate you on the victory obtained by the principles
of liberty, such as are broadly and indelibly laid down by the glorious
sons of '76; and are contained in the over memorable words prefixed
to the Declaration of Independence of these United States: viz. "We
hold these truths to be self-evident, that all men are created equal,
and endowed by their Creator with certain unalienable rights; and
among these are life, liberty, and the pursuit of happiness." A victory
obtained by these principles over prejudice, injustice, and foul oppression.

This day has the state of New-York regenerated herself—this day
has she been cleansed of a most foul, poisonous and damning stain. I
stand amazed at the quiet, yet rapid progress the principles of liberty
have made. A semi-century ago, the people of colour, with scarcely
an exception, were *all slaves*. It is true, many in the city, who remained here in the time of the revolution, (when their masters left at
the approach of the British) and many too from the country, who

became a kind of refugee, obtained their liberty, by leaving the country at the close of the war, or a few years respite from slavery; for such as were found remaining after the revolution, were again claimed by their masters. Yes we were all in the most abject state of slavery that can be conceived except *that* of *our* brethren at the South, whose miseries are a little more enhanced. Without going back to the time of the Negro plot, when a kind of fanaticism seized the people of New-York, something similar in its bearing and effect to the sad circumstances that took place among the people of New England in their more puritanic times, and about a half century before the fancied plot, when they put to death the good people for being witches.

Yes, my brethren, in this state we have been *advertised, and bought, and sold like any commodity.* In this state we have suffered cruelly; suffered by imprisonment, by whipping, and by scourging.

I have seen men chained with iron collars to their necks. I have seen——but hold! Let me proceed no farther. Why enter into the blood chilling detail of our miseries? It would only dampen those joys that ought to glow and sparkle on every countenance; it would only give vent to the feelings that would not be reconcileable with the object of our assembling. . . .

6

WOMEN:

In and Beyond the Household

Women were an important part of the work force in New York City during the early national period and consequently appear in documents throughout this book. Apprentice Alexander Anderson, for example, referred to his mother often in his diary and described briefly several other women, including a few prostitutes and an old beggar named Aunt Jenny, who danced for him for pennies. These references, when misread or hurried through, obscure the labor of these and almost all other women in the city. Women's work, as far as most documentation is concerned, was invisible work; women received mention and even description, but the fact that they might be in the midst of some labor often remained submerged. Anderson's mother obviously ran the household. Aunt Jenny may have been a beggar, but her beggary was her work and she eagerly and pitifully danced in order to elicit more money. The prostitutes flaunting their wares may have distressed Anderson, but they were plying their trade in an effective manner.

Several reasons for the difficulty in studying women's work present themselves. First, most of the documentation was created by men, even the documents in this chapter: all of them either passed through or emerged from the hands of men. Men set the type for advertisements, wrote the newspaper articles, penned the court and legal documents, and created most of the written record utilized by historians to recreate the past. Therefore most of the documents that describe working people concentrate on men.

Second, the nature of women's work makes documentation and study of it difficult. Women labored in the home, organized the household, raised children, and supervised servants. They took in washing and boarders, served food and drink, cleaned and cooked. Women worked as seamstresses, did piece work, labored in factories. They walked the streets vending a large variety of items, including food and small wares. Some women became prostitutes. All of these occupations, although crucial and central to the urban environment, remain poorly documented.

Third, the lack of documentation derives largely from the gender connotations of work in early national society. The new republic was a patriarchal world in which male definitions dominated. All of the documents in this collection represent an unusual view of that world, as compared to collections that focus on great men and great deeds, but that view usually stresses work that men thought was important: the production or movement of goods that led to the formation of capital. This gender definition became so powerful that even when women contributed in areas considered important to men, such as factories and textile production, they still received little attention. A full understanding of this subject, therefore, needs to break away from the gender-bound definition of work and examine the wide variety of activities in which women labored.[1]

The Age of Revolution had a profound impact on the status of women and female labor in the late eighteenth and early nineteenth centuries. Women contributed to the war effort during the American struggle for independence in a variety of ways. As camp followers numbering in the thousands, they cooked, cleaned, and nursed, fulfilling traditional functions. Women often held together the household or property, and sometimes the shop, while men were away from home fighting the war. Women also participated in boycotts, some crowd activity, and special rituals—such as "spinning bees"—they developed on their own. This association, along with the explicit attack on hierarchy and patriarchy imbedded in the independence movement, posed a serious threat to standard notions of social order.

1. Christine Stansell, *City of Women: Sex and Class in New York, 1789–1860* (New York, 1986).

Ultimately that threat remained unrealized as middle- and upper-class women redefined their role in society as republican mothers and wives who guarded moral and ethical values and took responsibility for sustaining the republic by rearing the next generation of proper citizens. This process of redefinition, however, led to a denial of the more radical gender meanings—including greater political awareness and economic independence—implied in the experience of poorer women who had sacrificed so much during the course of the war.[2]

As a result of the dislocation created by war and the emerging capitalist economy, women's place in society underwent significant changes. New employment opportunities appeared that helped to cut women off from many of the traditional bonds that tied them to patriarchy. A number of manufactories employed between ten and thirty women in such trades as tobacco processing and textile production. Many more women found positions in the service sector as domestics, washerwomen, cooks, and prostitutes. Some of these occupations were not new, but the expanding urban economy allowed more women to earn an income apart from a male provider. Despite the possibility of marginal independence, though, wages were low and workingwomen remained subject to exploitation.[3]

The legacy of the American Revolution was mixed for women. On one hand, middle- and upper-class women, fueled by their participa-

2. Linda K. Kerber, "'History Can Do It No Justice': Women and the Reinterpretation of the American Revolution," in Ronald Hoffman and Peter J. Albert, eds., *Women in the Age of the American Revolution* (Charlottesville, Va., 1989), pp. 3–42. See also Kerber, *Women of the Republic: Intellect and Ideology in Revolutionary America* (Chapel Hill, N.C., 1980); Mary Beth Norton, *Liberty's Daughters: The Revolutionary Experience of American Women, 1750–1800* (Boston, 1980); Jan Lewis, "The Republican Wife: Virtue and Seduction in the Early Republic," *William and Mary Quarterly*, 3d ser., 44 (1987), 689–721; Jacqueline Reimer, "Rearing the Republican Child," ibid., 39 (1982), 150–163; Kerber et al., "Beyond Roles, Beyond Spheres: Thinking about Gender in the Early Republic," ibid., 46 (1989), 565–585; Ruth H. Bloch, "The Gendered Meanings of Virtue in Revolutionary America," *Signs*, 13 (1987), 37–58; Joan R. Gundersen, "Independence, Citizenship, and the American Revolution," ibid., 59–77; Howard B. Rock, ed., "A Woman's Place in Jeffersonian New York: The View from the *Independent Mechanic*," *New York History*, 63 (1982), 435–459. See Norton, *Liberty's Daughters*, pp. 166–170, for "spinning bees."

3. For a negative assessment of the impact of the American Revolution on women, see Joan Hoff Wilson, "The Illusion of Change: Women and the American Revolution," in Alfred F. Young, ed., *The American Revolution: Explorations in the History of American Radicalism* (DeKalb, Ill., 1976), pp. 383–445; and Stansell, *City of Women*, pp. 20–30.

tion in the struggle and inspired by republican ideology, molded a new conception of womanhood that emphasized their nurturing and purifying role. On the other hand, poorer women, seasoned both by hardship and a new sense of independence, were more concerned with holding their own in the aggressive capitalist atmosphere of the new republic than in creating a new female role model. Measured against the middle-class republican ideal of womanhood, poorer women came up short. As a result, their contribution to work and the making of the new nation is difficult to document and often neglected.

"Training Up Women and Children to the Business"
FACTORY WORK IN THE 1790S

Relatively few New York City women in the early national period worked in factories, as New York's strength in this area of production, especially in textiles, did not develop until later in the nineteenth century.[4] The following selection by British traveler Henry Wansey (*The Journal of an Excursion to the United States of North America, in the Summer of 1794* [Salisbury, 1796], pp. 83–84) suggests that some investors, inspired by the promise of economic development implicit in American political independence, were investing in such enterprises. Along the East River in 1793 and 1794 rose a large and impressive manufacturing center packed with all of the latest machinery built from plans smuggled out of England. Using the power from the tides and the current at Hell's Gate, this textile factory not only modeled itself after English prototypes in terms of machinery, but also utilized a similar labor force by hiring a few skilled men to set up and operate the machinery, while relying upon less expensive labor of women and children to tend the machinery. The venture failed. The factory entailed too much capital, did not specialize in any one textile product, and may not have been able to retain its labor force. Even though this enterprise did not make it in New York City, similar textile factories quickly emerged throughout rural New England and even in nearby Paterson, New Jersey. By the 1820s a number of manufactories within the city, particularly textile enterprises,

4. Sean Wilentz, *Chants Democratic: New York City and the Rise of the American Working Class, 1788–1850* (New York, 1984), pp. 107–142.

Figure 54. Alexander Anderson, *Women at Work in a Small-Scale Loom Factory,*
BA

employed between ten and thirty women. But few factories existed in
the city because of the price of real estate, lack of power sources, and
foreign competition. As a result, those women who worked in crafts
tended to labor in small-scale enterprises.[5]

Went with a party to see Dickson's cotton manufactory at Hell
Gates, about five miles from New York. It is worked by a breast water

5. An attempt to set up a manufactory of gummed and medicated elastic employing
"400 women and girls" failed as well. A broad cloth manufactory, however, begun in
1810 with 250 spindles and five jennies and employing steam power continued in
operation until at least 1820. See Federal Manufacturing Census, 1820, Nos. 1317,
1321, and Howard B. Rock, "A Great Diversity: Artisan Crafts in New York City,
1820," a paper delivered at Clark Historical Library Seminar, Central Michigan University, April 1985. On women in the workplace see Stansell, *City of Women.* For a
discussion of women in factories elsewhere, see Thomas Dublin, *Women at Work: The
Transformation of Work and Community in Lowell, Massachusetts, 1826–1860* (New
York, 1979); Jonathan Prude, *The Coming of Industrial Order: Town and Factory Life in
Rural Massachusetts, 1810–1860* (Cambridge, 1983).

wheel, twenty feet in diameter. There are two large buildings four
story high, and eighty feet long. In one shop I saw twenty-six looms
at work, weaving fustians, calicoes, nankeens, nankinets, dimities,
&c. and there are ten other looms in the neighborhood. They have
the new-invented spring shuttle. They also spin by water, using all
the new improvements of Awkwright and others. Twelve or fourteen
workmen from Manchester. All the machinery in wood, steel, and
brass, were made on the spot from models brought from England and
Scotland. They are training up women and children to the business,
of whom I saw twenty or thirty at work; they give the women two
dollars a week, and find them in board and lodging; the children are
bound apprentice till twenty-one years of age, with an engagement to
board, clothe and educate them. They have the machine called the
mule, at which they have spun cotton yarn so fine as twenty-one
hundred scains to the pound, and they purpose making muslins.

"The Poor Widows Who Will Support Themselves"
THE PUTTING-OUT SYSTEM IN NEW YORK, 1810

If New York City did not become a center of factory production
during the early republic, it did start to develop its extensive textile
industry through other means. Entrepreneurs took advantage of the
burgeoning local and national markets, which were triggered by the
great economic revolution of the age, to engage in the production of
slop or ready-made clothing. These efforts depended on both larger
shops and out-work, or work hired out to a cottage industry. In the
latter system, individual tailors or seamstresses contracted to take
cloth, and in the confines of their homes, sew a finished product that
could be retailed at a hefty profit for the merchant supplier. As the
following selection reveals, the Reverend Ezra Styles Ely found this
practice both exploitative and objectionable. Commencing in 1810
Ely ministered to the poor and disadvantaged who resided at New
York City's almshouse and public hospital. This Presbyterian minister
discovered that the conditions of the people he met at these institutions were heart-rending, and he was particularly affected by the
plight of women struggling to survive in a city and labor market that
left them few options. Obviously the poor widow described in the

document fulfilled all of Ely's most sanguine hopes for the poor (Ezra Styles Ely, *The Journal of the Stated Preacher to the Hospital and Alms-house in the City of New-York for the Year of Our Lord 1811* [New York, 1812], pp. 33–34). She was both religious and pious; more-over, she demonstrated a responsibility that Ely found lacking in many of the poor he worked with: she paid the debt incurred from her husband's funeral and then struggled to house and feed her many children through honest work. Consequently, Ely expected her to achieve the ultimate in womanly success by rearing her children to become respectable independent mechanics and, by implication, good citizens.[6]

. . . *Sympathy* is natural and amiable; but *benevolence*, when exercised by a . . . man, is supernatural and holy. Would to God that the two were united in every human heart! Possibly both have been exercised in the relief of a certain poor widow, whose husband, a carman, died about a year since; leaving her, after she had defrayed the expenses of his sickness and burial, nothing for her support, but ten children. Four of these are able to provide for themselves, and one or two can give some assistance to the mother, by tending the four younger chil-dren, while the mother washes or sews for the necessaries of life. For eight months I have known this woman and her family. She is a professor of religion; and more, she is pious. Her children are neat and industrious. For a single room she pays twenty-five dollars, yearly rent; and earns part of this by sewing nankeen pantaloons and com-mon shirts, *for the eighth part of a dollar* for each garment. This I find the common price of job-work;[7] so that the poor widows who will support themselves, must be content with *one shilling*, while the pur-chasers pay *many shillings* for the same work. All who sell ought to have lawful gain, but the poor, who perform the work, ought to re-ceive at least half of that sum which is charged for making of apparel. Some of the children attend that benevolent Institution, "The New York Free School," and if the Lord shall spare them, I doubt not [that they] will make useful mechanics.

6. Carroll Smith Rosenberg, *Religion and the Rise of the American City: The New York City Mission Movement, 1812–1870* (Ithaca, N.Y., 1971), pp. 41, 52–53.
7. Like piecework, which paid by the piece, job work paid by the job, and, during this period, it was ordinarily performed in the home.

"She Is Sober, Honest, Industrious"
DESCRIBING THE IDEAL DOMESTIC SERVANT

During the early republic many women worked as domestic servants—nurses, cooks, maids, and general help who remained in the
household fulfilling so-called traditional roles. Usually poorly paid
and subject to both exploitation and abuse, most servants were either
immigrants from Ireland or blacks. Indeed, when the Society for the
Encouragement of Faithful Domestic Servants surveyed the city, they
counted 2,164 servants, 1,079 of which were Irish and 460 black.
Over three-fourths of the total were women (1652). Although these
numbers may underrepresent the full number of servants, the propor-
tions are probably accurate.

Finding a good servant posed a challenge to middle- and upper-
class homes as they strove to sustain a respectable life-style that limited the domestic duties of the household "mistress." The problem
was not so much finding someone to hire as finding the right person
to hire. The middle-class family wanted a servant to embody their
values of sobriety, hard work, and industry, while simultaneously acting complacent and subservient, eager for the most menial tasks. In
the new egalitarian atmosphere of the early nineteenth century, that
combination was difficult to find. Reformers organized the Society for
the Encouragement of Faithful Domestic Servants to help identify
and reward good servants.

The following document (Society for the Encouragement of Faithful Domestic Servants in New York, *Third Annual Report of the Managers* . . . [New York, 1828], 23) was intended as a recommendation
for recognition by the society of the individual described. The appen-
dices of the Society's reports were full of similar testimonials. The
one reprinted here describes the background of a typical domestic
servant, whose behavior, however, may very well have been atypical.
If this description represents the ideal servant in middle-class eyes,
careful reading of the document suggests that her willingness to work
at any chore, her honesty, sobriety, industriousness, thrift, religiosity,
and her avoidance of parties were unusual enough to be singled out as
attributes deserving of praise.

I take much pleasure in presenting the claims of one of my domestics
for such a reward from your institution as falls within your regulations.

Figures 55, 56, 57.
Many women worked
at home. Needlework
occupied much of
their time, as did the
difficult labor of
washing. *Women
Doing Needlework*, in
Samuel Wood, *Proof
Book* (New York,
1820), NYHS;
*Woman Washing
Indoors*, in Samuel
Wood, *Proof Book*
(New York, 1820),
NYHS; and
Alexander Anderson,
*Women Doing
Laundry*, BA

——— ———a native of Ireland, has been in this country about 4
years, and in our employ 14 months, as child's nurse. She is sober,
honest, industrious, and very faithful in her care of our children: She
is always willing to be called upon at night, if necessary. If we are
without a cook or waiter, she is ever ready to do the work of either,
even to going of errands or sweeping the streets; and in so doing she
never feels that she is conferring a favour, but on the contrary, is
merely doing her duty; and has frequently remarked that she is paid
for her time and services, and it makes no difference to her about
what she is employed. She has little or no company, and never
wishes to go out, except to church on Sundays, and occasionally to
see her sisters. She has no idea of poor girls either going to or giving
parties, and never has been to one since she has been here. Her
wages are $6, per month. Since she has lived with us, she has clothed
herself comfortably and respectably, has given the sum of $18 to her
needy relatives, and has laid up $33, which, with $12 she brought
from her last place, she has deposited in the Savings Bank. She is a
Catholic, but, we think, a conscientious one, and appears to have
much interest in reading the Bible. Your subscribers think her deserving of the approbation and rewards of your benevolent institution.

"I Guess, I Am a Woman Citizen"
THE DISTINCTION BETWEEN SERVANTS AND HELP

The Revolutionary idea of equality permeated all aspects of American society in the early nineteenth century. One of the reasons for
the difficulty in obtaining good help was that those who were hired as
domestics often believed they were the equal of their employers. The
result was that the term "servant," which in the eighteenth century
implied not only a form of bound labor but also a hierarchical relationship between servant and master, went into disuse. Instead the
less offensive and more egalitarian term "help" came to be used for
domestic labor. Henry Fearon probably intended to parody this lin-
guistic shift and the idea of equality it represented in the following
passage (Fearon, *Sketches of America* [London, 1819], 80–81). He no
doubt thought that a female domestic asserting herself as a "woman
citizen" was absurd, but the statement captures more of the spirit of
the times than he may have realized.

Servants, let me observe, are called "helps:" if you call them servants they leave you without notice. Englishmen often incur displeasure by negligence in continuing to use this prohibited word. The
difference, however, would appear merely verbal; for indeed I should
misrepresent the impressions I have received on the subject, if I
stated that the Americans *really* shewed more feeling, or were more
considerate in their conduct towards this class of society than the
English: every one who knows them will, I think, pronounce the
direct contrary to be the case. A friend of mine, the other day, met
with a rebuff at his hotel, which taught him the necessity of alter-
ing—not his ideas, but his words. Addressing the female "help" he
said, "Be kind enough to tell your mistress that I should be glad to see
her." — "My *mistress*, Sir! I tell you I have no mistress, nor master
either. I will not tell her, Sir, I guess; if you want Mrs. M——you
may go to her yourself, I guess. I have no mistress, Sir. In this country there is no mistresses nor masters; I guess, I am a woman citizen."

"Resolve to Employ Women Only Whose Proper Business It Is"

A DEFENSE OF FEMALE LABOR IN THE TAILORING TRADE

Gender was an important distinction in the workplace in the early
nineteenth century, and one sure way to taint any labor was to label
it as "woman's work." The following document appeared originally as
an item in a Philadelphia newspaper, but was then reprinted in a
New York paper as a means to lambast and insult the journeymen
tailors who were then out on strike (*New York Evening Post*, April 20,
1819). The author asserted that he was both manly and a friend of
women, and therefore found efforts by journeyman tailors to limit
female participation in their trade as particularly obnoxious. Opposed
to the turnout, the author attempted to taint the tailor's trade by
associating it with female labor. Note the contradiction here between
the author's defense of women and his use of gender as a weapon
wielded against the strikers. On one level he appears to have felt
some sympathy for poor women like the widow described by Ezra
Styles Ely. But on another level, his willingness to use the feminine

label as a slur against tailors indicates the author assumed that women's work was low and demeaning.[8]

The enclosed article from the *Aurora*, is, in my opinion, correct, liberal, and manly. Not seeing it in the *Evening Post*, I have presumed that it had escaped your attention, and I therefore inclose it, that you may insert it, and shew yourself to be what you always have been and, I am sure, always will be, the advocate of

WOMAN

"The devil among the Tailors." —The journeymen tailors in New-York, it appears, have had what they call a *turn out*—that is, they have combined not to work, unless conditions, which they prescribe, are complied with. Every man has a right to determine what he can afford, or what wages he will give; the right to refuse is equal; but combinations of one class, to force another class into any measures against their free will, is an usurpation which violates the first law of society; but there is an aggravation in this case, of the tailors in New-York, their *turn out*, is to *compel the master tailors not to employ women in any part of the tailor's work.* —The stupidity and brutality of this unmanly conspiracy, requires no coloring to mark its odium; these wretched men, whose conduct almost justifies the contempt that has become proverbial on the occupation—would shut out a numerous class of females from industry and bread, in order to enhance their own wages, which is more than three times the wages that the same class of men receive in England; indifferent to humanity and to equal rights which they possess, these wretches would consign women to indigence, that they might the more effectually impose upon the public.

The original cause of casting odium on the occupation of a tailor, and making him the *butt of ridicule* as only the *ninth part of a man*, arose out of a similar occurrence; in about two centuries ago, this trade of a tailor was performed wholly by women; it was scandalous and effeminate, for *men* to work at the needle— this occurred in England, about the close of the fifteenth century; the period when *doublet, tunic,* and *trunk hose,* began to give way to the *French* frock and skirted coat, with cape and collar, and the flapped breeches; when

8. Stansell, *City of Women*, pp. 106–115; Howard B. Rock, *Artisans of the New Republic: The Tradesmen of New York City in the Age of Jefferson* (New York, 1979), pp. 265–268, 280–281.

the name of a *male tailor* became as opprobrious as that of a male *milliner* in modern times. It is a curious instance of revolution in manners that the *men tailors* should now endeavour once more to injure women. If the master tailors are disposed to retrieve their trade from merited odium, they ought to resolve to employ women only; whose proper business it is."

"Women Are Very Inadequate"
THE TAILORS RESPOND

The journeyman tailors did not allow the attack on their trade to go unchallenged. A defense of their position soon appeared in the *New York Evening Post* (July 13, 1819), which is reprinted here. Although the gentleman from Philadelphia and the journeyman tailor who responded approached the strike from vastly different directions, they both shared one important, common opinion: the label of "women's work" denoted inferior labor. Indeed, the journeyman tailor took this argument to an extreme when he declared that women were incapable of doing the more skilled labor of the male tailor and therefore, in order to guarantee a full year's employment for the skilled male tailor, women ought to be excluded from even the simpler tasks.

Although in many ways this and the previous document are largely about male labor, some very important pieces of information about the place of women in New York's labor market can be gleaned from them. First, by 1819 women occupied a special niche in the tailoring trade by sewing pantaloons and vests. Second, entrepreneurs in the industry felt financial pressure to expand these areas of women's work in order to cut costs. Women were attractive workers because their work was cheaper than men's. In the changing market economy of the early republic this financial consideration became an increasingly salient factor. Finally, as more women entered the clothing industry, even before the introduction of factories and machinery, significant alterations began to occur in gender relations. The tailors were fighting a rear-guard action in challenging the feminization of their trade. As positions opened up for women in production, even though that brought a concomitant decline in the status of that position, opportunities expanded for women to work independently of the household and to support themselves and their families, albeit at an impoverished level.[9]

To the Public

We are now called upon, by the imperative mandate of nature, to develop to the world an act, unprecedented in its form, and intolerable in its oppression—I mean the unmanly and ungenerous conduct of the Merchant Tailors of New York, towards the Journeymen. It will be recollected that some two or three months ago the Journeymen Tailors were engaged in what mechanics call a turn out, by which is generally meant a contest with their employers for an increase in wages. This was not the object of the Journeymen Tailors in their turn out so called; though stated as one of their objects by the pragmatical interference of a gentlemen from Philadelphia whose billingsgate production on the subject in question, made its appearance in the city through the vehicle of the *Evening Post*.

This is an egregious distortion of fact, founded on ignorance or malevolent mendacity. The Journeymen only contended for the privilege of making Vests and Pantaloons, a right which belonged to them alone. The gentleman in question after advancing the preposterous and truly ridiculous idea that garments of every description ought to be made by women, very categorically asserts, that an employer has a right to determine what he can afford or what wages he will give. We say not; such are the contracted views of men in common life, who, when fortune so propitiously smiles upon them, as to enable them to commence and continue in, a profitable course of business; their only object is to accumulate money; in the aggregation of which, they were perfectly regardless of the wants of the Journeymen who they employ. The wretched helot is better qualified to feel the burden under which he labours than the merciless tyrant who inflicts it; hence the Journeyman is better able to decide upon the merit of his labour than his employer is for him. Believe me; in no part of America, are Journeymen Tailors so much oppressed as in New-York, and in no part of America are there so many wealthy Tailors, as their employers and oppressors. Not content with depriving them of a large proportion of their work to complete the climax of their illiberality, they have even determined to reduce their wages

9. Stansell, *City of Women*, pp. 106–129.

one dollar upon each coat, already very insufficient indeed. The gentleman above alluded to states that the wages of Journeymen Tailors in this country is tergeminous [threefold] to that of the same class of men in England. This is an evident mistake. A Journeyman Tailor in this country only earns from $10 to $12 per week, and that only about one half the year; the reason of which is that Vests and Pantaloons are made altogether by women in this country, (except in Philadelphia and Albany) whereas in England, all habiliments worn by men are made by men, for which they receive 37 shillings sterling per week, and that too, almost through the year, which certainly gives the latter an infinite advantage over the former. It is truly astonishing that any man should be so limited in his judgement as to pretend to say, that the whole business of a Tailor ought to be performed by women, because the simple and formless dress, tunic &c., worn by men, was made by women about the close of the 15th century. It is an indisputable fact that women are very inadequate to perform the work of a Tailor, which I shall endeavor to prove by the following syllogism. A Journeyman Tailor not above the level of mediocrity, cannot make a super fine plain coat to pass the ordeal of criticism, much less many of the garments that might be named; yet this very man can make waistcoats and pantaloons, and that too, with more judgement and solicitude than a woman can; hence we infer that women are incomplete, if incomplete they ought to disclaim all right and title whatever to the avocation of a tailor— What right has any man to interfere to the prejudice of another, or any set of men and publicly pretend to decide upon the subject, the merit or demerit of which he is perfectly unacquainted with? Suppose that I, an unlettered mechanic, should endeavor to soar to the sublime and unmeasurable regions of astronomy, you would laugh at my arrogance, and pity my ignorance. Hence it is reasonable to infer, that every man must be the sole judge of the nature of his peculiar avocation; Is it reasonable, I would ask, that the best of workmen should be unemployed half the year, and calmly submit to reiterated privations by the empiricism of women, many of whom have served but a few months at the business, aided by the mercenary support of employers, merely because women work cheaper than men? Certainly not? Nothing could be offered in justification of women asking, or employers giving, work to women, other than the long continuance of an unwarrantable practice, which is, indeed but a very slender excuse. A man after having served a septennial apprenticeship to a branch of business, (No matter what) has a right to all the profit accruing there from. In offering an address to the public, we necessarily appeal to all ranks of people, the rich and the learned, [as] well as the poor and unlearned. We are well aware that many of the former disdain even the prospective of the concerns of common life; but let such remember, that in a grand theater of human action each one must perform that part allotted to him, and that each is indispensable, and he whose humble lot it is to play a laborious but inconspicuous part, ought nevertheless to be justly supported, or the whole drama would fall into a scene of chaotic confusion.

"She Hopes for the Encouragement of Ladies in General"
MRS. CARNEY, A WOMAN ENTREPRENEUR

Despite the difficulties, some women managed to set themselves up as independent artisans on an equal economic footing with men. The following advertisement from the New York Evening Post, March 26, 1808, offers a glimpse into the business of one such extraordinary woman. Although we cannot determine with precision much about the life of Mrs. Carney, we can surmise a few key elements. In all likelihood she had previously been widowed, since the advertisement indicates a new married name for Carney and because divorce was almost unheard of at this time. Despite her new marriage, Carney continued an ongoing business. Of particular interest is the fact that Carney's shoe manufacturing includes a business relationship with a male shoemaker, Mr. Neal. The advertisement, however, also indicates that Carney not only worked on shoes, but also offered a variety of fine goods for sale in her shop. In this short document, then, we see a versatile and ambitious woman who continued an independent economic activity despite her apparent marriage.

Mrs. Carney, (formerly Mrs. Cunningham) has opened her
TICKEN SHOE MANUFACTORY
At the shop of Mr. Joseph Neal, No. 16 Bowery Lane,
nearly opposite the Watch House,
Where she hopes for the encouragement of Ladies in general, and particularly those who first patronized her. The shoes will consist of

Figure 58. This engraving of an all-woman millinery store reveals that women did play a rol in craft life within a few trades. The illustration unfortunately gives little evidence of th hierarchy within the shop. Alexander Anderson, Women Working in a Millinery Shop, An derson Scrapbooks, vol. 1, p. 78, NYPL

Sattin, Velvet, Nankeen, Jane, and Ticken. Patterns will be left with MR. NEAL, and he will attend punctually to all orders from those who may favor her with their custom. The work will be executed in the neatest manner.

MRS. CARNEY may be found at her Shop No. 16 Bowery Street, near Broad-street, where will be done all kinds of Muslin work. She will, for the accommodation of the Ladies, keep an assortment of Cottons, Threads, and Silks, for Needlework. Patterns of all descriptions, and frames, for Schools, if bespoke.

N.B. Ladies work'd dresses, gold and silver muslins, laces, and silk stockings washed and done up in the best manner.

"A Young Lady Just Out of Her Time"
A MANTUA-MAKER SEEKS EMPLOYMENT

Mrs. Carney represented a special type of economically independent woman, but the young lady described in this advertisement is more typical of workingwomen (from *Independent Mechanic*, April 25, 1812). Mantua-making (silk work) and millinery were two of a handful of trades in which women dominated. Having just completed her apprenticeship, the young woman was looking for work on her own. The advertisement is short and provides little detail about the individual in question, but her willingness to engage with a family indicates she wanted a household to which she could attach herself. Yet despite her concern for dependency, this mantua-maker was proud of her accomplishments and skill.

Mantua-Maker Seeks Work
WANTS EMPLOY

A YOUNG Lady just out of her time, in the Mantua-making and Millinery; acquainted with every fashionable branch of either. Will engage by the month or quarterly to a family; can produce sufficient satisfaction in regard of character. Apply at No. 47 Frankfort Street.

"Everything in Her Power to Extricate Him from His Difficulties"
WOMEN BREADWINNERS

Most craftsmen wanted their wives to stay at home in order to take care of their families and household. Some mechanics also wanted their wives to assist them in their trade. They preferred not to have to depend on their spouse's independent compensation for survival. In the capricious economic atmosphere of the early republic, however, many within the poorer ranks of artisans and of lesser skilled workingmen had little choice in the matter. The following two petitions sent to the mayor of New York illustrate the problem. The first (City Clerk Filed Papers, August 22, 1801, NYCMA) is the request of Elizabeth Kline to run a vegetable stand at the market because her rope-maker husband has had difficulty obtaining work. The second (City Clerk Filed Papers, August 26, 1816, NYCMA), seeking relief from a fine for selling liquor without a license, describes a manure cartman's spouse who, in search of needed income, set up a fruit stand in a grocery where she sold both wood and liquor. She planned to obtain a liquor license as soon as she could afford it. Her petition was denied.

Figure 59. An occupation available to women of lesser means was huckstering, in which women sold all sorts of produce, especially fruit and vegetables. Alexander Anderson, *Mother and Daughter Hucksters,* Anderson Scrapbooks, vol. 1, p. 66, NYPL

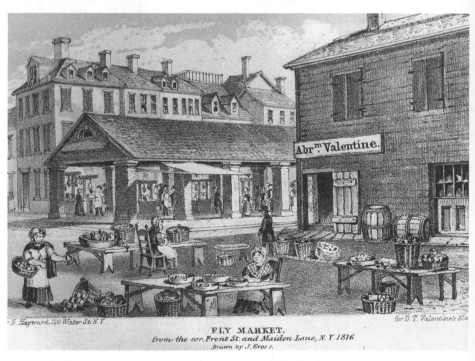

FLY MARKET,
from the cor. Front St. and Maiden Lane, N.Y. 1816.
Drawn by J. Evers.

Figure 60. At the Fly Market, the city's largest public market, women were permitted to set up tables to sell produce. Other women can be seen purchasing meat in the background. *Fly Market from the Corner of Front Street and Maiden Lane, 1816,* in *Valentine's Manual, 1857,* MCNY

Figure 61. On some occasions, independent craftsmen worked in family enterprises with their wife and children, as pictured here by Anderson. Alexander Anderson, *Woman Spinning, Husband Weaving, Anderson Scrapbooks,* vol. 1, p. 69, NYPL

To the Honorable the Mayor Aldermen and Commonalty of the City of New York in Common Council convened,

The Petition of Elizabeth Kline

Humbly sheweth,

That the petitioner's husband is a Rope Maker by trade and works as a Journeyman for the support of his family, but not having been able to meet with constant employment, he has got behind hand with his House Rent. and the petitioner finds it necessary to do everything in her power to extricate him from his difficulties and assist him in support of his family.

The petitioner therefore humbly prays that this Honorable board will be pleased to favor her with the privilege of Selling Coffee and

Chocolate in the Catharine Market where nothing of the kind is at present sold by any person. And as in duty bound the petitioner will ever pray &c.

Elizabeth Kline

We the subscribers do beg leave to recommend the within petition to the favorable attention of the Honorable the Mayor Aldermen and Commonalty of the City of New York.

James Mapes, John Wilson, Thos. Whittemore, James Smith

To his Honor the Mayor and Gentlemen of the Corporation,

The Petition of David Hay Humbly sheweth that your Petitioner is a poor man, and has a large Family to support by his hard labour carting Manure for Messrs. Furman & Dobbs— Your petitioner has been Complained of for selling Spirtous Liquors without license. It hapined his wife setting up a small fruit shop and sold some wood split up to other poor people, and as the place had been occupied before as a small grocery she sold some liquor with an intention to get Licence as soon as they could raise the Money to get them with—and your Petitioner begs that your Honours will be so good as to remit the fine and your Petitioner will be ever thankfull,

his

David + Hay

mark

We the subscribers are well acquainted with David Hay, and know him to be a very peaceable good Neighbour.

Stephen Burdett   Harry Griffin

"Frowning Ill-Humor and Slovenly Neglect"
THE BAD WIFE, AN EXAMPLE FOR OTHERS

For nearly all women, the most important work role was that of wife and mother. The middle and upper classes radically redefined these functions during the years of the early republic; traditional household duties became infused with civic meaning. The ideal woman served not only as a republican mother and hence guardian of the virtue of future citizenry, but also as the republican wife who fostered correct principles in her husband and maintained a proper home. Out of this development emerged the ideals of middle-class Victorian America that became so culturally dominant by the mid-nineteenth century.[10]

This ideal republican woman seemed to meet the needs and concerns of the middle class, but she did not so ably fit into the world of those of lower standing. The following account sketches out some of the components of this ideal as perceived by a young tradesman struggling to establish himself. When looking for a wife the mechanic stressed qualities of neatness, good temper, and "sufficient accomplishment"—the latter implying that she was capable of running a household. This particular match, made more in the kitchen than in heaven, started to fall apart when the wife, according to the husband, began to abandon these virtues and pursued luxuries not appropriate to her station. Her effort at gentility and middle-class status was foiled by the husband, and in reaction the wife abandoned all her pretensions and allowed the household, her person, and her marriage to fall into shambles.

Although the husband heaped blame upon his wife for not meeting his conception of proper female behavior, both of them were victims of a cruel contradiction posed by the nascent middle-class values of the early nineteenth century. Proponents of these values stressed virtue and the proper running of the household as central ideals. They also emphasized material possessions as a measure of gentility and social standing. The tradesman, the newspaper commentator ("Censor"), and the tradesman's wife recognized this. After all, the craftsman lamented the loss of comforts and the respectability that they entailed, as well as the loss of his home as a sanctuary after his hard day of labor. "Censor" decried the inability of the unfortunate tradesman to invite friends to his home to show off his domestic empire, while the wife pointedly commented that men who earned less than her husband were acquiring the possessions she desired. Her subsequent emotional collapse and abandonment of any concern for the household suggests the psychic cost that new middle-class values posed for those just at the edge of respectability.

10. Kerber, *Women of the Republic*; Reimer, "Rearing the Republican Child," 150–163; Kathryn Kish Sklar, *Catharine Beecher: A Study in American Domesticity* (New Haven, 1973); Barbara Welter, "The Cult of True Womanhood, 1820–1860," *American Quarterly*, 18 (Summer 1966), 151–174; Mary P. Ryan, *Cradle of the Middle Class: The Family in Oneida County, New York, 1790–1865* (Cambridge, 1981).

This document appeared in the *Independent Mechanic* (July 21, 1811), a newspaper that was published for tradesmen and that served as an important mouthpiece for the ideals and values of the upper strata of the mechanic community.[11] Perhaps the story of the tradesman and his wife was made up by a moral contributor or by the editor, but even if that were true, the tensions, concerns, and values imbedded in the selection still speak volumes for this group of workers and their wives. They tell a great deal about expectations of women's work and their role in the home in early nineteenth-century New York City.

> Marriage is Life's *lottery*, which hath many *blanks*;
> And he whom Fortune with a *prize* doth favor,
> The gift her choicest blessing should esteem.

THE following letter, from a discontented husband, I received a few days since, and which I have no doubt will be acceptable to some of my readers.

MR. CENSOR,
I am unfortunately a married man that can not live comfortably with my wife; and our uneasiness is altogether owing to her conduct.

Now, sir, as your paper comes regularly to our house, and is pretty generally read by her, I hope you will be so good as to publish a little wholesome advice in one of your numbers, that may tend to convince *her*, as well as any other woman, who may give their husbands like cause of complaint. That you may be the better able to feel for me, I will give you a fair statement of my case, from the beginning to the present time.

I am a mechanic, and am called a good workman, on which account I am able to keep in constant employ, and earn a good deal of money. While a single man, I was not fond of frolicking, and in about a year and half after I was free,[12] I had saved a pretty good sum. I then began to look about me for a wife, and pitched upon one what seemed to be every way calculated to make a fit companion for a steady mechanic. She appeared good tempered, sufficiently accom-

11. Rock, *Artisans*, pp. 126–127, 302–311.
12. That is, after he completed his apprenticeship.

Figure 62. One of the more common prejudices held against women in the early nineteenth century was that they spent their time unproductively engaged in slander and gossip. This engraving, showing women abandoning their spinning wheels for idle chatter, is indicative of that attitude. *Ladies Taking Tea*, in Samuel Wood, *Proof Book* (New York, 1820), NYHS

plished for a wife for me, *extremely neat* in her person, but without being *extravagant* in her dress; and to make all complete, she did not seem to be over fond of *company-keeping*. I accordingly made my addresses to her, and in a short time finally determined to ask her for my wife. I made her fully acquainted with my *then* present circumstances and my future prospects; and entreated her to maturely consider whether she would be content to live in the manner she might expect, if she accepted me for a husband; at the same time assuring her, that nothing should be wanting to make her life happy, that my industry could supply. She accepted the terms, and in a short time we were married.

All went well for about three months, when she began to form a new set of female acquaintance, some in the same circumstances with herself, but who were enabled, by foolishly squandering their husband's substance, to dress in all the extravagance of every new fashion, give tea-parties once or twice a week, resort [to] the theatre, and, in short, to launch into every kind of extravagance, unfitting for a mechanic's wife. She no sooner got well acquainted with the *ladies* in question, than she began to be very discontented. Our furniture was become too common. The *rag carpet* was a disgrace to the floor. Mrs. —— had a fine Turkey [Turkish] carpet, and her husband did not make as much money as I did. Our chairs were not fit a decent person to sit on, because Mrs. —— had a set of white and gold, with *painted rush bottoms*. Our *calico* curtains ought to be burnt; she was ashamed to look at them, after she had seen Mrs. ——'s white muslin ones with net fringe and *gilt* cornices. She was quite ashamed to ask a few ladies to tea, after having spent an afternoon at Mrs. ——'s, whose set of china cost *forty dollars*. In short our tables and irons, looking glass, and every article in the house ought to be sent to vendue, they were a disgrace to a decent family. I endeavoured to reason with her, but in vain; a remonstrance always produced a fit of the *pouts*, which generally lasted until I was forced to give her something which I was truly ashamed to do; further, she would refuse to be seen twice in the same gown or hat; she should be *known* by her *clothes*, always in the same dress. In short an article was scarcely soiled till it became so horribly old-fashioned that she could not possibly wear it until it was at least *altered* and *new trimmed*, to give it a change of appearance.

Scarce a week passed, in which the husbands of some of her extravagant friends did not appear in the lists of *insolvents*. Mrs. ——'s carpet, Mrs. ——'s china, and Mrs. ——'s curtains, were all sold by the hammer of the auctioneer. These instances I brought as warnings but in vain: and to save myself from a similar fate, I was obliged to lock up my money, and forbid her to run me in debt.

From this time she dashed into another extreme, she discharged our servant girl, declaring that if she could not appear like a Christian (as she termed it) she would not be seen out of the house, and would be completely the mope I wanted her. She now appeared continually in a state little inferior to the wench she had dismissed; she was always out of humor, and from being ashamed to be seen unless decked out in a manner unbecoming a tradesman's wife, she was now so careless of herself, that I was, in truth, ashamed that any one *should* see her. And thus has she continued to the present day. You must think, then, Mr. Censor, that my life is not very agreeably spent. We have a growing family, to make a decent provision for which, I work hard; and it is truly distressing to me, after my day's labour is over, to come home to a house, in which I had been accustomed to meet the smiling face of a sweet tempered wife, and could sit down to my comfortable supper, happy myself, seeing all contented about me; but which is now so sadly reversed, that I find nothing but frowning ill-humor, and slovenly neglect etc.. Instead of that neatness, which formerly proved my wife was anxious to make herself agreeable to me, I now find shameful inattention even to common and necessary cleanliness; which fully evinces a total disregard, as well of my good condition, or happiness, as of the opinion of the world at large.

Yours, &c.

A TRADESMAN

Scarce anything tends more to breed discontent between married people, than an avowed indifference, on the part of the females, to cleanliness, and neatness in their persons. Can it be supposed that a man in his senses could ever give the preference before marriage, to a girl who paid no attention to her appearance, but was always to be seen as if she employed in the kitchen? Everyone will answer—No. And where can there be a greater insult offered to a man, (one only excepted) than for his wife to so far deviate from that neatness of habit, which first fixed his attention, as to bring the blush of shame into his face when a friend calls at his house. Is it not a tacit declaration that she values not his love, or his good opinion; that she is joined for life to a man she dislikes, and that in his approbation there is no inducement of sufficient weight to balance the trouble she should have, in rendering herself agreeable. To this, everyone must answer—Yes.

I would recommend to all married ladies to think seriously on this subject, and some, perhaps, may find their own lives rendered more happy, from profiting by the example of the foregoing letter.

"Learn Them to Be Domestic"
RAISING REPUBLICAN WOMEN

The central issue in the following document from the *Independent Mechanic*, September 14, 1811, revolves around teaching young women their proper domestic role. "Poor Robert the Scribe" explored how a young virtuous woman should be trained for her work as a helpmate and guardian of the household. Rather than detailing the advice in his own voice, "Poor Robert" used a third person, "Aunt Tabitha," whose age and gender make her a more proper purveyor of information on the subject. The author mocked his aunt in an introduction (not included in the selection below) when he proclaimed Aunt Tabitha "an excellent reasoner" who "even if that shrewd old fellow John Locke was now alive . . . could prove to him . . . that her blue stockings were not white." While this humor almost brings Tabitha's credibility into question, the final discussion of raising young girls, placed within quotation marks to ratify its authenticity, reinforced the same middle-class values outlined in the tradesman's complaints in the preceding document. Youthful women are admonished to avoid frivolity and the "tinsel arts." A young lady need not be the "belle of the town"; far better for her to learn the pleasures and duties of her own house. This type of "solid" education would enable the young woman to choose the proper husband and assume proper domestic duties.

From the Desk of Poor Robert the Scribe . . .

"Girls," says she [Aunt Tabitha], "require much more care and attention in bringing up, than parents generally suppose. Some people think it sufficient if they can get their daughters early introduced into what they call good company, make them acquainted with all the newest fashions, and teach them a kind of flippancy of tongue and pertness of manners; but I am of a very different opinion. I never found that girls were generally esteemed for any of these tinsel arts. On the contrary, I have almost always found that the kind of assuming forwardness which belongs to some females, renders them disgusting to their associates; while a meek, modest deportment as often assure them to general esteem and respect. It has always appeared to me as one of the greatest misfortunes that can befall a young lady, to be tho't a belle of the town, and to be surrounded by a cavalcade of languishing admirers. I scarcely ever knew a lady of this character, who did not meet more than her full share of reproach. The lips of the malicious and envious are ever prepared with scandal, to endeavour, if possible, to bring such a person down upon a level with themselves in the public estimation. . . .

MATCHES!
"Will you have any Matches to day?
Twenty bunches for 6d."
Fine Matches! good Matches!
Will you please to have any,
In pity do take some,—
Three bunches a penny.

RADISHES!
"Radishes! Any Radishes!
"Here's your fine Radishes!"
Radishes! Radishes!
I hold them to view,
Turnip or carrot form,
As fine as e'er grew.

Figures 63, 64. Indigent women often became street peddlers, calling out their wares to passersby and to the more affluent residents secure in their homes. The upper and middling classes, who no doubt avoided these near-destitute beings, were also fascinated by them. The two figures here are from one small chap book, *The Cries of New York*, which had many editions published and became a popular children's book. This edition was engraved by Alexander Anderson. *Woman Selling Radishes* and *Woman Selling Matches*, in *The Cries of New York in Rhyme* (New York, 1833)

"To prevent girls from forming improper attachments, I know no better rule, than to learn them to be domestic. Girls that are fond of home will seldom if ever be troubled by the officious gallantry of a conceited fop. They will be likely, moreover, as I observed before, to make proper distinctions between the truly valuable and the artificial; between the man of real sense, and of imposing ostentation. It has always been my plan in bringing up my girls, to endeavour to make them pleased with home, and to furnish resources of amusement for them under my own roof; and I think I have succeeded very well, as every other parent may do. I have been desirous of giving them a solid, rather than a specious education; and have taken care to make them acquainted with household affairs. At the same time I have never wished to debar them of rational amusements abroad, but have always wished to make them prefer home to any other place."

The Strawberry Girl

Figure 65. This illustration of a strawberry peddler gives an insightful glimpse into her life. Niccolino Calyo, *The Strawberry Girl*, gouache, MCNY

"In the Practice of Receiving Men's Company"
WAYWARD GIRLS OF NEW YORK

The streets contained temptations for many young ladies from working-class families. Without much parental supervision and turned loose to fend for themselves, the choices were limited yet glaring. A meager and struggling existence might be eked out by selling items like hot corn or baked pears, or a young girl might turn to less decorous behavior, including petty thievery and prostitution. On the street the boundary between prostitution and merely seeking some treats in exchange for sexual favors was not distinct, as the cases of the two twelve-year-old girls described below suggests. The first clearly participated in "bad" behavior, and engaged in sexual activity with boys fourteen- and fifteen-years-old in return for apples and cakes. The second brazenly admitted to a long history of "receiving men's company" and proudly reaped the rewards, searching for customers at theaters and circuses seldom frequented by twelve-year-olds. Cut off from her family and rejecting her mother who struggled to earn a living by taking in washing and going "out to labor by the day," probably as a domestic servant, this young girl earned enough to rent a room of her own.[13]

These documents appeared in the *Fourth Annual Report of the Managers of the Society for the Reformation of Juvenile Delinquents in the State of New York* (New York, 1829), pp. 37–39. In both of the cases cited here, the Society was proud of the fact that these hardened and bruised girls found relief and assistance in the House of Refuge built for juvenile delinquents. Ultimately the Society aimed to send these young people to live with respectable families in the countryside, where they could learn virtue, the benefits of hard work, and Christianity.[14]

March 28th, 1828.

A. E. F.—From the Commissioners, aged she thinks, twelve years, the fourth of July last; born in B—— of Irish parents. Her father, she says was first partner and then foreman, to Mr. M'Q——, the founder, in D—— street; but a few months since went to the state of O——. Her mother, she says, used to drink so hard, that her father left her, and she then went to live in A—— street. This child went to live with a married sister, Mrs. N——, in C—— street, but was taken ill and went to Trenton. When this child went to live with Mrs. H——, in Y—— street, near A—— street, she says her step sister, T—— B——, had her sent here [House of Refuge], for going out and staying with different boys, about fourteen and fifteen years of age, in new buildings, at different times. She says that Mrs. H——'s daughter, M——, persuaded her to do so, and she used to

13. Stansell, *City of Women*, pp. 172–192; Timothy J. Gilfoyle, "The Urban Geography of Commercial Sex: Prostitution in New York City, 1790–1860," *Journal of Urban History*, 13 (1987), 371–393.

14. Robert S. Pickett, *House of Refuge: Origins of Juvenile Reform in New York State, 1815–1857* (Syracuse, 1969); Rosenberg, *Religion and the Rise of the American City*.

go also; and the boys would purchase cakes and apples for them—
they used to carry on bad in the streets. . . .

                                                    August 25, 1828.
    M.H.—From the Commissioners, aged twelve years, last spring;
born in B——, New-York, of English parents. Her father, J——
H——, put an end to his existence . . . , has no sister living, but five
brothers—the mother resides in T—— street, takes in washing and
goes out to labor by the day.

    The little girl has been three years, in bad practices, by going with
boys, in other girls' company first—speaks of many of the same age
and practices, then by degrees with larger boys. As small as she is,
and as young as she appears, she has been in the practice of receiving
men's company, for more than a year. In her time she has been very
active and successful in winning other little girls from the paths of
virtue. Had finally taken a room with Mrs. H——, in T——
street—frequently attends theatres, circuses, &c. La Fayette and
Mount Pitt. Enters Third Class. . .

"Where White & Black Persons of Evil Fame Resort"
CATHERINE AKENS IS CHARGED WITH KEEPING A "BAWDY HOUSE"

    As the previous document suggested, prostitution was widespread
in early national New York City. Indeed, recent studies have suggested that the exchange of sexual favors for some tangible benefit
may have marked the lives of thousands of working-class women. If
some women managed to move in and out of prostitution, others
accepted it as a regular means to earn a living. Catherine Akens, the
woman charged in this complaint with running a "bawdy house," fits
into the latter category (District Attorney Sessions Papers, June 7,
1819, NYCMA). The legal charge of maintaining a disorderly house
remained ambiguous during this period and included a variety of activities such as gambling, fighting, even allowing disruptive religious
meetings. But the bulk of disorderly cases involved prostitution.[15]

    15. Stansell, City of Women, pp. 172–192; Gilfoyle, "The Urban Geography of
Commercial Sex," 371–393.

Figure 66. Alexander Anderson, *House of Prostitution*, BA

William Sheehy of No. 63 Banker St. [and] Jasper Reed of No. 68 Banker St. being duly sworn say that Catherine Akens[,] a yellow [mullato] woman who occupies the upper part of 63 Banker St. keeps a disorderly house commonly call'd a bawdy house, where white & black persons of evil fame resort for the purpose of prostitution and while there fight and quarrel at all hours of the night to the great annoyance of these deponents and the neighbors.

Sworn the 7th June 1819—William Sheehy, Jasper Reed X his mark.

"Well May They Read Sin in Their Punishment"
ISABELLA GRAHAM'S REPORT TO THE SOCIETY
FOR THE RELIEF OF POOR WIDOWS
WITH SMALL CHILDREN

The following selection is an unusual document produced by an unusual woman—unusual for the period because it reprints a speech by a woman to other women about poor women. Represented here, then, is an interesting set of crosscurrents that provide an insight into the position of both impoverished and more affluent women in New York City during the early republic. The author of the document, Isabella Graham, was herself widowed in the West Indies in 1772, when she was thirty-one years old. A member of the middle class (her husband had been a military doctor), Graham was left mainly to her own devices and supported her children by establishing a school in Great Britain. Believing that America was a country blessed by God and the place where his work would be manifest, she moved to New York City in 1789, where she continued to work and teach school. She retired in the late 1790s after her daughters had married well and because she had made a shrewd real estate investment. She then turned her energies toward benevolent activities, spearheading the organization in 1797 of the first American women's reform organization (the Society for the Relief of Poor Widows with Small Children), served as its manager for a decade, and played an equally instrumental role in several other women's reform groups until her death in 1814.[16]

Although Graham and the women involved in these early reform efforts cannot be easily categorized as feminist, their activities launched American women into the public sphere in innovative ways. Republican ideas about womanhood after the American Revolution emphasized the nurturing and protective environment of the home and sentimentalized the family. Some women, energized by these ideals and by evangelical religion, began to project the new definition of womanhood into the greater society. To do so they asserted themselves in politics through petitioning and charity collections. This form of politics was, of course, both limited and deferential. By obtaining government support for their activities and by going into the streets of the poorer neighborhoods and aiding the destitute, however, these women gained an important visibility and established precedents for more radical reform activity in the 1830s.[17]

16. Isabella Graham, *The Power of Faith: Exemplified in the Life and Writings of Mrs. Isabella Graham of New York* (New York, 1816).

17. Barbara J. Berg, *The Remembered Gate: Origins of American Feminism: The Woman and the City, 1800–1860* (New York, 1978); Rosenberg, *Religion and the Rise of the American City*; Nancy F. Cott, *The Bonds of Womanhood: "Woman's Sphere" in New England, 1780–1835* (New Haven, 1977); Anne M. Boylan, "Women in Groups: An Analysis of Women's Benevolent Organizations in New York and Boston,

Figure 67. Women were commonly used to symbolize the republican spirit of America. In this ad for bleach, two classically garbed women representing Liberty and Equality stand on either side of the American eagle. Republican women were to hold the union together by serving as helpmates to their spouses and by raising children who would carry on the great experiment of the new nation. Alexander Anderson, *Bleach Ad*, Anderson Scrapbooks, vol. 3, p. 79, NYPL

The following document (Graham, *The Power of Faith*, pp. 395–398) is significant because it offers us a portrait of these reform activities, as well as a view of middle-class women's attitudes toward mechanics, the working class, and poor women. For women like Isabella Graham this effort to help the poor, with all of its religious and moral connotations, became their life's work. Given Graham's value system, which she articulated in her 1800 report, she fulfilled a very special function in society. The Society for the Relief of Poor Widows with Small Children selected the objects of their charity with care and took pride in its ability to manage the financial and charitable resources available to them. Finally, this document pro-

___

1797–1840," *Journal of American History,* 71 (1984), 497–519; Boylan, "Women and Politics in the Era before Seneca Falls," *Journal of the Early Republic,* 10 (1990), 363–382.

vides another glimpse, though through the lens of Isabella Graham's values and priorities, of working-class women made desperate through widowhood.

To the Society for the relief of poor widows with small children, in April 1800.

LADIES,

It is with pleasure we, your board, again mee[t] this benevolent society. With pleasure we announce the success of the Institution— its funds, its usefulness, and its respectability increase. We have on the books two hundred and seventy-four annual subscribers, thirty-nine more than at last meeting.

The Treasurer has received three hundred and thirty dollars from ladies in donations, and from gentlemen, six hundred and seventeen dollars, nearly double they gave us last year. Your managers have expended eight hundred and twenty dollars since last meeting, not quite five months. Perhaps this may surprise you, but there was no avoiding it. Though the winter has been mild, the price of wood moderate, the wants of the poor have been more pressing than in former years. We have on our books one hundred and forty-two widows, with four hundred and six children below twelve years of age, by far the greater part below six; besides many boys bound apprentices, for whom their mothers must wash, mend, and provide part clothing. Though the sum expended appears great, you will find, on calculation, that it is not quite six dollars to each family. Yet by prudent management, giving it to them by little and little, and in necessaries, nourishing, yet cheap, it went further than twice the sum given in money, and at once. Besides, cordials for the sick, and exigencies of different kinds, your managers have begged, and taken from their own pockets and pantries, (I speak within bounds when I say) to the amount of two hundred dollars more. Most of our widows have to learn economy from necessity: in the days of their husbands they lived not only plentifully, but luxuriously. Every class of mechanics in New-York could live well and lay up for their families, were they frugal; but the reverse of this is the case—the evil is general, and, I fear, not to be cured. The change to their widows greatly aggravates their misery—well may they read sin in their punishment, when meager want overtake them. But God forgives, and so ought we: We, who have so much to be forgiven, yet have our necessaries, our comforts, and even our luxuries spared. To us, our comfortable dwellings, cheerful fires, and convivial parties, give to winter its charms. Alas, for her! the new-made widow! to whom all these are lost forever—to her, the approach of winter is as the approach of death. Accustomed to spread the board by a cheerful fire-side, to welcome the companion of her heart from the labours of the day to bless and share the social meal, provided by his industry, drest with neatness and ingenuity, rendered savoury by health and appetite, and heightened in its relish by mutual love! The witty sayings of the prattlers are repeated, and the news of the household exchanged for the news of the city. The little ones too have their share; they tell the father the exploits of the day, who forgets his fatigue, and dandles them by turns on his knee, the mother's moistened eyes glisten with pleasure. Alas! the change! —Husband, father, support, provider, gone forever! The setting sun, the succeeding twilight, the rattling cars, the train of labourers, announce the approach of evening, when many boards are spread, many husbands return to bless their families;

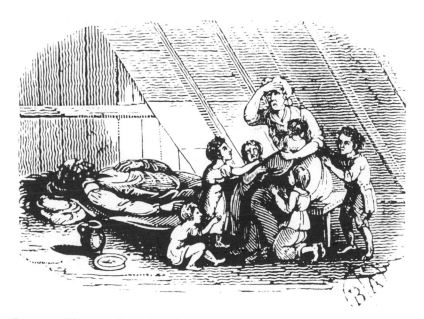

Figure 68. The city's limited welfare provisions, together with a woman's limited capacity for earning an adequate income, meant that the death of a spouse to a family of limited means was devastating. Alexander Anderson, *Woman in Garret with Children and Dying Husband*, BA

scarce can she believe that he is not in the crowd—fain would she persuade herself that she has been in a dream—fain would she fancy that yonder he is. Darkness pervades the earth; the neighboring doors shut in the happy families; the beaming fires illumine the windows. Back she staggers to her dreary dwelling, and wakes to all the realities of her widowed state. The once cheerful chimney scarcely emits a taper blaze. Her children cry for bread, but her empty pantry affords it not. Tired nature soon brings to *them* relief—they sleep—they forget. Not so the widowed heart; busy, cruel memory calls back and doubles her departed joys; comparison doubles also her present misery—every avenue to hope is shut. The deep-fetched sobs wring out the big round drops in blest profusion, (who can say the luxury,) till glutted with grief, she sinks among her babes. Time, that sorrow-healing balm, softens at length the pungency of wo[e]. The sympathising neighbors, the unrestrained complaint of tears, render her situation familiar; the wants of her children urge her to exertion for their support. Some sister-widow, pensioner on your bounty, consoles her with the news, that many benevolent hearts have united their efforts to relieve wants like hers. Hope steals in—she listens—is comforted, plans schemes of industry, and exerts herself to become father and mother to her orphans.

Many such, dear ladies, have eaten of your bread, been warmed from your wood-yard, clothed from your web—in sickness revived by your cordials, consoled and soothed by your Managers. Blessed office! —they are your agents, Ladies; they are also the agents of your God, by whose ministration he is the Father of the fatherless, the Husband of the widow, the stranger's shield and orphan's stay. . . .

INDEX

Library of Congress Cataloging-in-Publication Data

Keepers of the revolution : New Yorkers at work in the early republic
 / edited by Paul A. Gilje, Howard B. Rock.
     p.   cm. — (Documents in American social history)
   ISBN 0-8014-2665-0 (cloth : alk. paper). — ISBN 0-8014-9959-3
(pbk. : alk. paper)
    1. Labor—New York (N.Y.)—History—Sources. 2. Working class—
New York (N.Y.)—History—Sources. I. Gilje, Paul A., 1951–   .
II. Rock, Howard B., 1944–   . III. Series.
HD8085.N53K44 1992
331'.09747'1—dc20   91-55542